PRAISE FOR THE FIRST *URBAN APOLOGETICS* BOOK

Urban Apologetics is a much-needed, multifaceted tool kit that offers an interdisciplinary approach to promoting biblical faithfulness and gospel fluency. I plan on carrying this tool kit with me wherever I am called to give an answer for the faith within me, and I encourage you to do the same.

— **PASTOR RASOOL BERRY,** Bridge Church, New York City

Eric Mason and team have captured, in one sitting, the rumblings of the cultural winds that threaten to knock down the pillars of our truth that are lost in retweets and likes and memes. This book shouts loud to our times! Jesus is real! No cap.

— **KIRK FRANKLIN,** award-winning gospel artist

Urban Apologetics is about the defense of the faith and, more particularly, a contextualized defense of the faith, all with an irenic tone from brothers and sisters in Christ that will stir believers within and without the Black community to spiritual solidarity under Jesus our king and brother.

— **DR. MICHAEL S. HEISER,** executive director, Awakening School of Theology and Ministry, Jacksonville, FL, bestselling author of *The Unseen Realm*, cohost of *The Naked Bible Podcast*

It is my privilege to endorse this very timely and important work, full of information and insight. If you care about communicating to the rising generation, this book is worth your time.

— **DR. CRAIG S. KEENER,** F. M. and Ada Thompson Professor of Biblical Studies, Asbury Theological Seminary

The urban context of America warrants a fresh and fiery apologetic. With this text, Dr. Mason delivers! This book transforms defenders of the faith to be holistic disciples in their cities.

— **PASTOR CAM TRIGGS,** Grace Alive

Urban Apologetics shows the reader how God transforms persuasive ideological arguments into gospel opportunities, proclaiming Christ's victory over sin, error, and human insufficiency—for his glory and fame.

— **K. A. ELLIS,** director, the Edmiston Center for the Study of the Bible and Ethnicity

Urban Apologetics reveals the racial biases—evangelical and secular—that have been baptized as truth and masqueraded as the only right readings of history, theology, and Scripture. It is a masterful work that lays bare the weaknesses of the Black religious identity cults for those tempted to find hope and power in their teachings.

—**ERIC C. REDMOND,** PhD, professor of Bible, Moody Bible Institute, Chicago, associate pastor of preaching, teaching, and care, Calvary Memorial Church, Oak Park, Illinois

Urban Apologetics is a godsend, a book that is fully equipped to demolish the myth that "Christianity is the white man's religion" once and for all. Through scholarship that is irrefutable and writing that is engaging and understandable to laymen and academics alike, this work is a must-read for anyone interested in reaching people of African descent with the gospel.

—**CHRIS BROUSSARD,** founder and president, the K.I.N.G. Movement, internationally known sports broadcaster

Urban Apologetics is one of those rare books that will become a baton to be handed to men and women who are serious about global gospel transformation.

—**PASTOR JAMES WHITE,** executive VP of organizational relations at the YMCA

URBAN APOLOGETICS:

CULTS AND CULTURAL IDEOLOGIES

BIBLICAL AND THEOLOGICAL CHALLENGES FACING CHRISTIANS

URBAN APOLOGETICS:

CULTS AND CULTURAL IDEOLOGIES

BIBLICAL AND THEOLOGICAL CHALLENGES FACING CHRISTIANS

ERIC MASON

GENERAL EDITOR

ZONDERVAN
REFLECTIVE

ZONDERVAN REFLECTIVE

Urban Apologetics: Cults and Cultural Ideologies
Copyright © 2023 by Eric Mason

Requests for information should be addressed to:
Zondervan, *3900 Sparks Dr. SE, Grand Rapids, Michigan 49546*

Zondervan titles may be purchased in bulk for educational, business, fundraising, or sales promotional use. For information, please email SpecialMarkets@Zondervan.com.

ISBN 978-0-310-14299-7 (hardcover)
ISBN 978-0-310-14302-4 (audio)
ISBN 978-0-310-14300-0 (ebook)

Printed in the United States of America

23 24 25 26 27 LBC 5 4 3 2 1

I dedicate this book to Dr. Carl F. Ellis. In in the early and mid-'90s I went to Impact, a conference held yearly for Black college students from December 26 to New Year's Day. It was epic. Two thousand five hundred students in one place hearing the Word of God and fellowshipping. I heard Dr. Ellis ground faith in the gospel and give me language for my faith as a Black man. The '90s were a tough time to be a Black man and Christian. His work made it easier and gave me framework over the years for theological reflection. If I'd never had crossed his path, there'd be no Urban Apologetics. He is the godfather of all this. No him, no me.

CONTENTS

PART 2: CHRISTIAN SECTS AND CULTS

ACKNOWLEDGMENTS

God is an amazing God. In writing on urban apologetics, there is always a tremendous amount of spiritual warfare for me and the contributors. It's amazing that God has us releasing another work.

To the Most High: You have given us what is needed, and I just want to thank you for all your encouragement by the Spirit to stay the course.

To my amazing wife and children: You all help make this worth it. My prayer is that resources like this will aid not only the world but each of you in your own walk with Jesus. Yvette, you are a trooper! The space you give me to work on writing is amazing. Thanks for all your encouragement.

To the contributors, each of you have displayed that this is truly a labor of love for you. It's clear that you all understood the task of investing in the truth of the gospel of Jesus Christ, making it clear to struggling Christians and those who aren't. I pray that on earth and in heaven you experience the blessing of seeing, knowing, and feeling the fruit that will come from this great project.

Epiphany Fellowship: I am always thankful for you. For me, this is where we get to place boots to the ground. I'm looking forward to us continuing working on actually fleshing these issues out in community and in our city. Your support is a blessing to my family and me. Thanks to my sister Lisa Mason-Hobbs for assisting me in coordinating to get the work done as my executive assistant in this season.

To the team at Zondervan, Ryan Pazdur, Matthew Estel, Alexis De Weese, and everyone who had any hand in this project: thank you. Thank you for your labor and commitment to this project. To my agent, Andrew Wolgemuth, thanks for getting things connected to get this resource out.

Anyone else I forgot, please charge it to my head and not my heart.

CONTRIBUTORS

Thabiti Anyabwile is one of the pastors for Anacostia River Church. He has served as an elder and pastor in churches in NC, DC and the Cayman Islands. After a few years as a practicing Muslim, Thabiti was converted under the preaching of the gospel in the Washington, DC, area. Thabiti is the author of several books, including *Exalting Jesus in Luke*; *Reviving the Black Church*; *The Gospel for Muslims*; *The Decline of African-American Theology*; and *The Faithful Preacher*.

Anthony Bradley, PhD, is professor of religious studies and director of the Center for the Study of Human Flourishing at the King's College and serves as a research fellow at the Acton Institute. He has appeared on C-SPAN, NPR, CNN/Headline News, and Fox News, among others. His many books include *Why Black Lives Matter*; *Ending Overcriminalization and Mass Incarceration*, *Faith in Society*; and *John Rawls and Christian Social Engagement*.

Cristen Campbell, DMin, is a missionary, bible teacher, and speaker, who has primarily served in the Central African country of Cameroon for more than two decades. She is a graduate of Dallas Theological Seminary where she studied historical theology, cross-cultural ministry, and Christian education with a concentration in women's ministry and leadership.

Lisa Fields is one of the world's most sought-after Christian apologists. She is the founder and president of the Jude 3 Project, which has the goal of helping the Black Christian community know what they believe and why they believe.

She has a masters of divinity from Liberty University. She has also helped produce and create two documentaries through her partnership with Our Daily Bread: *Unspoken*, an in-depth look into the Christian heritage of Africa and people of African descent, and *Juneteenth: Faith and Freedom*.

Jerome Gay Jr. is lead pastor of teaching and vision at Vision Church. Jerome is also the founder and president of the Urban Perspective. Jerome has a master's degree in Christian studies and ethics from Southeastern Baptist Theological Seminary. He is author of four books: *Church Hurt*; *Talking to Your Children about Race*; *The Whitewashing of Christianity*; and *Renewal: Grace and Redemption in the Story*.

Elce-Junior Lauriston ("Thunder") was born in Haiti, grew up in the Bahamas, and now resides in Jamaica with his wife, Kahmal, and two children, Kah-El and Kah-Liyah. He is a Christian apologist with specialization in Seventh-day Adventism, the Sabbath, Sunday worship, and old covenant legalism. He has written several books, including *All Foods Are Clean and Every Day Is the Sabbath*; *The Sabbath*; and *Hiding In Plain Sight: The False Doctrines of Seventh-day Adventism*, volumes 1–3. He is a pastor in the United Church in Jamaica and the Cayman Islands.

Crawford Loritts, DD, is president and founder of Beyond Our Generation. Crawford has been a church planter, served for twenty-seven years on the staff of Cru (Campus Crusade for Christ) and served for fifteen years as senior pastor of Fellowship Bible Church in Roswell, Georgia. He has been the featured speaker at Super Bowls, NCAA Final Four Chapel, and the Pentagon with senior military officers. He and his wife, Karen, have been featured speakers at FamilyLife marriage conferences. Dr. Loritts is the author of nine books including *Your Marriage Today… and Tomorrow*, co-authored with Karen. He is the host of two national radio programs, the weekend program *Living a Legacy* and the daily program *Legacy Moments*.

Sarita Lyons, JD, PhD, is a wife, mother, speaker, women's bible teacher, and psychotherapist. She is on staff at Epiphany Fellowship Church in Philadelphia as the director of discipleship and women's ministry. Prior to full-time ministry,

Dr. Lyons was in private practice for eight years, where she provided counseling for individuals, families, couples, and groups for a variety of psychological needs. Some of her treatment specialties are recovery from trauma, depression, and anxiety, as well as marital and family therapy.

Eric Mason, DMin, is the founder and lead pastor of Epiphany Fellowship in Philadelphia, as well as the founder and president of Thriving, an urban resource organization committed to developing leaders for ministry in the urban context. He has authored four books: *Manhood Restored*; *Beat God to the Punch*; *Unleashed*; and *Woke Church*.

John Perkins, DD, is the founder and president emeritus of the John and Vera Mae Perkins Foundation and cofounder of Christian Community Development Association. He has served in advisory roles under five US presidents, is one of the leading evangelical voices to come out of the American civil rights movement, and is an author and international speaker on issues of reconciliation, leadership, and community development. For his tireless work he has received seventeen honorary doctorates.

Damon Richardson has a passion for helping to equip ministers, church leaders and all believers biblically, theologically and apologetically. Damon currently preaches itinerantly and is the founder of UrbanLogia Ministries, an online theological and apologetics resource which specializes in the field of urban apologetics. Damon Richardson is an ordained Baptist minister who has served over the past thirty-two years in various ministry roles including senior pastor and teaching pastor. Locally, he's a member of Blueprint Church Stone Mountain in Georgia. He is married to Nadine and they have four children. Damon holds an MA in religious studies and is a PhD candidate at Beulah Heights University in Atlanta, GA.

Kenneth C. Ulmer, PhD, DD, has been senior pastor of Faithful Central Bible Church in Los Angeles since 1982. He is the presiding bishop over Macedonia International Bible Fellowship and CEO of the Ulmer Institute. He is author of several books, including *A New Thing*; *Spiritually Fit to Run the Race*; and *Making Your Money Count*.

Brandon Washington is the author of *A Burning House* and lead pastor of Embassy Christian Bible Church in Denver. He holds a master's degree from Denver Seminary, where he studied systematic theology, apologetics, and ethics and now serves on the board of trustees. He lives with his wife, Cheri, and their two children in Colorado.

THE NEED FOR CONVICTION

ERIC MASON

Success, recognition, and conformity are the bywords of the modern world where everyone seems to crave the anesthetizing security of being identified with the majority.[1]

Nothing pains some people more than having to think.[2]

Most people, and Christians in particular, are thermometers that record or register the temperature of majority opinion, not thermostats that transform and regulate the temperature of society.[3]

We preach comforting sermons and avoid saying anything from our pulpit which might disturb the respectable views of the comfortable members of our congregations. Have we ministers of Jesus Christ sacrificed truth on the altar of self-interest and, like Pilate, yielded our convictions to the demands of the crowd?[4]

—DR. MARTIN LUTHER KING JR.

I t is impossible to think about the work of Dr. Martin Luther King Jr. and not think about him as a man of conviction. Today, more than ever before, we need men and women of deep conviction. A conviction is a belief or opinion about someone or something held with a measure of certainty that leads to significant adjustments in one's life to practically reflect that belief. There are people who have convictions about life in the womb. There are people who have convictions about what family is or about justice or systemic racism or Black identity and dignity. There are people who have convictions about the role and function of women in the church. And there are people on different sides of all these issues who have deep convictions.

The question isn't *whether* we have convictions. The question is, are they God-aligned convictions? Is the conviction we hold valid and true in the eyes of God?

BIBLICALLY ROOTED CONVICTIONS

There are some beliefs and opinions that we can consider nonessential—areas of preference or taste that we can agree to disagree on. But there are convictions that go deeper than this, beliefs that are universal because they are based on God's truth and the reality of his divine kingdom plans. Since Jesus made everything with an intended purpose (Col. 1:16), we should be united with his commitments.

Paul writes to the Corinthian church and encourages them to have unified convictions. Speaking to issues of tribalism in the church, he writes, "Now I urge you, brothers and sisters, in the name of our Lord Jesus Christ, that all of you agree in what you say, that there be no divisions among you, and that you be united with the same understanding and the same conviction" (1 Cor. 1:10 CSB). The word "conviction" he uses in this verse refers to "that which is purposed or intended, *purpose, intention, mind, mind-set.*"[5] It describes the direction of one's thinking, intention, disposition, and will.[6] Paul speaks of conviction again in 1 Thessalonians 1:5: "For our gospel did not come to you in word only, but also in power and in the Holy Spirit and with full conviction; just as you know what kind of men we proved to be among you for your sakes" (NASB). Here "conviction" means a full and complete confidence in someone or something. It describes certainty and full assurance[7] that is motivated by the Holy Spirit and rooted in God's Word. Elsewhere Paul urges God's people to be careful of letting their feelings lead their convictions: "Now these things, brothers and sisters, I have figuratively applied to myself and Apollos on your account, so that in us you may learn not to exceed what is written, so that no one of you will become arrogant in behalf of one against the other" (1 Cor. 4:6 NASB).

Today, many people, including many in the church, seem to have forgotten Paul's teachings. People's convictions are instead informed by their desires and cultural affirmations. They listen to deceitful spirits and the doctrines of demons. They accumulate teachers based on what they want to hear. They look for confirmation, not transformation, of what they believe and practice. We need clear prophetic voices leading to actions that plant the flag of gospel convictions in this fallen world.

BIBLICALLY INFORMED EXPERIENCE

We live in a world where people are led by experiential "conviction," the idea that my experience and my feeling are my truth, and my truth is ultimate—all that matters. Our experience may be real, but that experience is still interpreted through a lens of belief and values. So even our experience—though it may be factual and real—doesn't always amount to the truth. The fight we face today, in my experience as a shepherd of God's people, is helping this generation learn to have discernment that flows from God's Word and his truth. While many are responding well, others are being swallowed up by influences from their phone to their fellowship, drowning in the waters of cultural pluralism. I'm convinced that we are in a uniquely challenging time that requires followers of Jesus to be different. We must be people who show absolute faithfulness to Jesus—often despite the pull and sway of what we feel.

No one develops this kind of conviction in a vacuum. Often we have an experience and we need to make sense of it, figuring out how to deal with what has happened and how we feel. As believers, we do this by seeking God's truth in precept and principle—and we do this by reading and knowing his revealed Word in the Bible. Once we have clarity on what God's judgment is on an issue, we use that knowledge to inform our experience. We contextualize our feelings and our response based on God's truth for that particular issue. For instance, if people are experiencing an injustice, we look at what God says about it and then find ways to engage that issue that align with what God says. If there is sexual misconduct and sexism in our sphere, we don't turn a blind eye to it, protecting the guilty and shunning the victim. We deal biblically and honorably by properly investigating the matter through a biblical lens, through set-in-place disciplinary and protective measures we may have established (1 Cor. 6:1–6), as well as legal measures, contacting the authorities to help with the investigation (Rom. 13).

In the Black experience in America, we must be careful that we do not view our experience as revelatory, putting it on par with the Bible. That doesn't mean our experience is invalid. If we have experienced pain or suffered atrocities, we need to respond according to Scripture, just as we would engage any other issue in our world. Dr. Evans says it well when he writes,

> The black experience is real, but not revelatory. It is important, but not inspired. Recognizing this to be true during the social and theological revolution of the 1960s and 1970s placed theologians like me at the critical juncture of the emergence and development of black evangelicalism, in a position of being caught between two worlds. Holding tenaciously to a conservative hermeneutic of theology gave us, black evangelicals, a link to the white evangelical world. However, we also had to respond, both personally and on behalf of our calling given by God of faithfully and accurately shepherding those under our care, to the valid questions raised by the black revolution, black power, and black theology along with the inconsistencies taught by many of our white mentors.[8]

The Bible is our guide to interpreting and understanding our experience through the eyes of God.

BELIEF-LED ACTION

Conviction without action is hypocrisy. Is it even a conviction at all? Throughout this book, you will have your convictions challenged. You will learn about cults, errant beliefs, and cultural ideologies that are pervasive in our world. Many of these offer alternatives to biblical Christianity and are brushing up against our faith commitments every day. My hope as you work through this book is that you will be encouraged to walk in God-empowered conviction. I hope you will see that what the Bible says to us, while it speaks to our current challenges here in America, is also bigger than all that. You will be invited to examine how you form biblical convictions and to learn from sages who have spent decades observing, reflecting, and nurturing convictions in themselves and those whom they have led. My hope is that through reading and studying the material in this book you will be inspired to stand firm in the faith—no matter what madness you face on this terrestrial ball.

Biblical convictions that are applied well can speak to any issue in our world. In our previous volume, *Urban Apologetics: Restoring Black Dignity with the Gospel*, we addressed some of the false teaching of the Black "conscious community" and groups like the Hebrew Israelites, Black atheism, Egyptian (Kemetic) spirituality, and practitioners of African mysticism. Among these groups, revisionist history, conspiracy theories, and misinformation about Jesus and Christianity run rampant.

This work builds on that foundation and seeks to challenge and engage the convictions of Christian cults and several current cultural ideologies. In addressing these diverse beliefs in one volume, we are not suggesting that they are all equally aberrant. For example, those who embrace Christian nationalism are very different from those who hold to the beliefs of the Jehovah's Witnesses. We have chosen these belief systems and ideologies because of the way in which they have sought to influence and lead astray those in Black churches and Black communities. All have an interesting and relevant place in the Black religious and cultural narrative. We have sought to critically and honestly interact with these belief systems, examining them in light of orthodox Christianity and their influence and relevance for the Black community. Our selection is by no means exhaustive, but we hope it provides a springboard for anyone who seeks to engage one of these groups.

Along with a section on cultural ideologies (contemporary movements and belief systems that are influencing Black Christians and communities today) and a section on the cults (several groups that hold to unorthodox Christian doctrine), you will see several essays scattered throughout the volume. These are intended to help readers better apply the insights they are learning by vision and strategy, as well as general principles and some practical ways in which we can see the value of strong, biblical convictions. My hope is that readers will not only be convicted and gain confidence in the truth of God's Word but also develop healthy ways of applying what we believe through our interactions with others.

What we do (our ethics) flows out of what we believe (our doctrinal convictions). As Christians trying to live out our biblical ethics, we must first have biblical convictions. Speaking of Dr. Martin Luther King Jr., Carl Ellis reminds us, "Brother Martin was concerned about God's righteousness and justice wherever they were needed. He showed us that God's Word could be applied to other social issues, like the Vietnam War and hunger. He saw that biblical ethics must be applied to every area of life."[9] May we all be inspired to live out our faith in accordance with convictions rooted and grounded in the Word of God.

PART ONE

CULTURAL IDEOLOGIES AND MOVEMENTS

ONE

REDEEMING THE CULTURE

ERIC MASON

One of the best parts of my childhood was watching *Bugs Bunny*, *Woody Woodpecker*, *The Flintstones*, and *The Jetsons* after school and on Saturday mornings. I'd grab my favorite bowl of cereal and get to it. These shows were only on a few channels, and because some came on at the same time, I'd flip between them. Now that I'm a dad, I've begun introducing my kids to some of these older cartoons. And mostly it's been fun for us. But as I watch them as an adult, I realize that many of the jokes went over my head when I was younger. The writers creatively implanted mature themes in their scripts—topics most kids would miss. Yet now as I watch, in scene after scene, I am shocked at the sexual innuendo that's present in these children's programs. I've also begun taking a closer look at some of the other shows my kids watch today, and it's become clear to me that many of these programs have an agenda. They are shaping the hearts and minds of our children. In my childhood years, these "mature" themes were more subtle; today they are often obvious, even central to the plot of the episode. Let's call this what it is: blatant indoctrination.

I first heard the term "edutainment" listening to the work of musician KRS-One. The term is a merger of "education" and "entertainment" and is used to refer to the way entertainment and media actively promote an agenda.

The programs we watch and the shows we listen to have underlying ideologies. Many historians of contemporary culture credit the Disney company with developing the original concept:

> The term "edutainment" is something that was thrown around a lot through the mid to late 80's when Epcot was still a new concept in the theme park world. In contrast from other theme parks, Epcot, especially as it was in its early days, boasted more educational experiences than rides and other typical theme park attractions. As such, the term for entertaining, educational, ride/show sort of meant to be fun but still teach you something kind of experience has come to (unofficially) be known as "edutainment."[1]

When you consider the state of children's media today, as well as the pervasive influence of the internet and social media, it's fair to say that we are surrounded by organizations and entities trying to shape us through their influence. I can still remember a time when you had to wait for the news; you had to purchase or pick up a newspaper or a magazine. The news came in bite-sized pieces on a daily, weekly, or quarterly basis, and that was how you got your information. Now, however, we are constantly immersed in social media news feeds on Facebook, Twitter, Snapchat, Instagram, YouTube, and TikTok. And all of these channels of information are shaping how we think and feel and understand the world around us. Information that once took days to be reported and received can now travel to millions of people in mere seconds. This also means that any culture or ideology, from anywhere or anyone, can spread its influence—and they can do it quite quickly.

URBAN EXPANSION, GENESIS, AND GOD'S GLOBAL INTENTIONS

In God's eternal economy, he built his creative genius into the people he made, Adam and Eve. He created them in his image to reflect him to the rest of creation, and God called them to *subdue the earth*. The general meaning of this verb is roughly translated "to bring under one's control for one's advantage." We might paraphrase Genesis 1:28 to mean that you "harness its [the creation's] potential and use its resources for your benefit." In an ancient Israelite context this would suggest cultivating fields, mining mineral riches, using trees for construction, and domesticating animals.

As Adam and Eve and their descendants populated the earth with kingdom citizens, they would have had to develop ways to cultivate the earth beyond just growing vegetation. They would have had to develop ways to live in community; they would have had to build civilization—a city. In Roger S. Greenway's book *Discipling the City*, Harvie Conn has a chapter called "Genesis as Urban Epilogue." It is a theologically rich chapter that provides an excellent theology of urban ministry. Conn gives a theological overview of the Scriptures focusing on the Hebrew word for "subdue." He writes,

> The couple in the garden was to multiply, so providing the citizens of the city. Their cultivation of earth's resources as they extended their control over their territorial environment through the fabrication of sheltering structures would produce the physical architecture of the city. And the authority structure of the human family engaged in the cultural process would constitute the centralized government by which the life and functioning of the city would be organized, under God. The cultural mandate given at creation was thus a mandate to build the city, and it would be through the blessing of God on man's faithfulness in the covenanted task that the construction of the city would be completed.[2]

> In keeping with this urban intention of God, the images of the garden from Genesis become urban images. The river that waters the garden (Gen 2:10) is pictured in Psalm 46:5 as watering "the city of God." Zechariah combines the Edenic features of the river and life into "living waters" that go out from Jerusalem (Zech 14:9). And preeminently the Eden allusions reappear in the New Jerusalem of Revelation, "the holy city coming down out of heaven from God" (Rev 21:2).[3]

Despite all of this potential, the fall of the first humans into sin in Genesis 3 caused the separation of God and man and the corresponding separation between heaven and earth. This separation temporarily impacted how culture would be formed and developed, yet human beings did not lose the talents and gifts that God had bestowed upon them. Instead, those gifts grew distorted. People saw their talents and gifts as a means for attaining their own glory as

opposed to glorifying the one who made them. And in subsequent generations, as people moved further from God, they forgot where they came from
and the reason for their existence. Apart from hints and shadows of God's
redemptive work through the Old Testament, this knowledge would largely
remain forgotten by the peoples of the world until the coming of Jesus Christ.
Yet glimpses of our glory were still there as a mark of God's common grace. As
Conn concludes, "Despite sin's radical distortion of God's urban purposes, the
city remains a mark of grace as well as rebellion, a mark of preserving, conserv-
ing grace shared with all under the shadow of the common curse. Urban life,
though fallen, is still more than merely livable."[4] The people of God are called
to incarnate the good news of God into the cultures (where those cultural
values and distinctives are redeemable) and to be witnesses of the kingdom
of Christ as we represent his reign today. From the block to the boardroom
to social media to social clubs, we are called to engage. But before we engage
culture, we must understand it—how it forms us as individuals and societies.

CULTURAL HOUSES

What is culture? Carl Ellis says, "Culture embodies the cumulative effect of
history, destiny and consciousness in the life of a people. Although some have
defined culture as 'the patterned way in which people do things,' these visible
actions are more the manifestation of culture than culture itself. Culture itself
is made up of the underlying commitments, values, and beliefs a given group of
people have about the world and other people."[5] Culture represents the visible
and invisible systems that we use to relate to one another.

- **Everyone has a "core" that is a crucial part of their identity.** A person's
  core is made up of beliefs, behaviors, and values that they won't adjust
  or compromise.
- **Everyone has a "flex" portion of their identity.** This is composed of
  beliefs, behaviors, and values that a person is willing to adjust to better
  relate to others.
- **People with high cultural intelligence know their own core and flex.**
  They have a clear sense of what parts of their identity they will and
  won't adjust.

- **People with high cultural intelligence are able to move the core/flex boundary when appropriate.** They can examine their assumptions and adjust their behaviors to adapt to different cultural contexts without compromising their integrity.[6]

Culture, then, refers to the traditions and set ways of communicating and interacting with people in a particular context so they can understand and connect with one another. Culture distinguishes one group from another group, and over time culture develops into an operating system present in every society. As one grows up in a particular society or social group, those individuals will interact and learn how to live together, and the result is their unique culture.

A culture can be popular—reflecting the communication that happens more widely among large masses of people—but there are also numerous subcultures that can and will develop. Thinking of a cultural artifact like music might help make some of this more concrete. As music reflects various social groups, you will have pop music, but as you move into subgenres you will then have smaller groups like hip-hop, country, and rock. And even within each genre there are subgenres that indicate the presence of micro subcultures.

Culture isn't fundamentally bad; indeed, cultural formation is commanded and intended by God. Culture works as intended when it operates in the realm of God's freedom, reflecting his righteousness, and when all involved agree and operate within those intended means. However, when someone or a group of people seek to change that system in fundamental ways that impact God's intentions or the way humans relate healthily, it becomes a problem. Culture can certainly evolve and grow and change. But there are times when some of those changes deviate from God's righteous intentions. Consider modern technology for example. Technology is ever evolving, and as it evolves our culture will also change. Something as simple as shopping for groceries can dramatically change due to technological changes from generation to generation. From self-checkout to Instacart, to having your items pre-shopped and bagged for you for pick up, each of these changes represents a major cultural shift. But these changes don't always lead to fundamental changes that infringe upon or deviate from God's desired intentions. Some of them may be good reflections of his righteousness, leading to human flourishing and thriving.

Culture is housed in particular entities. The first and most basic home of culture is in the relationship between God and man. The second is the self as an individual, and the third is family. As culture grows, it is extended into society; smaller and larger social units lead to new relationships with neighbors, forming communities, which evolve into governments, institutions for work, and many others. More cultural houses are needed as ever more mechanisms are developed for people to interact with others, from our local interactions, to those nationally and internationally. The various houses of culture seem almost infinite.

However, when we talk about disruptions or attacks on culture, we are typically thinking of changes at the more fundamental and local levels. For example, if we begin redefining the family and its role and functions or we redefine genders, these are cultural changes that represent a fundamental disruption of the system—both from a natural and supernatural standpoint. This is why this unit of chapters is necessary and why we've included it in this book. We need to understand these cultural ideologies and how they affect us at these basic and fundamental levels as we process change and determine how best to engage those who are changing our culture.

CULTURAL DISTORTION: WHEN CULTURAL HOUSES BREAK AND CLASH

One of the best ways to disrupt a culture is to push the culture housed in one cultural house into another, or to force one house's culture onto another house. When another culture believes that other cultures are inferior or that their culture needs to be propagated within other cultures, we refer to that as cultural imperialism. Cultural imperialism can be defined as

the practice of promoting and imposing a culture, usually of politically powerful nations over less potent societies. It is the cultural hegemony of those industrialized or economically influential countries, which determine general cultural values and standardize civilizations throughout the world. Many scholars employ the term, especially those in the fields of history, cultural studies, and postcolonial theory. The term is usually used in a pejorative sense, often in conjunction with a call to reject such influence. Cultural imperialism can take various forms, such as an attitude, a formal policy, military action, so long as it reinforces cultural hegemony.[7]

Sadly, Christianity in the West has been a massive culprit of cultural imperialism.

Western culture once saw itself as the standard and viewed other cultures as fundamentally flawed—not flawed based on God's law but on man's preferences. This mindset affected Western Christians' relationships with other cultures it deemed less desirable. Many Western Christians saw themselves as doing the work of God by bringing other cultures up to their standard. Yet at the same time, they subjugated them, even when those cultures changed to meet their standards. In essence they were saying, "We civilized you; now we can utilize you."

Western Christians sometimes saw divergence from their accepted notions of "normalcy" as the result of unchecked sin in other societies. They assumed that if such peoples were to be won to Christ, they would first need to be "civilized" before they were evangelized (i.e., Westernized).

The legacy of cultural imperialism is still embedded in many parts of society today, though it may be present in other forms. It may be the redefining of the family or the false claims about critical race theory made by Christian nationalists and others who hold to hyperconservative rhetoric.

In the first section of this book, we'll be examining some of the cultural trends that are pervasive in society today and how these ideologies are affecting those in Black communities. Pastor Brandon Washington will help us better understand what critical race theory (CRT) is, what we can learn from it, and what we should be cautious about embracing. Thabiti Anyabwile will look at the history and growing influence today of Christian nationalism, why it is leading to the fracturing of evangelicalism, and why that may not be a bad thing. Anthony Bradley gives us a primer on Black liberation theology, explaining where it is helpful and why we need to know about it today. Sarita Lyons thoroughly overviews the LGBTQ movement, including one chapter on its history and then another on how Black Christians can respond to the growing influence of this ideology. Finally, I examine the growing phenomenon of deconstruction and some of the reasons this is affecting the Black church and how we can respond to it.

ENGAGING CULTURE AS BELIEVERS

Each of the topics we will discuss in this section of the book represent the influence of different, yet sometimes related, cultural ideologies. There are values, language, and assumptions about the world that sometimes align with God's truth and sometimes deviate significantly from that truth. As Christians, we are called to engage these cultures and not retreat from them.

Keep in mind that there are macrocultural movements and there are microcultural movements. The LGBTQ movement, Christian nationalism, and faith deconstruction are all trends that are happening at the macro level. Each has widespread influence and impact. Microcultures represent smaller cultural movements that swell into the mainstream. They may be widespread and well known, but they aren't as saturated or widely adopted into other cultural homes. CRT and Black liberation theology are examples of microcultural movements. Both have widespread impact in some ways—but typically not widespread influence. For some, CRT might seem to fit better in the macrocultural category, but as we will see in the chapters that follow, it better represents a microcultural trend.

Despite the importance of engaging other cultures, cultural trends, and cultural ideologies, we must always be careful as Christians. We must wisely discern how to apply our Christian worldview as we live and interact with others in society and in various subcultures. We must be "sober-minded" (1 Pet. 5:8 ESV) and resist being "tossed to and fro . . . by every wind of doctrine" (Eph. 4:14 ESV). We should take seriously the words of Colossians 2:8: "Be careful that no one takes you captive through philosophy and empty deceit based on human tradition, based on the elements of the world, rather than Christ" (CSB).

We are all products of particular cultures—your unique experiences and how those have shaped you, the culture of the family in which you were raised, the neighborhood in which you live and where you work, the country in which you reside. Your tastes and hobbies and activities likely reflect various subcultures as well. We are shaped by and create culture in good ways and in bad ways. And as our biblical worldview grows, we can see where we are healthy or unhealthy by examining our culture—our worldview and our values and actions—against the Bible. Scripture drives home this idea when it encourages us to pursue discernment and maturity: "Now everyone who lives on milk is inexperienced with the message about righteousness, because he is an infant. But solid food is for the mature—for those whose senses have been trained to distinguish between good and evil" (Heb. 5:13–14 CSB). Discernment is the ability to know the difference between the good, the grave, and the grey while navigating life in a fallen world and being led by God's Spirit, God's Word, and godly experiences and influences.

REDEEMING THE TIMES

At the conclusion of the Gospel of Matthew, Jesus came near to his disciples and said to them, "All authority has been given to me in heaven and on earth. Go, therefore, and make disciples of all nations, baptizing them in the name of the Father and of the Son and of the Holy Spirit, teaching them to observe everything I have commanded you. And remember, I am with you always, to the end of the age" (Matt. 28:18–20 CSB). This event came to be called the Great Commission, but it is really the Great *Recommission*. Jesus institutes disciplemaking as the means by which we are to be fruitful and multiply and fill the earth, fulfilling the creation mandate. Ultimately, Jesus fulfills this for us and through us, but until he returns we are called into the world to make his disciples. We are called to live in the culture we are in and to seek to be salt and light in it.

Our engagement as the church is the key to human flourishing. This is God's commission through his people. God designed the church to be the epicenter of culture, and the church's strength or weakness is a major determining factor in the success or failure of human civilization. When the church is strong, the culture is impacted positively—even if the "powers that be" in a particular place don't realize that impact and seek to marginalize and persecute the church. But when the church is weak, its influence deteriorates and so does the culture.[8]

Paul encourages us to redeem the time. The church should seek to be a community of communities. As Lois Barrett writes,

> The church as an alternative community can make a powerful witness when it chooses to live differently from the dominant society even at just a few key points. An important task of the church is to discern what are those key

points at which to be different from the evil of the world. For some, the key point will be authentic community in the face of the individualism of the dominant culture.[9]

Key images of God's alternative community, the missional church, are found in the Gospels' descriptions of the people of God as "the salt of the earth," a "light of the world," and a "city set on a hill." These images suggest that mission is not just what the church does; it is what the church is. Saltiness is not an action; it is the very character of salt. Similarly, light or a city on a hill need not do anything in order to be seen. So too it is with God's "people sent."[10]

As the church incarnates the message and the values and character of God into the world, we must "be wise as serpents and innocent as doves" (Matt. 10:16 ESV). We should isolate ourselves from evil but not from engagement (as Jesus states in John 17). We must speak prophetically, even using elements of the culture and affirming cultural values where appropriate to convey the message of the gospel, but parting from them where they are at odds with God's Word.

Jesus will come back one day and bring all cultures of the world from all time under himself, allowing for every cultural group to flourish while yet making us one (Rev. 7). Until then, we must engage one another across these cultural divides, sharing the truth of God through Jesus Christ and the Holy Spirit.

TWO

EVALUATING CRITICAL RACE THEORY

BRANDON WASHINGTON

In the spring of 2020, an acquaintance requested an "emergency get-together" at a local coffee shop. I asked for the meeting's agenda, but he was deliberately cagey. His use of the word "emergency" had tipped his hand, so he carefully concealed any additional information. I am always suspicious of such appointments; experience has taught me to expect a blindside hit. But I've known him for a few years, so, despite my reservations, I agreed.

I arrived early, retrieved a book from my satchel, and read while awaiting his entrance. The book was *The Color of Compromise* by Jemar Tisby, a work that reflects on the American church's active and passive "complicity in racism."[1] After about twenty minutes, my appointment arrived with another acquaintance, also a man I've known for years. I was not expecting them both, which contributed to my misgivings. As they took their seats, I unconsciously placed the book on the table between us. Unbeknownst to me, that mindless act affirmed their private burdens; for them, the book proved the "emergency."

After a few minutes, I grew tired of the hemming and hawing, the awkward exchange that usually precedes an uncomfortable conversation, so I pressed them to divulge their poorly hidden concerns. One of them revealed the meeting's aim by asking straightforwardly, "Brandon, are you abandoning the faith?" His query vexed me, but it did not surprise me.

I have been a pastor in one capacity or another for nearly twenty years. I graduated from an evangelical seminary, and my studies afford me confidence in my faith's defensibility. I stand unmoved on the kingdom gospel specially delivered by Christ.[2] However, my acquaintances observed my public struggles with American evangelicalism.[3] I believe it has abandoned the comprehensive gospel message, which is dutifully mindful of societal ills. The movement has demoted social justice to a poorly delivered punchline because, as the erroneous yarn is spun, *the church is responsible for the gospel, not social change.*[4] In my estimation, American evangelicalism has adopted what Carl F. H. Henry calls a "truncated" message.[5] We've turned a blind eye to some systemic sins—including institutional racism.

Spotlighting such transgressions is taboo. My acquaintances called me to a coffee shop to rebuke me, and Tisby's book only proved my infractions. Had they asked about my concerns, I would have readily engaged and would take no offense. But their question was an indictment cloaked by a disingenuous question mark.

They explained that I could not be an advocate of critical race theory (CRT) *and* a devout Christian. I took note of this because I'd never mentioned CRT. My reply was genuine with a hint of sarcasm, "I'm a critical race theorist? I did *not* know that." Oblivious to my attempt at light-heartedness, one of them lifted the book from the table and, as if showing *exhibit A* at my trial, asked, "What do you think this is?" He was posturing, which forced me toward monotone seriousness. I replied, carefully avoiding the remotest appearance of levity, "That is a credible record of some uncomfortable parts of American history. If it is outlawed, we become liars." It bears mentioning that he'd never read the book; he knew only that select Christian leaders marked its contents illicit.

I asked them to define CRT. They accused me of "hijacking the meeting" to avoid the compulsion to repent. I foolishly hoped to redeem the poorly framed conversation, so I asked a second time for a definition, adding that I needed to understand my sin if I were to repent appropriately. They replied obtusely, "We don't know what it is, but we know it when we see it." They took an uncompromising stand against a framework they'd never studied!

To be clear: I am not, and have never been, a critical race theorist. My acquaintances indicted me for violating the boundaries of Christian national-ism.[6] In reality, I am merely applying a hermeneutic that served as the backbone of the historic Black church and, consequently, the civil rights movement. I've had to familiarize myself with CRT because of clumsy interventions intent on saving my supposedly wayward soul. After repeated accusations, I do not have the privilege of saying, "I don't know what it is." This essay is a brief primer on CRT; limited space does not allow it to be exhaustive, but I pray it serves as a good introduction.

THE COMPLEXITIES OF EVALUATION

Polarizing notions have bastardized CRT, so evaluating it is complex. Typically, critics discard CRT as today's antipatriotic catchall.[7] At the lay level, far removed from intellectual ivory towers, most who reference CRT—adversaries and advocates alike—misrepresent it. Advocates take CRT to extremes and wield it beyond its design, which undermines any redeeming qualities. Adversaries brand CRT as a racist misrepresentation of America's history and values. CRT is the boogie man *du jour*; detractors believe it skulks in classrooms to rob us of our national virtue. Both extremes are suspect pre-cisely *because* they are extreme.[8]

In this chapter, I hope to offer a critique of CRT and consider its per-tinence to the church. Along the way, I will briefly articulate and illustrate some of CRT's foundational notions. Political tribalism plagues discussions of CRT—binary camps squabble like fighters from opposing corners of a boxing ring. But I believe the debate is too nuanced for pugilists, and that conviction shaped my approach. Prayerfully, when all is written and done, we will better comprehend a woefully parodied theory.

A BRIEF PRIMER ON CRT

Discussions of CRT can be counterproductive chiefly because interlocutors define it differently. Few things are as hopeless as feuding camps talking past one another. Therefore, it is necessary to define and describe CRT before con-sidering its vices and virtues.

A WORKING DEFINITION AND DESCRIPTION

CRT is a legal theoretical framework built on the observation that systemic racism exists, is pervasive, and was long preserved by the American legal system and national values.[9] Critical race theorists argue that racism is innate to the American ethos, *specifically its laws and institutions*. CRT is the brainchild of twentieth-century thinkers who asked why the accomplishments of the civil rights movement were manifesting so slowly—if at all.[10] We would do well to consider CRT a cordial but uncompromising evaluation of civil rights strategies. According to Richard Delgado and Jean Stefancic, early CRT voices like Derrick Bell and Alan Freeman were

> deeply distressed over the slow pace of racial reform in the United States. It seemed to them—and they were quickly joined by others—that the civil rights movement of the 1960s had stalled and indeed that many of its gains were being rolled back. New approaches were needed to come to grips with the subtle, but just as deeply entrenched, varieties of racism that characterize our times. Old approaches—filing amicus briefs, marching, coining new litigation strategies, writing articles in legal and popular journals, exhorting our fellow citizens to exercise moral leadership in the search for racial justice—were yielding smaller and smaller returns. As Freeman once put it, if you are up a tree and a flood is coming, sometimes you have to climb down before finding shelter in a taller, safer tree.[11]

Critical race theorists maintain that the innately racist nature of America's systems made civil rights strategies ineffective or unduly toilsome, so tangible progress was always just beyond reach despite apparent change during the civil rights era.

Any credible discussion of CRT recognizes the movement's preoccupation with the history of American laws and institutions.[12] For the critical race theorist, racialized values permeate American structures and policies. The racism is either de jura (lawfully sanctioned), de facto (extrajudicially practiced), or a mingling of the two (for instance, a federal law deliberately circumvented by state or local practices).[13] If this is true, embedded institutional racism explains the civil rights movement's trudging pace.[14] Under this definition, CRT is *not* a worldview but a methodological framework used to evaluate laws and systems.[15] Which explains why law schools use CRT to help students ponder history and assess any racialized intent behind some legal decisions.[16]

CRT AND THE CIVIL RIGHTS MOVEMENT

Critical race theorists' critiques of the civil rights movement are insightful. For instance, they deem *color blindness* and *assimilation* counterproductive. Their rejection of these civil rights strategies characterizes the CRT framework and uncovers some of the movement's foundational notions.[17]

Color Blindness

"Color blindness" is the pursuit of policies written without regard for cultural backgrounds or racial identities.[18] By and large, prominent civil rights leaders believed judiciously written color-blind laws would inevitably result in an egalitarian society. If the law is attentive to everyone's human dignity and worth, it need not specify race.

For critical race theorists, the idea of color blindness fails the viability test. It looks good on paper, but if a society is innately racialized, then color-blindness will fail.[19] The letdown stems from a history of willful racial bias. After centuries of a caste system prioritizing one race over all others, it is naïve to envisage color-blind laws that expunge longstanding racialized values.[20] To this point, Kimberlé Crenshaw asserts, "This belief in color blindness and equal process . . . would make no sense at all in a society in which identifiable groups had actually been treated differently historically and in which the effects of this difference in treatment continued into the present."[21] CRT underlines the injustice of drafting color-blind policies *after* centuries of color-conscious inequity and spotlights the human tendency to prioritize personal values over laws.

By way of illustration: Imagine a baseball game where one team cheats. The shady behavior is discovered during the bottom of the seventh inning after the cheaters amass a twenty-run lead. Upon getting caught, the tricksters commit to fair play for the rest of the game. The umpire, taking them at their word, bellows, "PLAY BALL!"—commanding both teams to take the field for the final two innings. The umpire deems the matter resolved. But is it that simple? The game's standard has not changed; the team with the highest score at the end is the victor, and the umpire will hold both teams to that standard. He expunged the history of cheating, but he did not erase the sordid score, a lasting effect that will undoubtedly impact the game's outcome! Ignoring seven innings of fraud only penalizes the defrauded team, who must now recover from an undue deficit to fulfill the game's unchanged standard. The umpire's decision perpetuates the offense and allows the cheaters to reap the mocking fruits of their shadiness. It all occurs in plain sight and under the umpire's authority.

Moreover, the umpire overlooked that the fraudulent team values winning so much that they were willing to cheat. Despite their newfound commitment to fair play, it is almost inevitable that they will resort to old tactics if victory is ever in jeopardy. Any revision of rules must be mindful of the game's history—namely, the dubious score and the cheating team's character. Overlooking these details *revises* or erases the game's first seven innings (history) and disregards the *ongoing implications* of the cheating team's fraud (present).

Color blindness troubles critical race theorists because it rescripts history by downplaying the implications of the racial caste system and inadequately weighs the continuing consequences of centuries of willful racial inequity. It obligates Black people to unchanged standards without considering the lead amassed by historical practices like slavery, Black Codes, Jim Crow, and redlining. Accordingly, critical race theorists aver that drafters of corrective laws must be mindful of the fraudulent history. Moreover, they must be vigilant against duplicitous policies sketched to circumvent civil rights laws. Critical race theorists argue that the circumstances require "race-conscious" instead of color-blind actions.[22] To this point, Crenshaw notes:

> The passage of civil rights legislation nurtured the impression that the United States had moved decisively to end the oppression of blacks. The fanfare surrounding the passage of these acts, however, created an expectation that the legislation would not and could not fulfill. The law accommodated and obscured conditions that led to conflict, countervision, and the current vacuousness of antidiscrimination law.[23]

In other words, color-blind advancements of the civil rights era provided the pretense of racial progress without genuine change. Moreover, the façade masked new segregationist policies—loopholes that undermined civil rights advancements. Color-blindness freed the populace to ignore race and, consequently, allowed institutions to turn a blind eye to ongoing racial discrimination.

Assimilation

The second rejected strategy, assimilation, logically follows from the first. Ironically, the ubiquitous imagery of a cultural melting pot illustrates the point. Whenever a collection of distinct ingredients melts together, the dominant one will be prominent and even overbearing in the final product. So if America prioritizes Euro-American culture, or "whiteness," then "melting" all cultures together will occur at the expense of nonwhite peoples; their identity and worth fade in the pot. Commenting on the downside of assimilation, Neil Gotanda writes,

> The abolition of a people's culture is, by definition, *cultural genocide*. In short, assimilation as a societal goal has grave potential consequences for blacks and other nonwhites. However utopian it appears, the color-blind assimilationist program *implies the hegemony of white culture*.[24]

Gotanda observes that the dominant group maintains its essential identity while the subdominant groups sacrifice their cultural selves to become part of the whole. It is neocolonialism disguised as virtuous nationalism. Just as color blindness allows the unique complexities of American Blackness to go unseen, assimilation makes racial and cultural distinctions appear trivial and even divisive. So, for instance, when a Black person voices discontent, their behavior may be judged as a selfish disregard for the melting pot's unity.

The combination of color blindness and assimilation allowed the dominant racial group to say, essentially, "We don't see color because we are all one." Theoretically, we've moved ethnicity and culture to the background and national identity to the foreground. But what if the national identity is cultural—namely, Eurocentric (white)? To be good citizens, all nonwhite people groups must abandon, to a measurable degree, their cultural identity and adopt the dominant culture's norms.

The notion of a melting pot is disingenuous. From the nation's inception, nonwhite peoples were at the bottom of the racial caste system, denied rights that would be foregone conclusions in a sincerely egalitarian society. Critical race theorists maintain that supreme court decisions like *Plessy v. Ferguson*, which sanctioned "separate but equal," proved the "melting pot" language insincere. A nation cannot simultaneously claim *the melting pot* and *segregation* as values; they are mutually exclusive. CRT spotlights such incongruities.

THE FRANKFURT SCHOOL AND CRITICAL THEORY

Most discussions of CRT hinge on critical theory (CT)—the work of the Frankfurt School, a group of Marxist-influenced European intellectuals. After World War II, they asked why the rational people of Germany abided by anti-Semitic genocidal policies. They concluded that national values could influence individuals and corporate structures. As Nazi values proliferated, German citizens either conformed or remained apathetic, allowing anti-Semitic policies to thrive. The Frankfurt School concluded that the populace frequently adopts institutional values, so critical theorists tend to have a pessimistic view of institutions.[25] They examine institutions with these assumptions in place.

CRT adapted select CT methods to examine racialized brokenness in America's legal systems. The adaptations are perhaps why critics treat CT and CRT as synonymous. To be sure, the former influenced the latter, so they share characteristics, but uncarefully conflating them is irresponsible. They developed in distinct settings and have correspondingly distinguishing markers. For instance, CT was initially devised to examine Nazi Germany, then institutions in general; CRT was tailored to one institution—the American legal system. This distinction is subtle but vital. CT's sweeping interpretation of institutions can be cynical, and its practitioners can assume systemic corruption before investigating. CRT, on the other hand, emerged from within Jim Crow America. Its framers did not assume institutional brokenness; they *observed* it in unhidden racist policies. CRT does not automatically evaluate all institutions negatively but critiques one society—namely, America—specifically targeting its values and laws.

Critical Theory and Free Will

According to detractors, CT denies human free will. Critics accuse the Frankfurt School of teaching that Germans adopted Nazi values involuntarily. This is a lazy oversimplification. CT is a method for examining the influence of institutions on individuals that comprise a society. This is not a denial of free will but an acknowledgment that societal values can sway individual decisions. The Frankfurt School concluded that, in Germany, the populace freely yielded to widespread Nazi values.

Consider this illustration: My notoriously independent ten-year-old son has long identified blue as his favorite color. For years, I've asserted that he came to that conclusion based on his ability to observe the superiority of *blueness*. On an occasion when he publicly touted an endorsement, I, on cue, shared my genuine belief that he'd independently arrived at his conclusion. My wife, following cues of her own, slyly asked my son why he likes blue. Having never considered it, he paused to give it thought, then replied, "It's because dad always wears blue." He is not wrong. He chose freely, but my values weigh heavily and are ever before him, shaping his interpretation of the world, including things as benign as color rankings. My values markedly increased his likelihood of adopting an affinity for blue. CT argues for widespread influence of this sort.

If an institution charmingly justifies malicious behavior, freethinking people will embrace it, sometimes unconsciously. Critical theorists argue that this occurred in Nazi Germany. So CT compels critical evaluations of societal norms and institutions to avoid blind embrace of bad ideas.

HISTORICISM AND DECONSTRUCTION

Historicism and deconstruction are two methods CRT adapted from CT and, ultimately, Marxism—an affiliation critics scrutinize. (Many of the criticisms have merit. Chief among them is that CRT, wittingly and unwittingly, inherited Marxism's functional atheism, which I will address later.) It bears repeating that CT and CRT are not wholly interchangeable; the former influenced the latter, so they share characteristics but are not synonymous. Though the link to Marxism is real, treating selective methodological *adaptations* as whole cloth worldview *adoption* is imprudent. Moreover, historicism and deconstruction are reasonable means of understanding a given society, and when used judiciously, they bear fruit.

Historicism

Historicism recognizes that our present is the direct result of our past. The alternative is *ahistoricism*, which disregards historical developments and history's role in causing the present. In my estimation, as it relates to the American ethnic rift, we are erroneously ahistorical. It is the reason Tisby's book provoked anger in the coffee shop. The book considers America's racialized history and consequences—events we'd rather forget.[26] In reality, we live in a moment that is the latest chapter in a long story, and all preceding chapters contributed to the present one. This is true of every moment. While many critical race theorists co-opted this idea from Marxism, it is not unique to Marxism! Frankly, it is a suitable and widely commended historical method sustained by both scholarship and common sense.[27]

Historicism is pertinent because examining present oppression should consider the series of events that culminated in the present. For the critical race theorist, any assessment of American institutions must ask, "Was historical racism systemic, and does it have ongoing consequences?" If oppressive circumstances endure despite competently organized attempts to change (e.g., the civil rights movement), it is rational to ask if racism is an institutionally sustained value.

In North America, the racial caste system dates to late seventeenth-century British colonialism. Even after America's eighteenth-century founding, the hierarchy was codified obliquely by the three-fifths clause and directly by the Fugitive Slave Act of 1793; both hinged on racialized slavery.[28] Moreover, tracking the nation's history through its founding constitution, federal laws, local laws, and supreme court decisions spotlights an unhidden theme of racialization. For the critical race theorist, history is consequential and needs analysis. It is almost impossible that the theme would have no consequences on today's society. The history requires examination.

Deconstruction

Critical examination of institutional history reveals racialized policies, language, and values. This brings us to *deconstruction*, which scrutinizes and reconsiders "traditional interpretations of terms, concepts, and practices, showing that they contain unsuspected meaning or internal contradictions."[29] For instance, America's touted language of equality boldly contradicts the institutions of slavery and segregation. Legal decisions like *Dred Scott v. Sandford* (1857) and *Plessy v. Ferguson* (1896) outright assume a racial caste system (the former declared Black people property with no rights; the latter declared Black people second-class citizens well into the twentieth century). If someone interprets history through the perspective of the touted language, they will assume America is an egalitarian nation. But if they read through the series of legal decisions, the contradiction between America's rhetoric and its laws is explicit. CRT, using deconstruction, spotlights the contradictions, underlines their inferred values, and considers the ongoing consequences of both.

Historical policies, not popular rhetoric, are indicative of national values. A society drifts toward its genuine values, even when they are outlawed. For instance, racist values openly determined legal policies before the Civil War. After the Civil War, despite three new constitutional amendments intended to reverse racial inequities, society acted according to embedded values. In the South, local and state administrators drafted policies to circumvent the Thirteenth, Fourteenth, and Fifteenth Amendments, which ostensibly abolished slavery, guaranteed citizenship, and affirmed voting rights (for Black men).[30] Still, the amendments had no bearing on practices when the populace decided to honor racialized values over legislation. For instance, the Fifteenth Amendment afforded Black men the right to vote, but it was utterly toothless. In his commentary on post-Civil War conditions, Derrick Bell notes:

> Southern government stripped blacks of political power. Given meaningful if unspoken assurance that the federal government would not protect black civil rights, conservative southerners regained power utilizing racial fear and hatred to break up competing populist groups of poor black and white farmers. In addition to the disenfranchisement of blacks, whites sought to secure their power through intensive anti-Negro propaganda campaigns championing white supremacy. . . . In this hostile climate, segregation laws that had made a brief appearance during Reconstruction were revived across the South, accompanied by waves of violence punctuated by an increase in lynchings and race riots.[31]

Critical race theorists analyzed (deconstructed) the institutions that would allow such circumstances to occur so consistently. They observed that, initially, the brokenness was overt—embodied by transatlantic and chattel slavery. After the Civil War, it was insidious—epitomized by Black Codes and Jim Crow laws. They concluded that the pervasive oppression could not be incidental; it had to be a national value that shaped corporate behavior and institutional policies.

The Frankfurt School first used CT to examine the pervasiveness of Nazi anti-Semitism; following suit, the mid-twentieth-century architects of CRT deployed CT's deconstruction to critique the American ethnic rift. CRT was not searching for racism but investigating objectively racist institutions. To do so, they read history with an eye fixed on racialized norms to consider their ongoing implications. Their approach recognizes the past as a historical narrative and examines (deconstructs) the narrative to discover national values.

EXAMPLES OF CRT METHODOLOGY IN ACTION

CRT considers the implications of poorly diagnosing the American ethnic divide. Civil rights leaders sought to work within the legal systems, believing they were indicative of America's genuine, though unrealized, values. This belief hinged on documents like the Declaration of Independence, which asserts that "all men are created equal and endowed with certain unalienable rights." Civil rights leaders, recognizing the disparity between the Declaration and reality, sought to close the gap. Critical race theorists argued that the discrepancy was deliberate, so expecting good fruit from a system that is inherently racist is futile. According to Delgado and Stefancic, "Unlike traditional civil rights discourse, which stresses incrementalism and step-by-step progress, critical race theory questions the very foundations of the liberal order, including equality theory, legal reasoning, Enlightenment rationalism, and neutral principles of constitutional law."[32] Progress toward racial equity is a battle of wills—a fight between racial progress and the institutional status quo. So as racist policies were overturned, they were replaced with new, equally effective policies that remarginalized Black people.[33]

BROWN V. BOARD OF EDUCATION

For the critical race theorist, innately broken systems are beyond simple repairs and immune to superficial changes, which explains why some civil rights accomplishments lacked the intended outcome. For instance, in 1954, the supreme court issued the *Brown v. Board of Education* decision. On paper, the decision should have been the end of "separate but equal," but it wasn't. A decade after the decision, public schools were *less* integrated.[34] In many districts, strategic fund reductions devastated public schools occupied by Black students after integration and the white student exodus. As a result, many public schools had to shutter their doors, remaining closed for years.

Brown v. Board and the consequent mass exodus of white families resulted in the mid-twentieth century's private school boom. While reducing the funding to public schools, some districts issued school vouchers to white students who enrolled in private schools to seek refuge from integration. Observing these consequences, Derrick Bell concludes that *Brown v. Board* was impotent. A legal decision can be "holy writ" but still go unheeded because it violates national values. When racial supremacy is a value, a law for the rights of Black people will only succumb to new policies that maintain white hegemony. To this point, Bell writes, "As had happened in the past, the law employing the vehicle of a major judicial decision offered symbolic encouragement to the black dispossessed. The substantive losses so feared by its white adversaries evolved almost unnoticed into advances greater for whites than for blacks."[35]

POST-RECONSTRUCTION AND JIM CROW ERA

Racialized practices were public. For instance, in the aftermath of the Civil War, the country entered the Reconstruction era. For the first time in the nation's history, it was an attempt at an egalitarian society that witnessed the election of Black politicians in Southern states. It lasted for approximately a dozen years. Historian Allen Guelzo asserts that Reconstruction was "overthrown" as it thrived.[36] The opportunity to kill Reconstruction occurred after the 1876 presidential election. The election's outcome was in dispute, so Rutherford B. Hayes made a dubious agreement with Congress that prompted them to settle the election in Hayes's favor. Hayes repaid the favor by removing Union soldiers from the South. Historian Paul Johnson calls the arrangement "legalized fraud."[37] The consequences were devastating; Union soldiers were responsible for, among other things, overseeing elections. In their absence, this responsibility fell to Confederate segregationists.[38]

One would think the Thirteenth, Fourteenth, and Fifteenth Amendments, all ratified during Reconstruction, would be adequate protection for Black citizens of the South. Ostensibly, the revised Constitution abolished slavery, secured Black citizenship, and ensured voting rights (for Black men). However, Southern states drafted new policies—loopholes that followed the letter of the law but upheld the value of white supremacy. They could not deny the right to vote based on race, but they had the freedom to create new racialized standards, which they did in plain sight.

For instance, the Grandfather Clause denied the right to vote to anyone whose grandfather could not vote.[39] While avoiding the straightforward language of racial discrimination, the Grandfather Clause made voting a matter of inherited legacy. The problem with this policy should be obvious; the grandparents of most late nineteenth-century Black people never had the right to vote because of denied citizenship and slavery. In a nutshell, Southern states used the legacy of Southern slavery to openly disenfranchise emancipated Black citizens as the federal government sat idle. They further bolstered Black disenfranchisement with poll taxes, literacy tests, and the requirement to own property. The Fifteenth Amendment was rendered moot.

Black people celebrated the Reconstruction amendments but could not reap the benefits because racial values resulted in state and local policies that superseded federal laws. W. E. B. Du Bois, commenting a half-century before CRT's codification, writes, "The slave went free; stood a brief moment in the sun; then moved back again toward slavery."[40] CRT examines such recurrent moments in history to discern institutional values and their consequences.

NUANCE AND COMPLEXITY

Critics tend to relish binary categories because simplicity makes critiquing easier. Unfortunately, the world hardly works that way. A movement can genuinely possess both good and bad qualities, and CRT is no different. Instead of manufacturing simplicity, it behooves us to recognize nuance and embrace the complexity, considering CRT's vices and virtues. Having done this, I cannot be a critical race theorist, but I openly affirm at least two of its central tenets with a clear conscience.

DETRACTORS

Detractors accuse CRT of categorizing all white people as hopelessly xenophobic and American history as wholly racist. I concede that this behavior is typical at the lay level, but, respectfully, laypeople are often poor representatives of a framework. For instance, I've met many (too many!) seminary graduates who cannot adequately discuss the Trinity. Their blunders are self-disqualifiers, but they have no bearing on the integrity of Christian doctrine.

Unfortunately, critics often cite popular definitions of CRT to characterize or, more accurately, mischaracterize it. They poorly represent the movement's methodological framework. By definition, CRT evaluates systems. It gives most attention to laws, policies, and institutions to determine their implications on racialized social norms, and any consideration of individuals is oblique. Treating CRT as a direct assessment of individuals is a distortion of the methodology and its domain.

ADVOCATES

Advocates can undermine CRT by improperly deploying it. It is a methodology designed to uncover systemic brokenness—namely, racism. Because of its characteristic historicism, CRT is a credible diagnostic tool, but it is not a means to redemption. By way of illustration, it may be necessary to demolish part of a building in preparation for remodeling. During that process, a sledgehammer may be the tool for the job. But once demolition is complete, qualified builders replace the sledgehammer with the proper instrument.

When used judiciously, CRT effectually deconstructs broken systems. Unfortunately, it does this so well that wielders are reluctant to replace it with rebuilding tools—an error exaggerated at the popular level. Overlooking CRT's specialization, lay theorists continue to use it as a wrecking ball, devastating even the redeemable parts of a system. This well-intended misappropriation of the theory leads to ongoing deconstruction and perpetually delays our divine imperative to restore. We tear down when necessary, but rebuilding is always the goal. CRT is a suitable means of analysis, but once that phase of the process is complete, theorists should seek institutional redemption.

THE GENETIC FALLACY

Those who point out the influence of Marxism and the Frankfurt School's critical theory on CRT are *not* wrong, and informed critical race theorists concede this. But in my estimation, citing Marxism and CT as disqualifying predecessors without carefully weighing the nature of their influence commits *the genetic fallacy*, which is the whole-cloth dismissal of information based solely on its origin. A potentially dubious beginning does not automatically falsify the final product.[41] For instance, atheistic scientists have made objectively true observations of the universe. Their flawed worldview does not blind them to common-sense observations. Racism is objective and discernable; Marxists and students of the Frankfurt School can observe it credibly.

Moreover, critics charge the Frankfurt School with *presupposing* systemic brokenness. As the accusation goes, CT is a method used to manufacture evidence to prove their unfounded assumptions, so they see oppression and dispossession where they do not exist. While I can appreciate how CT can be accused of institutional cynicism, I have never read an argument that capably accuses CRT of the same problem. CRT came about amidst Jim Crow segregation and disenfranchisement, after centuries of sanctioned racialized slavery and the "overthrow" of Reconstruction. Critical race theorists did not presuppose America's racialized injustice; they honestly observed it! At the time of CRT codification, legal segregation was an objective reality. It is irresponsible to shun critical race theorists without regard for their hermeneutic and historical context. Worse yet, it is intellectually irresponsible to conflate CT and CRT haphazardly, imposing the errors of one on the other.

A CRITIQUE

By and large, Christian critiques of CRT have resulted in whole-cloth dismissals. However, I maintain that this results from Christian nationalism, an unwholesome alignment between American evangelicalism and American institutions. Unexamined nationalism can obscure debased national values and their pervasive, ongoing implications. So the conclusions of critical race theorists are automatically offensive. I'm reminded of an assertion from my coffee shop interrogators, "CRT is an unholy attack on the godly history of a Christian nation." Looking to the past, they do not see repeated marginalization of subdominant groups ("minorities"). They are missing part of the historical story, and an incomplete understanding of American history results in a flawed interpretation of the American present. CRT excels at highlighting these overlooked events and, therefore, has the ire of Christian nationalists.

That said, I do not believe we can blindly embrace CRT. Instead, we must evaluate it through the lens of the Christian worldview. It has vices, and where it falls short, we must speak up. To do otherwise is unchristian and poor apologetics.

CRT VICES

I am troubled by some vital characteristics of CRT. Most of my struggles hinge on our fundamentally different worldviews. While some critical race theorists are theists, CRT's methodology is functionally atheistic. So CRT has a flawed perception of the temporal world, resulting in notable defects that are inconsistent with a Christian worldview. To spotlight a few:

1. Doctrines of Last Things and Sin

CRT does not consider the total restoration of creation, which will occur when Christ returns. Nearly all of my criticisms stem from this one point. While CRT excels in recognizing the historical experiences of marginalized peoples, its evaluations do not include the doctrine of final things (eschatology). CRT does not account for the Christian kingdom that, once consummated, will embody wholeness, including justice. The absence of this future hope distorts their temporal mission. For radical critical race theorists, the material world is all there is, so they seek the ideal from human-made institutions. They anticipate the impossible from fallen humanity—evidence that CRT also has an erroneous doctrine of sin (hamartiology).

These weaknesses explain some of their critiques of the hard-fought advancements of the civil rights movement. Christian civil righters were making incremental progress toward the promised eternal kingdom.[42] Critical race theorists are not wrong to strive and advocate for ethical ideals; Christians should share this imperative (Matt. 25:31–46). But CRT seeks an immediate utopia that is impossible in a fallen world. They have a romantic view of creation that continuously disappoints. So they are always in the act of deconstruction to the exclusion of incrementally rebuilding as we await the return of our just and holy king.

2. No Gospel and Poor Deployment

CRT has no gospel! The movement excels at spotlighting problems—a history of racist policies and institutions. And I maintain that the church is obligated to ponder, at least, the conclusions of critical race theorists. It can equip us to observe and confront besetting sin. I'd also maintain that many of CRT's historical observations are credible, and the church would do well to weigh them. But popular-level critical race theorists attempt to use CRT methodology toward a solution when it is equipped only as a diagnostic tool. Just as a doctor's stethoscope can discover a heart ailment but cannot heal it, CRT can spotlight systemic racism but has no treatment. It is in a perpetual state of diagnosing (deconstruction). Without a redeeming message and corresponding mission, CRT will perpetually demolish and never build. Among some leaders of CRT, there are efforts to develop strategies toward redemption. These efforts are relatively recent responses to critiques and are still in development. But as of this essay, I maintain that CRT has no full-orbed message that culminates in redemption.

CRT'S VIRTUES

Despite my inability to fully adopt CRT, it has my attention because of two strengths: its insistence on a comprehensive historical narrative and its handling of historical racism. To my mind, these strengths make CRT relevant to all discussions regarding race in America as long as we deploy them carefully.

1. The Historical Narrative

CRT has not changed the American story; it has only underlined woefully under-weighed parts. It spotlights uncomfortable moments from our past and examines how they shaped the present. Critical race theorists ask why slavery and segregation were institutional policies. Their questions are uncomfortable but merited—even obligatory! In pursuit of the truth, comfort should never be an inflexible prerequisite. Ignoring the complex parts of the story leads to historical myths and falsehoods. Dismissing CRT's methods and credible observations may occur at the expense of our integrity.

2. Institutional Racism

It is noteworthy that Christianity, which teaches original sin, would have spokespersons who deny the notion of systemic racism (Rom. 64:6; Rom. 8:7; Eph. 2:5). I maintain that institutional brokenness is all but a foregone conclusion. Sinful humanity is incapable of untarnished systems, which explains why American institutions and policies bear the patina of racialized sin. Fallen human beings tend to prefer homogeneity and marginalize those who are *other*. It is peculiar that platformed Christian leaders willingly concede these iniquities but soften them and deny their ongoing implications.

Critical race theorists recognize racism as a historically corporate offense. While we can identify individual transgressors, it bears mentioning that American racism was generally an institution upheld by national values and, more to the point, unsubtle laws. Unwittingly, CRT embodies the biblical notion of communal guilt and the need for corporate change (2 Chron. 7:11–22). They've inadvertently discovered the biblical idea of corporate sin. Instead of providing the gospel, the part of the story that CRT does not have, we've publicly spurned them. Any methodology that plausibly discovers corporate sin should receive a hearing. Disqualifying it out of hand is willful self-delusion.

RELEVANCE TO THE CHURCH

If we hope to be good apologists and missionaries, we must first be good historians. Whether we concede it or not, a racial rift plagues America. It is longstanding and has many contributing factors. Among them is conflict over the nation's racialized history. Because we must contextualize our gospel message, we should familiarize ourselves with our past and its ongoing implications. We do not have the privilege of crying ignorance.

Usually, the American narrative depicts the perspective of the white male aristocracy that founded the country. Their lauded opposition to oppressive England and the founding of the United States is essential to the story. But is it the whole story? The critical race theorist considers the American narrative from the perspective of those outside the aristocracy. For instance, Black and white people did not experience America's independence in the same way; they share a past but have different historical stories. While white America rejoiced in their newfangled freedom, Black people lived under the burden of sanctioned slavery. More to the point, their enslavers obliviously celebrated national liberty.

Upon being invited to speak at an 1852 celebration of American independence, Frederick Douglass observed the boldfaced irony of asking an escapee from slavery to celebrate national liberty. He delivered a speech entitled, "What to the Slave Is the Fourth of July?" Among many uncompromising remarks, he said:

> What, to the American slave, is your Fourth of July? . . . To him, your celebration is a sham; your boasted liberty, an unholy license; your national greatness, swelling vanity; your sounds of rejoicing are empty and heartless; your denunciations of tyrants, brass fronted impudence; your shouts of liberty and equality, hollow mockery; your prayers and hymns, your sermons and thanksgivings, with all your religious parade, and solemnity, are, to him, mere bombast, fraud, deception, impiety, and hypocrisy—a thin veil to cover up crimes which would disgrace a nation of savages.[43]

Douglass delivered these words nearly a century before CRT codifiers were born, but astute readers will observe that he shared their hermeneutic and concerns. Douglass lamented the reality that obliviousness to the experiences and history of Black people makes his appeals for social justice unduly hard. His concern was legitimate, and it persists to this day.

SOCIAL ETHICS

As the embassy of the heavenly kingdom, the church is the organization ordained to embody kingdom ethics. We are ambassadors of the eternal kingdom (2 Cor. 5:20), which is the epitome of justice. To sit idle amid injustice is an abdication of our divine calling. A reasonable and thorough interpretation of history is relevant to the church because it clarifies social ethics and mission. If history reveals systemic oppression, then the church is compelled to confront any ongoing sinful fruits.

Instead of leaning into our calling, the American church has taken sides in the debate. By and large, American evangelicalism concedes, somewhat unenthusiastically, our racist history but not its ongoing implications. The denial negatively affects our ethics and missions. For example, many American Christians feel little compulsion to take a gospel stand against racial injustice, deeming it beyond the pale of our Christian mission. The world is watching, and our Christian integrity is under scrutiny. So I would argue that mission and social ethics, especially regarding racial injustice, are *the* most significant apologetics issues of our day. It is simply negligent to ignore or deny the defensible observations of critical race theorists. If they are correct, we have a divine task ahead of us, and complacency is ungodly.

CONCLUSION AND SUMMARY

Before ending our "emergency get-together," I was sure to provide my coffee shop interrogators a chance to clarify their concerns. They summed, "CRT has corrupted you. You are digging up forgotten things and fighting long-dead battles." In their estimation, CRT breathes life into past events that have no bearing on our present. Here's what they missed: I was not functioning under the influence of CRT. My observations of the racial rift result from my hermeneutic and historical method, which predate my introduction to CRT. Critical race theorists and I arrived at the same conclusions because we observed the same history. Systemic and pervasive racism have plagued us since the nation's inception, and we exist in its ongoing implications. Willful blindness to this reality will never remedy the American ethnic rift.

They also miss my unwavering commitment to the gospel. I've observed some of the same institutional frailties as CRT, but I have a comprehensive message that confronts all brokenness. In Christ, I am equipped to rebuild and redeem. Instead of joining me, they argued for apathy. I cannot honor their request; God's commissioning carries too much weight (Matt. 28:16–20).

Good apologists recognize the need to expose themselves to historical narratives that accurately clarify the story of our mission field. Without a comprehensive historical story, we will fall woefully off mission. Some CRT tenets help to discern the narrative; carefully incorporating them will benefit believers seeking understanding. But adapting CRT methodology requires due diligence as we navigate its unchristian vices. If we neglect this responsibility, we surrender the divine imperative to think well (2 Cor. 10:5).

The American racial rift desperately needs authoritative confrontation that can come only from the church. But because we are willfully blind to the circumstances, we sit voluntarily idle. Meanwhile, CRT, which credibly notices systemically racist conditions, has no gospel to brandish. Critical race theorists have settled for perpetually swinging the sledgehammer of deconstruction. What would happen if the church recognized the valid observations of CRT and fittingly wielded the gospel? Imagine the witness it would be and the lives it would change both temporally and eternally. We have a message that equips us to confront sin, but because it was critical race theorists who spotlighted the offense, we've holstered the gospel and cried ignorance. May God have mercy on our hubris and complacency.

SURVIVING AND THRIVING IN A MULTIETHNIC CONTEXT

CRAWFORD LORITTS

For more than fifty years I have had the unspeakable privilege of serving in full-time vocational ministry. It has been the joy of my life to both pursue and experience God's call, plan, and work in and through me. Yes, there have been seasons of suffering, disappointment, and discouragement along the way. But Jesus has met me and carried me during these times. Looking back, I realize that his calling for my life has not just been the primary way in which he wants to work through me but a primary way in which he wants to sanctify me so that I look more like him. On my way to doing something, I must become something.

Through the years God has given me various assignments, but the core calling and context has been remarkably consistent. God called me to preach and teach his Word, and the context has been in ethnically diverse environments. And I want to say a few words about the context of my calling.

CONTEXT

Before I was a follower of Christ, God began to shape the trajectory of my life and future ministry. My parents were from North Carolina and, as part of what has been called the Great Migration, in 1942 they left the South and moved to the central ward of Newark, NJ. I have two older sisters, and our family lived in a multiethnic working-class community. We lived, played, and went to school in this environment. Our friends were Black, Hispanic, Italian, Greek, and various other ethnicities. This would be an anchor influence in my life.

But there were two other powerful, identity-shaping influences in my life. First, our family. Our parents made sure that my sisters and I understood, appreciated, and valued the price that those who came before us paid. We heard the stories about my great-grandfather Peter, the former slave. We heard firsthand some pretty amazing stories about the accomplishments of my uncles and aunts in the face of violent, vicious racism. Our parents were not perfect, but largely because of their commitment to Christ, they were not bitter. They were open, loving people. I would like to think that this, too, shaped us.

Secondly, there was our church. Back then virtually everything about my world was ethnically diverse except our family and our church. We faithfully attended Trinity AME Church every Sunday. It was a block from our apartment building. Although I couldn't put words to it then, looking back, there was this profound sense of affirmation and belonging whenever we gathered together for worship. There was a sweet life-giving fellowship that was grounded in the gospel, our common history, and the current reality of our struggle. I remember the smiles, hugs, and celebration that was a part of our church experience. The message was that we mattered to each other and we mattered to God. We had dignity. Worth. Value.

Monday through Saturday my world was diverse. I am a member of a Black family and a Black church, and I am very proud of my heritage. But for whatever reason, I never felt conflicted or that I had to choose between either loving my people—which I do—or loving my white friends. God gave me a gift in those formative years. I experienced loving friendships and relationships in both "worlds." This would prove to be huge in the years ahead.

At age thirteen I surrendered my life to Christ. My teen years coincided with the height of the civil rights movement. I was a young follower of Christ with a desire to know and understand God's Word, my place in this historic moment, and how all of this "fit" within the context of my background—a foundation God had sovereignly laid. It was and, in some respects, still is a journey.

But as I read the Scriptures, I was captured by the compelling vision of the apostle Paul in Ephesians 2. He describes the church as one body, one people, having been reconciled first to God and then to one another through the death of Christ on the cross. This took me on a journey through the New Testament in which I further discovered that his church is to be the visible demonstration before a watching world of the power of the gospel to produce authentic, supernatural unity. This points to more than just a universal, spiritual unity. The fact that there is not a church in the New Testament that is not visibly multiethnic strongly indicates that whenever possible this should be our reality, our norm, as well. I was gripped and I guess even branded by the vision.

MULTIETHNICITY AND THE CHURCH

I am not suggesting that every church needs to be multiethnic. However, I am saying that every church should reflect the demographic makeup of its community. And when that happens, it demonstrates the deep, rich integrity and power of the gospel. That being said, I am not suggesting that the context of my calling is what everybody else should do.

But if you are Black and serving in these contexts, it is important that you do not succumb to either of the following two pressures: The first is white idolization. This is the damaging notion that your presence in these contexts is to underscore, affirm, and validate the "rightness" of white leadership and, thus, devalue the gifts, talents, and experiences God has given to you and wants you to use to advance the mission and bring gospel value to where he has placed you. This is a strong statement, but we insult and dishonor God by devaluing who we are and what he has placed in us to advance his cause. Keep in mind that we cannot impact that which we worship. It will inevitably change us and not for the good. You have a seat at the table because God put your chair there. Take your seat, and act like you belong at the table.

The second temptation is to be dominated by the need to prove our ethnic authenticity. Let's face it, no one wants to be seen as abandoning our people, betraying the pain and suffering of the people whose shoulders we stand on or ignoring or minimizing the racism and injustice we still experience. It still stings to be called an "Uncle Tom." And when those words or similar comments are made, we are driven to prove just how Black we are.

I have been accused of either not being "Black enough" or not being authentically Black because I served on the staff of a predominately white organization and served as the senior pastor of a multiethnic church. When I was younger, I would bristle at these comments and become defensive. I then felt compelled, even forced, to prove that I am just as Black as those making the accusation. But somewhere along the line, it dawned on me that my defensiveness didn't make sense. I allowed myself to be drawn into something that drew me away from what God called me to do.

Don't misunderstand. I am a follower of Christ, and I am proud to be Black. And it is right to be called to task if I or any other Black leader, no matter what context we serve in, ignores or denies the reality of racism and injustice. Further, there is a stewardship responsibility to use whatever influence God has given us to open doors for others. But my primary focus must be on obeying and fulfilling what God called me to be and to do. In the end, seeking to prove how Black I am as a core motivation is a self-defeating distraction. It is nice to get the validation and approval of others. But it is wrong to be "guilted" away from where God placed you.

As I write these words, I am seventy-two years old, and I realize that I have more road behind me than I do in front of me. But my heart is filled with praise to our great God for His goodness. Yes, in recent years I have been profoundly disappointed in some of my white evangelical siblings who have, in my view, attached barnacles to the gospel and acted in such a way that makes identifying as an "evangelical" unappealing. But what encourages me most is this rising generation of Black Christian leaders like Eric Mason, my sons, and so many others who are deeply committed to Christ, the gospel, and the expansion of his kingdom. They represent different callings and different emphases but a balance and mutual support that is refreshing. I shed tears of joy and gratitude when I hear their vision, listen to them preach, or read their books. Father, keep your hand on them and multiply your impact and influence through them far beyond anything they could ever dream or imagine (Eph. 3:20–21).

THREE

EVANGELICALISM AND WHITE CHRISTIAN NATIONALISM

THABITI ANYABWILE

Most Americans have images of the January 6th insurrection emblazoned on their memories. Pictures of men dangling from and climbing up the walls of the US Capitol Building. Shouting crowds gleefully bursting through doors and windows. A handful of Capitol Police in riot gear being trampled. And in their midst, several crosses standing high. Placards declaring "Jesus saves." Declarations that their actions were God's will. This strange conglomeration of images, feelings, and rhetoric crystalized in a single moment the growing threat of white Christian nationalism (WCN) to the American democratic experiment.

But to understand WCN, we must understand its parasitical relationship to American evangelicalism. White Christian nationalism thrives in the sacred spaces, rhetoric, and symbols of evangelicalism, where it siphons much of its religious fervor and legitimacy. In some instances WCN has transformed American evangelicalism itself into a cult of race, power, and politics. This essay traces the historic relationship between white evangelicalism and the cult of WCN. In doing so, I hope to reflect on both the weaknesses and choices that make WCN possible as well as whether evangelicalism can be a nurturing community for Black Christians.

WHAT IS EVANGELICALISM?

The term "evangelical" or "evangelicalism" is originally derived from the koine Greek word translated "gospel" in our English Bibles (see Rom. 1:16, for example). At the most basic and biblical level, evangelical religion is gospel religion. It is religion that focuses on the good news of salvation in the person and work of Jesus Christ.

In the English Middle Ages, "evangelical" was used to describe the message of salvation and to refer to the four Gospels. During the sixteenth century's Protestant Reformation, "evangelical" became a way to contrast Roman Catholic and Protestant views of salvation. The term could be used both as an insult by Roman Catholics and as a mark of authenticity by Protestants. In time the word "evangelical" became a synonym for "Protestant."

As a synonym for "Protestant," the term "evangelical" stood for several theological convictions, including justification by faith, the sole sufficiency of Christ for salvation, the once-for-all sacrifice of Christ on the cross, the final authority of the Bible, and the priesthood of all believers. Today, David Bebbington's quadrilateral[1] is often used as a simple way to define the theological emphasis of evangelicals. According to Bebbington, evangelicals focus on the necessity of conversion (conversionism), the authority of the Bible (biblicism), the centrality of the cross of Christ (crucicentrism), and the necessity of good works (activism).

AN EVANGELICAL ORIGIN STORY

But to understand evangelicalism today we must look beyond the label, and so it's important to understand where American evangelicalism *as a movement* originates.[2] That origin story helps us recognize why evangelicalism can so easily be bastardized into white Christian nationalism—and why it's often problematic even when it's not bastardized.

Here, I want to focus on what we might call the "classical period" of evangelical development. I distinguish this period from what some might call the "modern" or "neo-evangelical period" beginning in the 1950s under the leadership of Billy Graham, Harold John Ockenga, Fuller Theological Seminary, and Carl F. H. Henry, breaking off from American fundamentalism. We're going back further, to the founding, classical period, because that's where the problems begin.

English Puritanism

Four streams flow into the ocean of evangelism. The first is English Puritanism.

Puritanism was a movement of dissent from the established churches of Europe. The Puritans sought church reform and revival from the 1550s to 1660s (and a little longer in America if you count Jonathan Edwards as an American Puritan). The Puritans wanted to rid the established Protestant churches of any traces of remaining Roman Catholic faith and practice. They emphasized preaching for conversion, search for personal godliness, and the layperson's study of the Bible. They wrote extensively on the nature of the Christian life with the goal of personal growth in holiness.

Theologian and Puritan scholar J. I. Packer (1926–2020) describes Puritanism as a holiness movement in ecclesiastical form. According to Packer:

> Their dream was holiness in their own lives and in the lives of those around them. The Puritans didn't talk about the "state"; they simply talked about conducting all of life in a way that honored God and respected other people. That was their idea of community. The perfect church was a church containing families that practiced holiness and worshipped with a purged liturgy under the leadership of a minister who was a powerful preacher of the Bible.[3]

Packer's description captures the Puritan *spiritual* ideal. However, Dr. Packer's statement misses the fact that while Puritans may not have *spoken* often about the "state," they nevertheless *interacted* a great deal with the state, including the founding of state colonies when Puritanism made its way to the New World in the early 1600s. Those Puritan-founded colonies eventually became a part of the United States of America.

If Packer's summation is accurate, then it suggests that one contribution to the formation of American evangelicalism is a Puritanism that habitually overlooks or discounts its state activities with subjective religious language. In other words, both Puritanism and American evangelicalism are religious movements that *talk* piety but *practice* politics. The consequence of this is an American evangelicalism that began and continues its life without sufficient theological resources to justify its political practices. As we will see, this has left American evangelicalism especially vulnerable to a white Christian nationalism that wants to control the church's political vision and life.

European Pietism

A second river flowing into the lake of American evangelicalism is European Pietism. Pietism begins in 1675 with the publication of *Pia Desideria* by Philipp Jakob Spener. Spener and others were concerned about religious formalism and nominalism in Germany. They thought the church had lost its vital power and significance. In *Pia Desideria*, Spener proposed six corrections for combatting religious formalism and nominalism in Germany:

1. Return to the Scriptures.
2. Laypeople must become active in the life of the church.
3. Move beyond correct beliefs to active godliness.
4. Stop arguing and start loving all unbelievers and heretics.
5. Ministry and ministers must be truly converted.
6. Students training for ministry must be well versed in the practices of godliness.

Like the Puritans before them, the Continental Pietists from Lutheran Germany influenced later evangelicalism through their emphasis on "true religion," organized philanthropy, conversion, and assurance of salvation. The Pietists provided later evangelicals a way of talking about the spiritual condition of churches as either nominal, formal, heady, and control-conscious on the one hand *or*, on the other hand, as true Christianity engaging heart and mind, motivated by love to action.

The German Pietists produced the first wave of Protestant missions and helped stimulate the evangelical revivals and awakenings in the 1700s and 1800s. From the Pietists we get Zinzendorf (1700–1760), Selina Hastings, Countess of Huntingdon, and the rise of the Moravians or Brethren—all of whom were vital to the spread of evangelicalism on both sides of the Atlantic.

Primitivism

English primitivism was a third stream with formative influence on what would become American evangelicalism. The High Church Anglicans of the late 1600s stressed "primitive Christianity," which they thought of as the pure faith practiced in the first century. High Church Anglicans emphasized imitating the faith and life of early believers, asceticism, discipline for society, and regular observance of the Eucharist. Samuel and Susannah Wesley were both diligently committed to this primitivism. They catechized their children (John and Charles Wesley), insisted on personal morality, and frequently celebrated communion. From these Anglicans came organizations like the Society for the Propagation of the Gospel in Foreign Parts (SPG) and the Society for the Propagation of Christian Knowledge (SPCK). The Anglicans established the pattern for later evangelical development of parachurch groups and volunteerism, and they laid the groundwork for later evangelical interest in reforming society as a whole.

The Anglicans of the 1600s saw significant overlap between the church and state. Membership in one equaled membership in the other. Later, American Christians and secular politicians would formulate and clarify the separation of church and state. While they saw such a separation as essential for both the health of the church and the state, early American Christians did not abandon their desire to reform society according to their principles, a desire they inherited in part from their English Anglican forefathers. As much as American evangelicals concerned themselves with the spread of the gospel, they also concerned themselves with the question of shaping civic and social life.

Privilege

When we reflect on the origins of American evangelicalism, we must also note how evangelicalism sought and often achieved a cozy relationship with aristocrats. This is the fourth stream flowing into evangelical development.

The rich and influential of society became the financial patrons of the early movement. This benefactor relationship with power influenced early evangelicals' engagement with questions of institution and authority. In many instances, evangelical dependence on wealthy patrons guaranteed the movement would normally look favorably on and stand in solidarity with those in power. That was true during the Puritan era in its battle to control who was king or queen in England and Scotland. It was true during the persecution of Pietists in continental Europe. And it was no less true as early American evangelicals began the work of developing a new nation.

Whitefield and Wesley both received financial and church-building support from Selina Hastings, Countess of Huntingdon. The much-celebrated William Wilberforce was himself an aristocrat who did not question the class privileges and status he enjoyed, nor the poverty and deprivation "commoners" suffered. In the New World, Jonathan Edwards was socially an Old-World slaveholding aristocrat who held the same sense of entitlement and privilege for his social and ministerial class.[4]

THE UPSHOT

Classic evangelicalism, at its founding, was primarily concerned with the *heart* or *inner man*, not with the body and social concerns. It is true that early evangelicals founded philanthropic organizations and were involved in the transformation of society. However, those organizations were founded *mainly* as vehicles for gospel advancement—*not out of theological and ethical reflection on the biblical requirements of justice.*

In other words, evangelical philanthropy was instrumental but *not* essential. Evangelicalism was primarily a "heart religion"—not a "body and soul religion." As historian Mark Noll puts it:

> Evangelicalism in its origin was *overwhelmingly a movement of spiritual renewal.* The first evangelicals concerned themselves with social, political, institutional or intellectual arrangements *only as these matters seemed to promote or threaten personal faith.* . . . Evangelicalism was a pietistic movement in which the relationship of the self to God eclipsed all other concerns.[5]

The upshot of this emphasis on inward renewal left American evangelicals without sufficient resources to frame a robustly biblical vision for social, political, and institutional engagement. In much of its preaching and writing, American evangelicals relegated social and political matters to a distant second or third place when compared to the priority of gospel mission. Yet despite the priority of the gospel, the movement never ceased being politically concerned and engaged. It simply did so without a coherent ethical system or well-developed political theology.

With regard to institutional power, early evangelicals largely sought to control the institutions around them. They wanted to be kingmakers, and the movement benefitted and grew through its association with power and privilege. Today, this desire to wield public power remains. We see it expressed in evangelicalism's love affair with presidential politics, including calls to vote for and defend Donald Trump, a move many onlookers recognized as a significant betrayal and departure from evangelical convictions about the character of politicians. Absent sound public theology, power-seeking efforts make evangelicalism susceptible to the worst cultic impulses, resulting in developments like white Christian nationalism.

IN WHAT WAY IS CHRISTIAN NATIONALISM "WHITE"?

In the previous section, we considered the origins of evangelicalism. Knowing the origin story of American evangelicalism helps us reflect on the "Christian" in white Christian nationalism. It also helps us to identify which weaknesses in evangelicalism the cult of WCN can attach itself to. But what about the "white" in WCN? How are we to understand "whiteness" and the ways it contributes to the "cultification" of evangelicalism? To answer those questions, we will consider the construction of race and whiteness in the American context.

THE MAKING OF RACE AND THE LEGALIZATION OF INJUSTICE

Rebecca Anne Goetz in *The Baptism of Early Virginia* sketches the historical development of race and whiteness among early English Anglicans in Virginia. Goetz coins the term "hereditary heathenism" as a way of describing how European settlers and colonizers thought of indigenous and African persons. Goetz writes:

> Over the course of the long seventeenth century, Anglo-Virginians transformed their meanings [Negro, Christian, Englishman, heathen, infidel]. Not only did they effectively reimagine what it meant to be Christian but *they also invented an entirely new concept—what it meant to be "white."* In courtrooms and legislative chambers, in their homes and in their public spaces, and while at war with themselves and with Indians, Anglo-Virginians *redefined the meanings of these words and created new racial categories.* They increasingly *connected physical differences such as skin color with a budding idea of hereditary heathenism—the notion that Indians and Africans could never become Christian.* As they began to think of Indians and Africans not as potential Christians but as people incapable of Christian conversion, Anglo-Virginians *laid the foundations for an emergent idea of race and an ideology of racism.*[6]

"Hereditary heathenism" is Goetz's shorthand for the ways Europeans simultaneously regarded indigenous and African peoples as "uncivilized" and attributed that condition to their heredity as indigenous and African people. To be "civilized" meant being white and Christian. Goetz continues: "In deciding that Indians and Africans could not truly become Christian and that their heathenism was hereditary, Anglo-Virginians *asserted a new definition of human difference that was written both on the body and in the soul.*"[7]

Thus began the construction of race and whiteness in the New World. A new social, biological, religious, and political category (i.e., whiteness) was formed and a new ideology sprang from it (i.e., white supremacy). In both the church and the government, to be white meant being civilized and Christian and therefore entitled to rule over others.

Famed sociologist W. E. B. Du Bois reflected deeply on the construct of whiteness in much of his work. Perhaps his most seminal writing on this was his 1935 book *Dark Waters*. Many have found Du Bois's definition of "whiteness" as a "public and psychological wage" helpful in understanding the racial caste of America. But as Ella Myers points out, Du Bois's conception of whiteness goes well beyond just the wage concept. Myers understands Du Bois to also frame whiteness as *dominion*, a "title to the universe." In this conception, rooted in the chattel principle of slavery and expressed in violent Jim Crow and colonialism's dispossession of land from darker peoples, whiteness is a "pervasive, taken-for-granted perspective" that the world and its darker peoples *belong* to white people as a property. In addition to American chattel slavery, Du Bois saw this principle at work in "the scramble for Africa," the subjugation of India, and the exploitation of China and Japan. In Du Bois's view, whiteness-as-dominion is lived as a comprehensive worldview or "religion" that marks the "darker world" as property—both land and people—to be owned, used, and disposed of by white people.[8] Du Bois, of course, is reflecting on more than three hundred years of American history at that point—a history in part shaped and "theologized" into existence by white evangelical Christians.[9]

It's important to recognize that racism and white supremacy were not external, distorting factors affecting the growth and development of American evangelicalism. Rather, American evangelicalism itself was *giving birth to* whiteness, race, racism, and white supremacy. The religious movement was the parent not the child in this relationship. American Christians—and in this case Anglicans in Virginia—invented whiteness as a protected privileged class with religious sanction, political power, and an unquestioned sense of entitlement to own peoples and lands. Over the following centuries, American evangelicalism as a movement questioned these views at times, but also furthered their development. Whiteness and white supremacy became the de facto ideological orientation of the New World and the American evangelical church for much of its four-hundred-year history.

THE EVANGELICAL STALWARTS OF RACIAL EXPLOITATION

The construct of whiteness and race could not have survived without the sanction and preaching of evangelical clergy. Had preachers *en masse* condemned racial heresy and fought for the full equality of indigenous and African people, these views would have been less likely to become mainstream. But as it was, many of the leading evangelical pastors and theologians of the day put the concept of whiteness to work on behalf of their personal and professional projects.

We see this ideological whiteness at work in the lives of early evangelical champions like George Whitefield (1714–1770). A leader of the First Great Awakening, Whitefield traveled several times across the colonies preaching the necessity of new birth, including preaching to enslaved Africans. But historian Mark Noll observes:

> During 1740, [Whitefield] criticized Southern slave owners for mistreating slaves and took special pains on several occasions to preach to slaves. But he also decided on the spur of the moment that, since Europeans were unable or unwilling to work the land supporting his orphanage, it would be 'impracticable' to survive in Georgia without purchasing 'a few Negroes' as slaves. Whitefield, who preached so willingly to slaves, *hardly gave a thought when he became a slaveowner himself.*[10]

When his interest in human property changed, so also did Whitefield's preaching against slavery. Whiteness offered him a social and economic platform to justify owning and exploiting his African neighbor for "humanitarian" purposes.

Jonathan Edwards, an early American pastor and theologian, also owned slaves. Though he wrote volumes on nearly every subject, Edwards left comparatively little written evidence of his views on slavery. What evidence we do have comes from Edwards's defense of a fellow clergyman who was about to be fired by his congregation for owning slaves. Edwards enjoyed the privileges of an Old-World aristocrat while living in the New World, and he was repulsed by the notion that laypeople would dare fire a clergyman. This was a greater concern than what he knew to be the wickedness and unrighteousness of the transatlantic slave trade. He could turn a blind eye to slavery while shouting "touch not the Lord's anointed" when a fellow pastor was about to be fired over it. To make matters worse, the pastor he defended was a theological opponent of Edwards and the revivals. Whiteness took sides with other white people and their "property" interests instead of taking sides with the truth, with justice, and with the oppressed.

Samuel Davies (1723–1761) provides another example of racism and whiteness taking precedence over truth and justice. "Davies was not a social radical, and in fact like Whitefield became a slaveowner himself. But he was also a determined advocate of literacy among blacks, and he had no qualms about admitting converted slaves to full church membership."[11] So an enslaved African could be a full member of Davies's church and would be taught to read and write, but could not have his Black body go free with Davies's support and advocacy. Davies "was not a social radical" because Davies benefitted from the social structure. In other words, his understanding of whiteness kept him from seeking the full liberation of the enslaved.

Whitefield, Edwards, and Davies were mainstream leaders, not outliers. They were not exceptions to the norm. They were the norm. They characterized the everyday views of American evangelicals. Historian Mark Noll summarizes this period of American evangelicalism with a string of revealing observations:

- In America, evangelical anti-slavery *failed because there were so many slaveholders and so many of them were evangelicals.*[12]
- The limitations of evangelicalism appeared most clearly *in challenges requiring either systematic and comprehensive analysis or cooperative and coercive actions.*[13]
- Changing the world was never as important for the early evangelicals as changing the self or as fashioning spiritual communities in which changed selves could grow in grace.[14]

- *They could turn so obsessively inward as to ignore the structures of social evil.* Most important, evangelicals *could trivialize the Christian gospel by treating it as a ballyhooed commodity to be hawked for its power to soothe a nervous, dislocated people* in the opening cultural markets of the expanding British empire.[15]

One of the long-developed habits of white evangelicalism has been to "care" for the souls of Black people but to abuse, exploit, and destroy the bodies of Black people. The most charitable interpretation would be to say that American evangelicalism has suffered from racial blindness, not seeing the hypocrisy and compromise that has gone on for so long. But such charity seems unwarranted in the face of so much historical evidence that evangelicalism's *best luminaries* knew full well of the injustice but decided to profit from it anyway.[16]

Whiteness, when understood as a form of property or public compensation, allowed them to commit these compromises without risk.[17] To be white was to enjoy the status of being "not-Black." Being white also involved actively devaluing Blackness while elevating things "not-Black." Whiteness conveyed not only monetary but also psychological and social benefits to those who claimed it—benefits that were to not only be enjoyed but protected. It functioned like a religion or worldview wherein white people were entitled to own the bodies, labor, and lands of people of color. This religion of whiteness made the evangelical movement vulnerable to cultic forms (like today's WCN), which would begin to frame America as a Christian nation, seeing it as a nation under assault by a host of nonwhite "others" who had no claim to it.

WHAT IS WHITE CHRISTIAN NATIONALISM?

To this point, we've seen that white Christian nationalism has clear roots in historic, mainstream American evangelicalism. From its founding, the evangelical movement emphasized the interior spiritual life over the social and physical life, sought a comfortable relationship with wealth and power over any identification with the poor and marginalized, and participated in the creation of whiteness as a new racial category, viewing nonwhites as property to be used for racial advantage. Each of these assumptions left room not only for error but provided fertile soil for cults to grow. White Christian nationalism is one such cult.

It is difficult for many white Christians to identify white Christian nationalism as a cult. Several factors create this difficulty, from the confusion of nationalism with patriotism, to the conflation of Christian ethics with Republican politics, to the association of white cultural norms with a "biblical" or "Christian" worldview.

But perhaps the greatest difficulty many white evangelical Christians have comes from white Christian nationalism's ubiquity. As one recent book on the subject remarks:

> White Christian nationalism is one of the oldest and most powerful currents in American politics. But until the insurrection, it was invisible to most Americans. It was invisible to most conservative white Christians, *because for decades it has been the water they swim in and the air they breathe.* It was invisible to most secular progressives, because they live in a bubble of their own in which white Christian nationalism seems "fringe" rather than mainstream.[18]

The ubiquitous yet largely undetected presence of WCN raises some terribly important questions for us to consider. How can we distinguish WCN from the orthodox Christian faith? And if WCN is "the water they swim in and the air they breathe," can evangelicalism be rescued from it? As we look to answer these questions, we will begin with a clear definition of WCN.

DEFINING WHITE CHRISTIAN NATIONALISM

Sociologists Philip S. Gorski, Samuel L. Perry, and Andrew L. Whitehead are leading researchers on Christian nationalism and white Christian nationalism in particular. In *Taking America Back for God*, Whitehead and Perry define WCN as "a cultural framework—a collection of myths, traditions, symbols, narratives, and value systems—that idealizes and advocates a fusion of Christianity with American civic life." The authors are careful to distinguish historic orthodox expressions of Christianity from the "Christianity" of white Christian nationalism. They continue, "The 'Christianity' of Christian nationalism represents something more than religion. As we will show, it includes assumptions of nativism, white supremacy, patriarchy, and heteronormativity, along with divine sanction for authoritarian control and militarism. It is as ethnic and political as it is religious."[19] This characterization, unsurprisingly, shares much in common with Du Bois's whiteness-as-dominion and Frederick Douglass's distinguishing of "slaveholding Christianity" from the "religion of Jesus."

At the risk of being overly simplistic, we can define Christian nationalism as the story white Americans (both Christian and not Christian) tell themselves about the founding of America, American identity, and the political future as it *should* be. This "racial imaginary"[20] predicts a range of attitudes and behaviors for those holding them. The amalgamation of these narratives and values is something other than Christian in the historic sense and debatably American. It is essentially a religious *cult* that assigns its own meanings and eschatology to American life while co-opting the language, symbols, and tropes of evangelical Christianity.

In another book on the subject, Philip Gorski and Samuel Perry write:

> White Christian nationalism is our term for the ethno-traditionalism among many white Americans that conflates racial, religious, and national identity (the deep story) and pines for cultural and political power that demographic and cultural shifts have increasingly threatened (the vision). . . . The term "Christian" in white Christian nationalism is often far more akin to a dog whistle that calls out to an aggrieved tribe than a description of the content of one's faith.[21]

In this sense, WCN is a myth, a "deep story" that provides a "white power" vision for white people. "White Christian nationalism idealizes the power of white Christian Americans. It is rooted in white supremacist assumptions and empowered by anger and fear."[22] It is a picture of khaki-clad, tiki-torch carrying white men marching in support of Confederate monuments shouting, "You will not replace us!" It is both a story about white America's past and a longing for its future. It makes cherished assumptions about what it was and is to be an American and a Christian by blending and idealizing American and Christian identities for white Americans. Gorski and Perry explain at greater length:

> White Christian nationalism's "deep story" goes something like this: America was founded as a Christian nation by (white) men who were "traditional" Christians, who based the nation's founding documents on "Christian principles." The United States is blessed by God, which is why

it has been so successful; and the nation has a special role to play in God's plan for humanity. But these blessings are threatened by cultural degradation from "un-American" influences both inside and outside our borders.

Like any story, this one has its heroes: white conservative Christians, usually native-born men. It also has its villains: racial, religious, and cultural outsiders. The plot revolves around conflicts between the noble and worthy "us," the rightful heirs of wealth and power, and the undeserving "them" who conspire to take what is ours. Sometimes, the conflicts culminate in violence—violence that restores white Christians to what they believe is their rightful place atop America's racial and religious hierarchy. The heroes are those who defend the purity—and property—of the white Christian nation: with violence, when necessary.[23]

Again, this "deep story" is a *myth*. At most every point, the story fails the tests of facts and history. But it draws upon selected Christian stories and phrases for a patina of legitimacy. And like many mythic stories, there are clear ways in which this story speaks to the realities of life. WCN's myth impacts American popular culture, fuels the political imagination, leads to contentious debates about the good life, and seeks to redefine cherished American ideals like freedom and order. It does all of this with the religious sanction of Christian symbols, teaching, and participation—to disastrous effect.

The urgent task facing us today is to recognize WCN as an aberration and distortion of biblical Christianity. Simultaneously, however, we must acknowledge that WCN springs from the chosen weaknesses and compromises of American evangelicalism in place since its founding. It is an oddly familiar cult to many (especially white American Christians), yet it should also be a shockingly foreign distortion for all true Christians. The final question we need to ask is this: Can white Christian nationalism be separated from evangelical faith and practice?

CAN AFRICAN-AMERICANS ENJOY A HEALTHY PARTICIPATION IN EVANGELICALISM?

Christian historian Dr. Thomas Kidd begins his book *Who Is an Evangelical?* by writing, "This book seeks to show how historically peculiar a partisan and ethnic definition of evangelicals is."[24] Dr. Kidd sets for himself the task of distinguishing historical, orthodox evangelicalism from its "partisan and ethnic" knock-off. Though he does not mention "white Christian nationalism," his choice of "partisan and ethnic" overlaps considerably with the way I am using this term.

Dr. Kidd understands that the American evangelical project is currently in a crisis driven by four overlapping factors:

1. Confusion about the term evangelical itself;
2. An impression that "evangelical" may just mean white Republicans who consider themselves religious;
3. A sense that political power may be the essential evangelical agenda; and,
4. The inability of evangelicals of different ethnicities, especially whites and blacks, to agree on basic political questions.[25]

I appreciate Dr. Kidd's attempt at clarifying historic evangelicalism from "partisan and ethnic" knock-offs. But I'm afraid his book only succeeds at further demonstrating why a partisan and ethnic definition of "evangelical" is *not* very peculiar at all. It is indisputable that racial and partisan aspects of the evangelical movement have been commonplace in the movement from early in its history. I believe it remains an open question whether the American evangelical church can separate itself from WCN or begin to resolve some of the overlapping factors Dr. Kidd rightly understands as creating a crisis. Here are five reasons I have a less-than-optimistic view that American evangelicalism can be redeemed from the cult of white Christian nationalism.

I. ASSOCIATION WITH WHITENESS

First, the term "evangelical" continues to be highly associated with whiteness. Who can be known by and embrace this label? History and contemporary observation tell us the answer is *only white Christians who hold a variety of conservative leanings along with a few nonwhite Christians—but only when it benefits white people.* Ethnic minorities are only able to comfortably identify as evangelicals to the extent that they "don't get too political" and they confirm the "deep story" of WCN. The historical narrative doesn't really tell the story of *welcomed diversity* as much as it tells the stories of episodic *detente* and occasional assimilation at the cost of Black identity and political vision.

2. DIVERGING DEFINITIONS

There remain questions about how to understand evangelicalism as a *movement* and whether "others" have a place in it. Is it to be understood in terms of its theological commitments? Or is it to be understood in terms of its prominent and influential leaders (a kind of celebrity evangelicalism)? Or should evangelicalism be understood in terms of its institutions (denominations, publications, etc.)? These viewpoints overlap, of course. But what should have the primacy?

For example, if we adopt a theological definition of evangelicalism, it's quite true that evangelism is a diverse movement.[26] A theological definition seems to provide the movement its best chance at reform and inclusion. Under this definition of evangelicalism we would include white evangelical churches along with historic Black churches as well as Hispanic charismatic and Pentecostal communions. However, even when African Americans hold to a common evangelical belief *and* score high on measures of Christian nationalism, they do *not* hold the same political views of their white counterparts.[27] The differing political outlooks and the boundary-keeping habits of white evangelicals[28] tend to force Black Christians from their ranks.

Chances at reform and inclusion are not greatly improved if we define the movement either by its leadership or its institutions. Very few African American Christians recognize common cause with prominent white evangelical and Christian nationalist leaders—and for good reason if WCN represents an essentially anti-Black view of life. For most of their history evangelical institutions participated in slavery, supported and defended segregation, and allowed no ethnic senior leadership in their ranks—which is not surprising given that the institutions were shaped by the "deep story" myth of WCN and the evangelicalism that birthed it. While the theological definition is more inclusive, in practice the movement is far more *ex*clusive.

3. RELIANCE ON ASSIMILATION

Optimism about evangelicalism being a diverse movement relies almost entirely on people of color assimilating into white-controlled contexts. Thus far, the multiethnic evangelical church remains an "elusive dream."[29] Where it exists, it exists largely through the willingness of African Americans and other people of color to overlook ensconced and intractable aspects of white America's "deep story" and its effects on persons of color. Increasingly, Black people are unwilling to make that sacrifice.[30] Continued references to evangelicalism as a "diverse global movement" may be obscuring on-the-ground migrations away from white evangelical churches in America.

4. UNBALANCED POWER DISTRIBUTION

Any rescue of evangelicalism from WCN requires interrogating evangelical uses and distributions of power within the movement and the country. The monopolization of power by white men in evangelical institutions replays the same monopolization of power by white males in American institutions at large. This power concentration means very few African Americans can be long-term insiders to the evangelical movement. Rescuing evangelicalism from its cultic offspring would require destroying evangelicalism's power table and remaking it to genuinely reflect global and national diversity. We'd have to dismantle the "property rights" assumption of whiteness-as-dominion. We'd have to stop centering white hegemonic sensibilities, concerns, and culture to include the legitimate and diverse perspectives of others *as owners* together of the Christian enterprise and not merely as tolerated junior managers. It's not yet clear that white Christians are interested in that project. Until they are, rescuing evangelicalism from WCN seems highly improbable.

5. HISTORY OF ANTI-BLACK STANCES

Evangelicalism as a movement has generally and consistently taken anti-Black positions. Recall that Dr. Kidd's book focuses on evangelicalism more broadly rather than white Christian nationalism specifically. He does a wonderful job documenting some of the social and political positions that have become definitional in evangelicalism. Historically, the movement has been generally proslavery and prosegregation, anti-affirmative action and anti-immigration. What's the common denominator for these positions? The common denominator is the servicing of whiteness and the disadvantaging of Black people. From an African American viewpoint, the social and political positions are the *determinative* factors in cooperation and unity because those factors have been *deadly* factors for us, while serving the social and political causes of whiteness.

If I'm correct about what's central to evangelical concerns, then evangelicalism will consistently perpetuate the harm of Black people unless its deep story is radically rewritten. Without that historical revision, Black participation would be tantamount to spiritual, social, and political suicide. For that reason, evangelicalism is not likely to become more diverse until this dynamic is radically and demonstrably changed. That would require *at least* identifying and rejecting WCN as a cultic force, but would need to also go on to radical repentance for centuries of ethno-traditional idolatry. If evangelical reaction to *The 1619 Project* is any indication, we won't see any revisions to its deep story happening anytime soon.

CONCLUSION

In the American church, mere formal theological agreement remains insufficient for maintaining Christian cohesion and solidarity. Theological agreement only holds the movement together in times of peace and quiet, when outcomes benefit whites as much or more than others and others overlook the basic disenfranchisement in the movement. Where there are noncorrespondent outcomes—winners and losers—theological agreement dissolves in a flood of difference.

We are not yet socially and politically the one people—with a shared Christian identity as the people of God—that the Bible tells us we are and calls us to live out. Until there's a defining *we*—multiethnic in nature, one new humanity in Christ—that replaces the default *me*, unity will be elusive. Until there is a defining *us* that replaces any sense of "them" among Christians, unity will be hard won. As long as "Christian" and "American" remain racialized as "white," and "whiteness" continues to be a property that devalues Blackness, then American Christianity lingers dangerously close to the cultic abyss.

The evangelical and WNC movements are perceived to be racialized because the movements are and always have been racialized. A different future requires we respond to this reality not merely with theological affirmations but ethical practices that produce the egalitarian life of the kingdom of God. In America, the main thing in the way of a biblical vision for the church and society is the cult beliefs and practices of white Christian nationalism and—to some extent—of evangelicalism itself. We can easily distinguish the two on paper, but we may not be able to make deep and wide distinctions between them in practice.

If, as Black Christians, we want to worship the Lord with the dignity and embrace that comes from being his chosen and redeemed image bearers, it's possible to find such inclusion in a smattering of enlightened and self-sacrificial evangelical churches. However, I suspect the majority of us will find an easier time maintaining dignity and following Jesus if we avoid the cult of white Christian nationalism altogether. This may mean avoiding evangelical churches that continue to have much in common with its cultic offspring.

FAITH, HOPE, AND LOVE

JOHN PERKINS

I came into this world on a hot Monday morning in June in New Hebron, Mississippi. The year was 1930, and life was hard for poor folks in the Jim Crow South, especially poor folks who were Black. I don't know how hard it was for my mother to bring me into the world, but she used all the strength she could muster to help me survive. I nursed at her breast for seven months, depleting her energy and draining her very life from her. She died of pellagra, a disease caused by a lack of niacin. To put it bluntly, she starved to death. I still wrestle with the thought that any person in America could starve to death. In 1930, the systems in place kept Blacks at the lowest level of existence. Some of these systems exist today.

While slavery eventually came to a halt officially, the system of sharecropping proved to be an extension of slavery in disguise, continuing many of the same norms. People who had been slaves had no property, no land, nothing to call their own. It was clear fairly quickly that while sharecropping gave former slaves work to do, this new system denied them the full benefits of their labor and was a mere stepping stone above the slavery system. Not surprisingly, most of the "fruit" of the sharecroppers' labor went to the man. Rather than protest, the sharecroppers learned to make do with the little that they had and to quietly accept that they were being taken advantage of.

In *Letters to a Birmingham Jail*, I shared this story that captures well the plight of many Black people:

> When I was about eleven or twelve years old I worked a whole day hauling hay for a white gentleman. I was expecting to get a dollar or a dollar and a half for that day of work. But at the end of the day he gave me a dime and a buffalo nickel . . . one dime and one buffalo nickel. What I really wanted to do with it was take it and throw it on the ground, because I had value and worth. My value and my worth were well placed in my labor. I wasn't asking for him to give me anything. So, I was completely affronted. It affronted my whole being. That's when I discovered that I had dignity, but I didn't have any way to protect it.[1]

I'm not the only one who has been insulted and slighted. As Black folks in America, many of us have experienced similar situations repeatedly throughout our lives. We've had to "suck it up" and move forward as best we could as a people in America. We had dignity, but we had no way to protect it. Yet our strength has been renewed again and again as we acknowledged what deep in our hearts we knew: God created us in his own glorious image. We still believe he created us in his image: "So God created mankind in his own image, in the image of God he created them; male and female he created them" (Gen. 1:27). Faith in that truth has kept us moving forward, despite many obstacles, hardships, and plain old feelings of just being "tired and fed up" with the ways of the world.

FAITH AS AN ANCHOR

> Through many dangers, toils and snares
> I have already come:
> 'tis grace has brought me safe thus far,
> and grace will lead me home.

My son Spencer used to say, "You play 'Amazing Grace' on the black keys, and you play it at the tune of the sound of the groan of the dying slaves." The groan of the slave was a lament. As he bent to the ground to pick cotton in the blistering heat of the day, slaves would sometimes cry out from the depths of their souls, "Soon I'll be done with the troubles of the world, troubles of the world, troubles of the world. Soon I'll be done with the troubles of the world. Going home to be with my God." Spencer's lament was for a world gone evil. It was his cry to the God of heaven who he knew held the balance.[2]

We always had faith, even when some folks tried to deny our faith. African American Richard Allen is known as the founder of the African Methodist Episcopal Church (AME) in America. He was a freed slave who joined the St. George United Methodist Church in Philadelphia, Pennsylvania, in 1787. He got frustrated with having to deal with segregated pews and mistreatment of his people. Since that day, one denomination after another decided that worshiping God together as people of many nationalities was not required. We're still not worshiping God together, continuing to splinter not only physically but also spiritually. Eleven o'clock on Sunday morning still is the most segregated time of the week. Some of us have worked hard to encourage the church to get together, and clearly some progress has been made. Unfortunately, not nearly enough progress has been made. We fought hard to end segregation in the school systems across the nation. The fight to end segregation in our churches has not been fought nearly hard enough.

Yet we believe that our God will make all things right in his own time. Our faith is strengthened when we look back and remember all that God has already done on our behalf. "God of our weary years, God of our silent tears. Thou who has brought us thus far on the way. Thou who hast by Thy might, led us into the light. Keep us forever in the path, we pray." Yes, he has been faithful. And our faith in him is unshaken. We still trust him. "Faith is the substance of things hoped for, the evidence of things not seen" (Heb. 11:1 KJV). Our faith is fearless because we still have hope.

HOPE UNDAUNTED

Hope keeps our hearts beating. It helps us see the light in the darkness. It gets us up in the morning. Jesse Jackson would say, "Keep hope alive." Hope on. Don't ever stop hoping. Our ancestors were slaves who hoped for a better day when their children's children would one day be free. During the civil rights movement, we hoped to one day arrive at the dream that Dr. Martin Luther King Jr. talked about—that day when all of God's people would be judged by the content of their character rather than the color of their skin. We can't let go of that hope.

To lose all hope would be devastating. Langston Hughes ponders that in his poem "Harlem." He asks, "What happens to a dream deferred?" What do you do when you have nothing left, not even a dream of things getting better? I know something about that. There was a time in my life when, after the beating I suffered in jail, I lost hope. I lost all hope for a better life for my family and for my people. It was as though the cruel beatings crushed all the hope I had for better days to come. In the hospital where I struggled to keep living, I was full of anger. I wanted to die. Then I wanted to go after the people who had treated me so violently. I wanted revenge.

Suicide and genocide are the fruit of hope lost. My heart breaks as I see what is happening in the streets of many of our cities today. It's not pretty: Young people have lost hope. The gangs, violence, and anger are signs of hopelessness. We must rekindle our hope, following the instructions of our ancestors. Our hope is not in political systems. Our hope is not in financial means. Our hope is in Jesus alone! Our ancestors would sing, "On Christ the solid Rock I stand! All other ground is sinking sand. All other ground is sinking sand!" Yes, Jesus Christ is our hope. He has brought us thus far, and he will carry us on.

We still claim the promise that God spoke through the prophet Jeremiah to the Jewish people who had been carried away to Babylon: "'For I know the plans I have for you,' says the LORD. 'They are plans for good and not for disaster, to give you a future and a hope'" (Jer. 29:11 NLT). We must hold on to hope, moving forward at the direction of the One who made us, loves us, and has good plans for us.

LOVE IS THE FINAL FIGHT

It warms my heart to think about what happened when the slaves were finally emancipated. The years of captivity had served to teach them how to suffer well. Rather than hating their oppressors, they learned by the grace of God to forgive and love them. They fought the war right alongside white folks and chose to love this country, even though promises made to them were broken without the slightest remorse.

During the civil rights era, the thing that set the movement apart was the willingness to love our enemies. We learned how to sit at lunch counters where they would not serve us and to be spit on without striking back. We learned how to march in the face of police officers with dogs and billy clubs and chose not to fight back. We learned the power of love and to recall that God means what he says in Exodus 14:14, "The LORD will fight for you; you need only to be still." God smiled on those sacrifices and opened doors that no man could close. He opened doors of education, doors of opportunity. He fought on our behalf.

Faith is our anchor. Hope is what gets us up every morning. But love is the greatest of them, because God is love. It's been my life's work to say that the church must take the lead on this. We are his body—black, white, brown, and all others—all blood-washed believers in Christ. Personally, I dream of a day when the church will look like heaven. As I wrote in *Dream with Me*:

> I want the white police officers to be sitting next to the young black boys in church on Sunday, singing songs and praying together, learning to be members of the same family of God. I want the single black mother and the family that recently emigrated from Latin America to go up and take Communion together. I want the older widow, who has been living out a lonely life in a nursing home, to be visited and cared for by the young man whose third-grade test scores said he would end up in prison someday. I want this to be the picture of the church. I want to see a real community of love.[3]

I still have hope that we can get there. I still have faith in the unfailing promises of our God. He is the God who forgives us of all our sins and wipes the slate clean, allowing us to go forward as though we never sinned. I've drunk deeply from that fountain of forgiveness, and it has compelled me to forgive everyone who has ever harmed me. As I prepare to meet my Savior soon—and very soon—I've settled all accounts in my heart. We all have to do that if we want to fix this mess we're in. We have to forgive. It's mandatory because God has promised he will forgive us "as we forgive others." And we've got to love. Love is the balm that will heal all our brokenness, our hurts, and our division.

Now we see things imperfectly, like puzzling reflections in a mirror, but then we will see everything with perfect clarity. All that I know now is partial and incomplete, but then I will know everything completely, just as God now knows me completely.

Three things will last forever—faith, hope, and love—and the greatest of these is love. (1 Cor. 13:12–13 NLT)

FOUR

UNDERSTANDING BLACK LIBERATION THEOLOGY

ANTHONY BRADLEY

Christianity is an Eastern religion, including east Africa. However, many African Americans were introduced to Christianity through the Western European expression characterized by white supremacy, racism, and the oppression of Africans and African Americans during slavery. The experience of white racism and the oppression of Black Americans was inaugurated in the Americas during slavery and extended through Jim Crow and the civil rights movement. Some argue, however, that this oppression ceases only when one's particular community of white Christians is willing to confess and repent of their complicity in the subjugation and oppression of Black Americans and Christians of African descent. How, then, do we make sense of the Black experience and history of oppression meted out by white conservative secularists and white Christians? This is the question Black theology seeks to answer.

WHAT IS BLACK THEOLOGY?

When discussing Black theology, it can mean many things to many people, so a precise definition is extremely useful. The 1969 National Committee of Black Church Men offers a concise definition of Black theology:

Black theology is a theology of black liberation. It seeks to plumb the black condition in the light of God's revelation in Jesus Christ, so that the black community can see that the gospel is commensurate with the achievements of black humanity. Black theology is a theology of "blackness." It is the affirmation of black humanity that emancipates black people from white racism, thus providing authentic freedom for both white and black people. It affirms the humanity of white people in that it says No to the encroachment of white oppression.[1]

This definition was forged following the murder of Martin Luther King Jr. At this time, many Black church leaders began helping communities transition from Jim Crow to face the challenges of new social and political freedoms. They also worked hard to help African Americans navigate the Jim Crow resistance by whites and apply the Christian tradition to the particular issues facing Black America into the 1970s and 1980s.

The most prominent figure in the development of Black theology was James Cone, who taught systematic theology at Union Theological Seminary (New York, NY) from 1969 until his death in 2018. Although the themes for Black liberation can be traced back to the beginning of the Black church in America on slave plantations and among freed Blacks, it was James Cone who systematized this theological framework into an academic discipline. It became the starting point of reflection for several generations of Christian reflection on Christianity and the Black experience.

DEVELOPMENT

In the late 1960s, James Cone was rightly frustrated that at no point in his seminary or PhD studies at predominantly white institutions was there any discussion about racism and segregation in America. To put this in perspective, this would be the equivalent of a seminary discussing the state of the world in 2020 but not referencing the COVID-19 pandemic or the murder of George Floyd. Both Martin Luther King Jr. and Malcolm X had been murdered in the struggle for racial justice, yet predominantly white seminaries were talking about abstractions that had nothing to do with the day-to-day Black experience on the ground. Cone, who had been raised under Jim Crow in Arkansas, was frustrated by his professor's refusal to see "racism as a *theological* problem."[2] Consequently, he worked to apply all of the resources of the Christian tradition in the West to make sense of the intersection of Christianity and the Black experience. The outcome was the academic formulation and crafting of Black liberation theology. After completing his PhD at Northwestern University, Cone published *Black Theology and Black Power* in 1969, which began a series of deep reflections on what the experience of Christianity means in light of Black suffering in the United States.

AIMS

While Black theology explores what Blackness means in the light of God's redemption of the world through Jesus, the theology should not be construed as "woke" or "antiwhite." Cone's project was constructive, seeking to address the glaring absence of theological application to the Black experience. When Cone speaks of "Blackness," he is not merely referencing skin color; rather, "Blackness" is a metaphor for the social location of oppressed, marginalized communities. Thus, it can apply to all persons of color who have a history of being oppressed, as well as to other marginalized groups, such as the LGBTQAI+ communities.[3]

Black liberation theologians seek to apply theology in a way that affirms the previously denied theological anthropology of Black people. They want to declare God's "no" to Black oppression by declaring, in a sense, that Black lives matter to God and, as such, white people can no longer normalize white supremacist, patronizing, or paternalistic orientations toward Black lives. As such, Black theology begins with the life experience of Blacks within the context of oppression and formulates theology from there.

The overall emphasis of Black liberation theology is the Black struggle for liberation from various forms of white racism and oppression. It locates the imperatives of the Christian gospel to that end. Cone, in seeking to develop something unique for the Black experience, was eager to develop a theology that went beyond nineteenth-century liberalism and neo-orthodoxy. He often clearly states his departure from each tradition at key points, dealing with issues specific to the Black community.[4]

LIBERATION AS THE STARTING POINT

In *A Black Theology of Liberation*, Cone develops Black theology as a system. He begins by identifying liberation as the starting point and content of theology as it relates to the Black experience.[5] Many of Cone's initial formulations serve as the background for later developments of Black theology as a theological system.[6]

A THEOLOGY OF LIBERATION

According to Cone, Christian theology is a theology of liberation—"A *rational study of the being of God in the world in light of the existential situation of an oppressed community, relating the forces of liberation to the essence of the gospel, which is Jesus Christ.*"[7] Harry Singleton expands this view, noting that a God whose nature is freedom brings the "good news of God's historical intervention in oppressive relationships, and given that Black skin has come to symbolize oppressed humanity in our time . . . transforms God into a God of Black liberation."[8] God specifically takes on the struggle of Black people.[9]

In this framework, the meaning of the work and person of Christ is to show that God is at work in the Black community as it seeks to restore its dignity in a society that is committed to the advancement of Black suffering. The God of liberation instills in Black people the necessary resolve "to relentlessly fight for freedom; to restore freedom with which God created the world."[10] In fact, according to Singleton, Black people, "unable to place any trust in whites to guide them to freedom, have had to depend on another source—and one greater than white supremacy—a free and liberating God."[11]

Black theology seeks, then, to understand and apply the implications and applications of the gospel of Jesus Christ in light of the history and experience of Black oppression. The gospel is the good news that God came in the person of Christ to liberate Blacks from white oppression and to bestow upon them the power to break free from oppressive social structures and relationships experienced in white supremacy and white condescension toward Black humanity. Christian theology, then, is understood in terms of systemic and structural relationships between two main groups: the oppressed and the oppressors.[12] One of the most defining implications of Christ coming was to free African Americans from the centuries-old tyranny of white racism and oppression in the forms of slavery, Jim Crow, and resentment of Black humanity.

For Cone and others, the biblical grounds for the liberation narrative of redemption emerge from these key features in the history of God's people:

1. God chose Israel because they were oppressed.

2. Old Testament prophecy targets the lack of social justice as God is revealed as the God of liberation for the oppressed.

3. Jesus reaffirms the preeminence of God as liberator by locating his ministry among the poor and the oppressed (Luke 4:18–19).[13]

INTERACTION WITH WHITE PEOPLE

Black theology highlights the ways white Americans and white Christians (mainline Protestant and evangelical alike) consistently fail to recognize Black humanity as demonstrated in their support of slavery and their willingness to turn a blind eye during Jim Crow.[14] White theology and European theology, when formed in isolation from the Black experience of suffering, always tends toward white supremacy and becomes a vehicle of white oppressors. White mainline and white evangelical theology fail to relate to the experience of Black suffering, and therefore lose their association with the theology of the Bible, rendering them no longer Christian.[15]

There is one guiding principle in Black theology: an unqualified commitment to the Black community as that community seeks to define its existence in light of God's liberating work in the world.[16] Black theology is a survival theology that seeks to say "no" to white supremacy and "yes" to God.[17] The decision to be in union with God "is a decision by the Black community to walk by faith and not by sight—the human longing for deliverance under the whip for white rule."[18] Black theology sends a clear message from God to white secularists and white religious folks alike that "Black lives matter." Those who perpetuate racism and white resentment of Black people's existence need to know that it is God's will for Black liberation to come to pass on earth as it is in heaven. Regardless of anti-Black attempts to exterminate the world of Black people, Black theology is here to remind the world that "the God of liberation has always been on the forefront of the Black struggle, leading black people to the freedom that is God's essence."[19]

THE ROLE OF THE BLACK EXPERIENCE IN BLACK THEOLOGY

For Cone, the central reason for God's activity in the lives of human beings is to free them from political and economic oppression. If human relationships were not socially or politically oppressed, however, one might conjecture that, according to Black theology, Jesus's work would not be necessary. Black theology, then, is limited to "language about God's liberating activity in the world on behalf of the freedom of the oppressed."[20]

Sociopolitical oppression is the core problem with the human community and is the central interpretive theme for all of Black theology. The whole of the biblical story is, in fact, focused on God's "liberation of slaves from sociopolitical bondage."[21] This is the message of both the Old and New Testament. There are three main issues that shape much of the reflective discourse among Black liberation theologians: slavery, racism, and systemic injustice.

SLAVERY

The focus on the issue of slavery by Black liberation theologians makes sense, given that the religion through which Africans and African Americans experienced oppression was Christianity. Raboteau contends, "From the very beginning of the Atlantic slave trade, conversion of the slaves to Christianity was viewed by the emerging nations of Western Christendom as a justification for enslavement of Africans."[22] Cone introduces the background of Black religious thought by noting:

> Black religious thought has been primarily Christian, but strongly influenced by its African background and the struggle of Black people to liberate themselves from slavery and second-class citizenship in North America. Because it has been developed in response to the involuntary servitude of Africans and subsequent Black struggle for equality in the United States, it has never been exclusively Christian or primarily concerned with the explication of creeds and doctrines as found in the dominant theologies of Europe and America.[23]

Black liberation presents Black Christians with the theological tension of this question: "Why did God permit millions of Blacks to be stolen from Africa and enslaved in a strange land?"[24] Cone observes that "if religion is inseparably connected with life, then one must assume that slaves' and slaveholders' religious experiences did not have the same meaning because they did not share the same life. . . . Their social and political realities were radically different."[25] Slavery, with its legacy of racism, is one of the reasons for the formation and continuation of Black liberation theology.

RACISM

The Black church in America has been on the frontlines to restore Black dignity and humanity in a society that organized itself around race.[26] From slavery to Reconstruction to the Jim Crow era and beyond, Blacks in the United States have experienced a particular kind of modern racism—one where society was organized on the basis of racial hierarchies. During slavery, white supremacy and slave ownership were mainstays of Calvinist and Puritan religious communities; even religious leaders such as Jonathan Edwards owned slaves, and the sentiment of white superiority was promoted by evangelicals throughout the entirety of Jim Crow.[27] It was the white Christian silence regarding the suffering and oppression of Black Americans that would ultimately motivate the creation of Black liberation theology.

Cone believes that white theology's "amnesia about racism is due partly to the failure of Black theologians to mount a persistently radical race critique of Christian theology—one so incisive and enduring that no one could do theology without engaging white supremacy in the modern world."[28] The Black church exists in part to help Blacks deal with the "demonic racism destroying Black America."[29]

SYSTEMIC OPPRESSION

Cone is clear that if white Christians want to be taken seriously in their claims of human dignity, they must act immediately to address systemic issues of racial oppression within Christianity in America and within the culture at large.[30] If white churches claim to be Christian institutions, and "if Jesus Christ is the Lord of the church and the world as white confessions claim, then church institutions that claim the Christian identity must reflect their commitment to him in the congregational life of the church as well as in its political and social involvement in society."[31] In the early years of the development of Black theology, Cornel West says that Black theology needs to press the systemic sin issues even further because

> [its] absence of a systematic social analysis, which has prevented Black theologians from coming to terms with the relationships between racism, sexism, class exploitation and imperialist oppression . . . [and] its tendency to downplay existential issues such as death, disease, dread, despair and

disappointment which are related to yet not identical with suffering caused by oppressive social structures.[32]

American society continues to be a place rife with racist structures.[33] Blacks continue to be victims of such structures in the areas of banking, mortgage appropriations, disability benefits, small-business loans, education, and so on.[34]

WOMANIST INTERPRETATION

One expression of Black liberation theology uniquely recognizes that Black women live at the intersection of race, class, and gender and require special reflection in light of God's liberative activity. This development came to be known as womanist theology. Black women's unique experience is brought to bear by asking specific questions like: Where is God in the experiences of Black women? By what name should this God be called? What does it mean to live a life of faith? How should Black women respond to God's call?[35]

Womanist approaches to theology seek to develop a range of theological constructions "in which black women are the main subject."[36] It seeks to understand everything about Christianity from the lived experience of Black women. Because of the oppression of gender entrapment, African American women often suffer from low self-esteem, damaging relationships, and so on. Black women needed their own theological discourse because white feminists have a consistent history of marginalizing "black women's needs and realities."[37] Delores Williams defines womanist theology as

a prophetic voice concerned about the well-being of the entire African American community, male and female, adults and children. Womanist theology attempts to help black women see, affirm, and have confidence in the importance of their experience and faith for determining the character of the Christian religion in the African American community. Womanist theology challenges all oppressive forces impeding black women's struggle for survival and for the development of a positive, productive quality of life conducive to women's and the family's freedom and well-being. Womanist theology opposes all oppression based on race, sex, class, sexual preference, physical ability, and caste.[38]

Womanist theology is both an affirmation and critique of Black male theologians in the struggle against white supremacy. Womanist theologians criticize Black male theologians for ignoring the devastating effects of patriarchy with important women voices like Delores Williams, Katie Cannon, and Cheryl Sanders.[39] In order to explicate the unique experience of Black women, womanists look to resources like the work of Alice Walker and Zora Neale Hurston. The writings of Alice Walker have been particularly formative for self-identified womanist theologians. Her book *In Search of Our Mother's Gardens: Womanist Prose* (1983) is the aegis of the term "womanist."

In Williams's own words, the appropriateness of womanist theological conclusions "will ultimately reside in [their] ability to bring black women's history, culture, and religious experience into the interpretive circle of Christian theology and into the liturgical life of the church. Womanist theological language must, in this sense, be an instrument for social and theological change in church and society."[40] That social change has important roles in forming and shaping the constructive roles that Black women play in the church and in society at large. Stephanie Mitchem summaries the key points of womanist theology as follows:

- Womanist theology uncovers and incorporates the ordinary theologies of black women's lives.
- The communal dimension of black women's experiences includes the values of social activism and the creation of safe spaces. This communal dimension extends into the methodology of womanist theology itself, where theologians and ethicists collaborate rather than compete.
- Alice Walker's definition sets important parameters of discovery and implies a methodology that is interdisciplinary while remaining centered on all aspects of black women's lives.
- Ethics becomes a starting point from which to build a womanist theology, particularly in its continuing critical social analysis.
- Ongoing dialogue and openness are essential, particularly because womanist theology breaks with some of the dynamics of Western theological construction.[41]

Womanists situate themselves both as a corrective to the oversights, blind spots, and weaknesses of Black male theologians and as a liberative theology in dialogue with Black and feminist perspectives.

BLACK THEOLOGY AND CONTEMPORARY FAITH

How is Black liberation theology lived out in daily life in the twenty-first century? What does it mean for a life of faith today? For that, we turn to Harry H. Singelton III and his 2022 book *Forever in Thy Path: The God of Black Liberation*. In this framework, to have a personal relationship with Jesus as Lord and Savior fails as proper conversion narrative because it is confined to personal triumph in spiritual terms and does not extend to global problems, nor does it explore how Christianity has contributed to global problems.[42] The personal relationship approach grew out of a white proslavery theology and reduces faith to an inward condition that fails to make "the world of oppressive relationships a key component of faith."[43] It does not "call whites to conscience about the highly oppressive way in which they have used Black people as commodities to obtain wealth and status."[44] Traditional Black churches mirror the failures of white churches when focusing on personal conversion frameworks and not addressing issues of injustice and oppression in their songs, prayers, sermons, and so on. In these Black churches, "Jesus is still white." Instead, what is needed is a conversion to a faith of the God of Black liberation.

The first task of the Black Christian conversion is to "[uncover] the truth of African/Black history and oppression at the hands of white people."[45] Conversion exposes the falsehoods of white Christians about Black people and restructures Christianity to impress upon the convert "that the new life of faith is a commitment to reimagining the liberating essence of being a Christian."[46] For Singelton, Jesus was not looking for the convert to praise necessarily but to emulate him in his absence. Thus, "The life of Jesus was not meant to be a historical event but a paradigm for change."[47] That work begins by restoring Black dignity and "through a liberating conscience given by God to never tire of deconstructing white theories about black bodies."[48] The Christian life needs to be a "militant religion" centered on liberation and freedom that bears witness to the fact that Jesus was indeed a Black man from Africa and not a white man from Europe. Singelton maintains that "the path of conversion becomes authentic only when the falsehoods of racist Christianity are exposed and replaced with the truth of the liberation reign of God."[49]

Under Black liberation theology, "issues of human liberation now have to take precedence over the religious individual and otherworldliness."[50] God seeks to return Black people back to their original state of freedom in God—a state that is free of white oppression. Black people are still subjected to systemic bigotry and random acts of violence at any time and, therefore, they need a God of liberation. In the wake of George Floyd's murder, what the Black community needs is the Jesus as liberator of the marginalized and oppressed.

By extension, "Christian obedience is the commitment to move an oppressed community to its God-appointed liberation; any other activity ceases to be Christian obedience."[51] We know God and his will insofar as it is defined by God's intervention on "behalf of the lowly and despised, making the struggle of the oppressed God's struggle."[52] God intervenes through the work and person of Jesus Christ. The essence and meaning of the Christ event is that "God demonstrates his love for freedom through his identification with the despised in their struggle for self-determination."[53] God has revealed himself in the social context of Black oppression: "The God of Black liberation comes to us as a God of social righteousness."[54]

Divine righteousness reveals to the world God's plan to liberate Black humanity and not allow white people to have a clear conscience about their "racist rule."[55] In our contemporary society, biblical revelation is the expression of God's love for freedom of humanity and God's disdain for systemic oppression and white privilege.[56] As such, we understand the importance of the resurrection—that is, that God assures victory over oppression and the overcoming of oppressive death. Therefore, "The truth of the gospel is that the crucifixion represents the passion and death of an oppressed people who are resurrected not in heaven but on earth."[57] Because of Black experience in America, "God comes as liberator to realize what white men have prevented in history—freedom, justice, and equality."[58] Therefore, "No approach to Christian faith has relevance in our time unless it is grounded in Black liberation."[59] In the end, becoming a true Christian, a true person of God, means embracing the God of Black liberation—a God who demands an abandonment of the old status-quo theology that has privileged white Americans and has sentenced Black people to the worst forms of physical and mental abuse in modern history."[60]

ASSESSMENT

Theological formations are always subject to imperfections and errors because they originate from the imaginations of imperfect humans who cannot help but bring some presuppositions to the task of biblical interpretation and application. Christian doctrines are formulated by identifying particular problems and issues that exist in real time and formulating principles to address those in the most faithful way possible. In this sense, real-life tensions generate theological reflection. When evaluating any theological system, especially those with ethical implications, it is best to approach them with the same set of questions:

1. What facets of God's creation have they rightly focused on to identify as worthy of praise?
2. What does the framework view as a source of evil?
3. What does the framework offer as the source of salvation from its conception of evil?
4. What are some inconsistencies, internal tensions, or blind spots within the framework itself that might undermine its ability to achieve the proposed solutions?[61]

Applying these questions to Black liberation theology broadly—from James Cone, to womanist theologians, to the most recent expressions in the work of Harry Singleton—we can proceed as follows:

1. **What facets of God's creation have they rightly focused on to identify as worthy of praise?** Black theology rightly identifies the failures of Christianity to acknowledge the inherent dignity of all people of African descent. It rightly acknowledges the presence of evil in white societies that provided the context for the violent and systemic oppression of Blacks. It rightly acknowledges that God seeks to restore the dignity of African Americans in the face of white oppression and liberate people of color from social and political oppression. It rightly acknowledges the history of Black women's unique subjugation at the intersection of race, class, and gender.

2. **What does the framework view as a source of evil?** Black liberation theology views oppression and white supremacy as the source of evil. As Singleton observes, "Spiritual death [comes] through the imposition of white supremacy."[62]

3. **What does the framework offer as the source of salvation from its conception of evil?** For Black liberation theology, God, the liberator of the oppressed, is the source of salvation. Jesus came to liberate Blacks from sociopolitical oppression, white supremacy, and racialized dehumanization.

4. **What are some inconsistencies, internal tensions, or blind spots within the framework itself that might undermine its ability to achieve the proposed solutions?** Space does not permit a full treatment, but there are two main issues that introduce limitations for Black theology's goals. The greatest irony of Black liberation theology is that, in the end, it remains Eurocentric and white-centric, and it is not comprehensive enough.

EUROCENTRIC AND WHITE-CENTRIC

Christianity began as an Eastern and North African religion. Thus, a robust practice of Christianity today does not need to be in dialogue with white Christianity in America or European Christian history. There are robust Eastern and North African Christian resources from the early church tradition that provide rich understandings of what it means to be a Christian that are not centered on "white" theological conceptions of faith.

Ironically, Black theology remains in theological captivity to whiteness by limiting the identity of God and the mission of Jesus to freeing Blacks from the oppression of whites. In this regard, Black liberation theology is not radical or liberative enough. Its framing centers Black faith as a corrective to bad white theology and a faith of resistance against white supremacy. Bad white theology should not be the starting point for Black biblical and theological reflection on faith and life.

The constant focus on what white Christians believe inadvertently reifies white supremacy and keeps Black Christianity incarcerated to Western Eurocentric dogmatics. What it means to be a Christian of African descent should be unrelated to white people, Eurocentric theological priorities, or persuading white people to think a certain way about X or Y. Black people are not called to be the caretakers of white minds. Keeping "white people" in Black Christian mouths contributes to an internalized othering that may distract Black Christians from holistic liberation.

The Coptic Christians of Egypt have been persecuted by Europeans and Muslims since the third century.[63] Egyptian Christians know oppression and dehumanization.[64] Yet Christians in the Middle East and across Africa are not limiting God's activity to sociopolitical liberation. They are declaring the good news that, in Christ, the Spirit liberates God's people from the powers of sin, death, and the devil, inaugurating new-creation life and moving towards the eschatological glorification of the whole cosmos.[65]

UNCOMPREHENSIVE

The Achilles' heel of Black liberation theology is that it does not go far enough in addressing the root cause of all evil. White supremacy is evil, but it does not encompass cosmic evil. Racism exists, but it is neither omnipresent nor the cause of all tragedy, pain, or trauma in the lives of Black people. Holistic liberation is more than freedom from temporal oppression. In the cosmic battle between the Trinity and Satan, there is so much more happening in the lives of Black people than systemic obstacles and bad white theology. The devil is trying to kill Black people (1 Peter 5:8). Spiritual warfare at the supernatural level is real (Eph. 6:12). Jesus specifically came to undo the work of the devil (1 John 3:8) in every area of life. Jesus conquered more than the evils of the created order (like racism and white supremacy)—he conquered Satan himself (Col. 2:13–15).[66] Comprehensive liberation, therefore, includes freedom from sin and the power of death in the lives of God's people, in addition to issues of racial injustice.[67]

What sins do Black people need to repent of? Black liberation theology leaves that as an open question. Ancient Christianity, however, was adamant that Jesus also came to liberate us from sin and to call us to a life of repentance and prayer.[68] Repentance is the liberation from slavery to sin, the devil, and the passions of the inner life.[69] The personal relationship approach did not grow out of white theology, it grew out of an ancient faith that teaches the importance of our union with the Holy Trinity.[70] Black liberation theology does not provide a framework for spiritual formation in the path of personal holiness.[71] It's true that God wants to free his people from injustice, but he also cares that we petition for their daily needs and wants us to care for the needs of the disadvantaged.[72]

DISCUSSION

Unlike many other cultural movements in the Black community, churches that preach and teach Black liberation theology are Christian churches. They simply have a unique theological emphasis. Churches that teach Black liberation theology are more likely to be associated with progressive Protestant mainline denominations and will be much lower in adherents than other expressions of Black Christianity to date. The pastors that preach are likely to have graduated from a Protestant mainline seminary or a progressive evangelical one. In many of the mainline churches where Black liberation theology is found, one will also find openness to progressive views on sexuality, gender, marriage, and so on. Levels of openness to progressive ideas, however, depend on the particular congregation and cannot be universalized. In our current era, Black liberation theology is also largely confined to churches that serve the Black middle class in large metropolitan areas. The prosperity gospel and Black Pentecostalism are exponentially more widespread and pervasive in the Black church today than Black liberation theology. Black liberation theology tends to emerge in the public discourse when Black politicians refer to it, as we saw during President Barack Obama's first presidential campaign and his relationship with Rev. Jeremiah Wright and Senator Raphael Warnock (GA), who studied Black liberation theology in graduate school. White evangelicals wrongly believe that Black liberation theology is a current, widely accepted theological confession of traditional Black churches. That is simply false. One is not likely to find a church that focuses on Black liberation theology in most Black communities in America outside of mainline denominations and affiliates. When one does encounter this theology, ask the four interrogative questions listed above and make a decision about whether or not this particular theological emphasis with its concomitant limitations, blind spots, and weaknesses is disqualifying.

Black liberation theology remains highly dependent on European theology and philosophy for its categories. Therefore, if we are looking to make a distinction between biblical Christianity and white Western Christianity, Black liberation theology will not do the job. What really matters is our analysis of the strengths and weaknesses of this theological tradition so that church goers can make the best decisions about placing ourselves and our families in a context for spiritual formation that cares more about what the Bible teaches than the concerns of Western society, culture, and philosophy.

THE REVOLUTIONARY PULPIT

KENNETH C. ULMER

Do you want a revolution? Do you want a revolution?" was both the clarion call and challenge to the church world issued by my spiritual son and former youth pastor, Kirk Franklin. It was a declarative, defiant, and descriptive depiction of a time that was evolving. It echoed the theme song of one of the musical sages of the ages, the late great Josephine Baker, in her signature song of an era—but not a truth—gone by: "The Times They Are A-Changin'."

"Do you want a revolution?"

The prophet Isaiah uses the language of a revolutionary in Isaiah 43:19. I love the way our modern-day revolutionary exegete Eugene Peterson says it: "Be alert, be present. I'm about to do something brand-new. It's bursting out! Don't you see it?" (Isa. 43:19 MSG). The phrase "something brand-new" is Peterson's contemporized verbiage for the Hebrew word *chadash*, an adjective meaning "new" or "fresh."[1]

Both in Hebrew and in Greek, there are two words for "new." One means new in *time*. This would describe what a person has when they replace a Ford car made in 2000 with one made in 2022. The person still has a Ford—but one that is redesigned, updated, and remodeled. The other word for "new" means new in *kind*. New in kind would be like replacing a 2000 Ford with a 2022 Mercedes Benz. It is a brand-new car, a totally different design. It is a new car, but new in *kind*. When God says he is doing a new thing, it is new in *kind*. You can't compare it to the past. It is brand new, creatively new, never-seen-before new—revolutionary new!

I fear too many of us have missed this majestic memo. So many are looking for, hoping for, even praying for a return to a pre-COVID world. But this is a new world—new in *kind*. God is doing a new thing! This new thing requires faith without a point of reference. In the words of the book of Joshua, we "have not passed this way before" (Josh. 3:4 ESV).

CULTURAL REVOLUTION

Culturally, boundaries have not only shifted and expanded, but in many cases they have dissolved and disappeared. The voices that mold, make, and shape this contemporary culture are no longer voices echoing the divine document; these voices no longer reflect what was once upon a time referred to as a "Judeo-Christian ethos." Often, culture is being shaped by the voices, the images, the "influencers" with the most followers and likes.

Never has society been more technologically connected and less relationally committed. No longer do people go to church or even clubs to find friendships and relationships. Now, more and more are seeking friendships online. Similarly, spiritual connections and experiences at a distance and online have become a viable option for many. Discipleship is more and more being done online than in the pew. This generation is increasingly being discipled, one way or another, by TGIF: Twitter/TikTok, Google, Instagram, and Facebook.

No longer do the masses feel a sense of urgency to get to the house of the Lord on Sunday. We used to "go" to church. Now we "sign on" to church. Sincere church minds have realized that they can do church with a cup of coffee and slippers on rather than endure the rituals of preparation for the journey from house shoes to the house of God.

Historian Jon Meacham, in his documentary compliment to his best-selling book *The Soul of America*, highlights this cultural metamorphosis, tracing political history from the age of the radio during the presidency of Franklin Roosevelt, to the emergence of TV spotlighted in the Kennedy and Reagan years, where hair and makeup became necessary preparation for the eye of the camera reaching the masses, to the present dominance of the digital, cable era, which became headquarters for the Trump phenomenon. Meacham says we are in an age where the people do not engage the "text," referring to print media and printed methods of communication; rather, one's worldview and philosophy of life is more emotional and visual, more passionate than reasonable.[2]

Contemporary visionary Dr. Len Sweet, who echoes and paraphrases Meacham, would say we have gone from Gutenberg to Google. Sweet prophetically declares that our culture is driven more by visuals and optics than by chapters and verse. In fact, Sweet would encourage modern homileticians and pulpiteers to be healed of "versitus," zoom our lens out, and move to preaching with the relevant narrative "narraphor" structure that always aims toward placing the worshiper, hearer, student, parishioner into the biblical story.[3] This is a visual generation. Why do you think more and more "small churches"[4] have huge TV screens? In many of them, the preacher is standing just feet away from the congregation, but most of them are watching him on the screen anyway. This is a revolution!

PASTORAL REVOLUTION

The contemporary kingdom is populated with throngs of frustrated pastors who followed the historic Black evangelical pattern of instructing, inspiring, and encouraging the saints to "not forsake the assembling of yourselves"—in other words, "Come to church! The doors of the church are open." Enter COVID-19. COVID-19 revolutionized our invitation. Instead of "Come to church, come to church," we said, "Don't come, don't come; stay home, tune in." And then, after two years or so of "Don't come, don't come," things changed.

Several pastors I know are struggling with how to regain their credibility for standing on the scriptural exhortation, "Come to church," then saying, "Don't come," then having to say, "Come back, come back." Their congregants are asking, "*Please*, what do you want us to do? What does the text say and mean? Why do we have to come back? We can get you online." Or as one lady, intending to compliment me, said, "Bishop, you are one of my favorites. I watch you every Sunday. In fact, you are my second stop. I tune in to five churches every Sunday. I start on the East Coast, and with the time changes, you are my second stop every Sunday!" So much for brand loyalty!

We used to sing an old gospel song with the line, "Let us all go back to the old landmark." I fear that many of my fellow pastors who are going back to the old landmark are going back by themselves. They are desperately emphasizing community and fellowship more than ever in veiled attempts to encourage and exhort the saints to come back into the building. But I surmise that the times have changed so much that things will never be the same. No one is going with them. It will never be the same. We are incarnating the words written in Joshua: We "have never been this way before" (Josh. 3:4).

Fast forward to a (hopefully) post-COVID era, and I see myself in a platoon of fellow spiritual soldiers—including those of us who have endured long enough to timidly, sometimes frighteningly, yet proudly wear the title "generals" in the kingdom army. We preacher/pastor/ army-chaplain-type soldiers are struggling with the challenge of finding balance and creating hybrids to minister to and serve those in the pew and online—an unheard-of challenge a few short years ago. Most of us have had to learn and adjust to a new style, new rhythm, new approach to standing before the camera congregation, with no emphatic "Amen! Say it! Preach, Preacher!" No longer can we ride with the rhythms of the carefully placed and anticipated verbal encouragements we had grown accustomed to. We now must look at the few before us in the pews, and the greater number beyond us through the camera lens. I suggest the future dynamic requires not either-or, but both-and.

This is a revolution!

MINISTRY REVOLUTION

We are thrust into the revolutionized, glamorized, moderately spiritualized, not necessarily godly culture. As we attempt to incarnate the Christ and imitate the exhortation, "And I, if I am lifted up from the earth, will draw all people to Myself" (John 12:32 NASB), we are in a tug-of-war between authenticity and attractiveness. We are faced with the tension of being authentic, or unapologetically lifting the Christ, and being attractive—that is, doing so in such a manner that he does the drawing (not us) in a magnetizing, authentic way so that men and women come to him. Most of us will lean to one side or the other. To echo a word of wisdom I heard over forty years ago, "God is seldom at the extremes where we are; he is usually somewhere in the middle."

We can often be so fundamentally orthodox in presenting the authentic Christ in an authentic manner, and we lean so far in our orthodoxy that we are unattractive to the very world we are called to reach and penetrate. Our orthopraxy is often so lost in our orthodoxy that we repel those we attempt to reach. Or, on the other hand, in our attempt to be so attractive and appealing and "dope," we will lean more to orthopraxy and minimize orthodoxy. Our Christ of the cross is obscured by our attempts to make him and his church more attractive and relevant. We send Jesus to our contemporary wardrobe and makeup departments, and we put him on stage before a generation that is attracted and captured by the comfortability of his spiritual sartorial splendor; they seldom, if ever, come to see the scars and blood stains of his cross.

This new culture is influencing the present kingdom generation to minimize the authority of God's Word, compromise the lordship and messiahship of Christ, and marginalize the power and presence of the Holy Spirit. We risk being like the church of a friend of mine, whose response to "How was church today?" was "It would be great if we could hear about Jesus every once in a while." This guy was minister of music in one of the largest churches in Los Angeles, arguably the most socially relevant, justice-preaching, community-impacting church in town. It could be said that they were attractive but minimally authentic in their presentation and emphasis on the genuine Christ of the Bible. You were more likely to hear an invitation to join a movement than serve the Master.

ECCLESIASTICAL REVOLUTION

The revolution has contemporized our approach to God and colloquialized our address to him. We used to say and sing, "I need thee every hour, most precious Lord." We used to sing of our awesome God by declaring his omnipotence: "How Great Thou Art." In the revolution, the "awe" of the majestic God has been reinterpreted into a more familiar, casual, colloquial God who will "blow your mind!"

Today we hear fewer majestic musical similes and less biblical nomenclature such as "King of kings and Lord of lords." The revolution has changed our vernacular—but this should not be interpreted as a sign of an apostate generation. This generation still loves the Lord, but they might be more inclined to rap about his righteousness than sing 'til the power of the Lord comes down. No longer is "dope" limited to stuff you push or snort. I witnessed a young lady who was obviously declaring her allegiance to Almighty God with the revolutionary designation on her sweatshirt: GOD IS DOPE! Kanye reinterprets the gospel plea, "Walk with me Lord" to the spiritual war cry, "Jesus walks with me," and walks to the top of the charts.[5]

Today's generation still loves the Lord, but rather than singing about it in the choir, they are prone to rap about it in the praise team (the traditional choir's successor), add some choreography, and then post it! Praise the Lord! The most popular gospel songs used to be those heard on any Sunday morning from the choir. Much of today's music appeals more to one's earphone and device playlist than the A and B selection in the building of the House of the Lord. Much contemporary music is more adaptable to personal meditation and worship through earphones than to Sunday morning participation in the pew.

What used to be called the "invitation" is less likely to be a call to walk down an aisle or shake someone's hand or even lift your hands and repeat a brief salvific prayer. Following Christ is more a private and personal decision than a public, responsive action. I am seeing churches still growing in attendance with fewer public baptisms and lagging official membership rolls. This is a generation with a greater emphasis on "walking the walk" than walking the aisle. More and more, this present generation prioritizes a practical demonstration of love, justice, compassion, and equity than a positional act of walking an aisle. There seems to be more hunger for practical community than membership on paper.

The resulting revolutionary challenge is that the church has, for over two years, worked hard at increasing the number of online participants; we have restructured and, in many cases, eliminated some now-irrelevant staff positions to increase our viewership and production quality, only to face the frustrating inability to build disciples.

This revolution is upon us. The revolution spoken of by the young prophet Franklin has invaded, influenced, and been initiated into the pulpit legacy passed down from stacked crates and makeshift podiums of the slave church. My personal religious, spiritual, biblical journey—which included four earned degrees, three in the areas of biblical investigation, theological study, and academic achievement—*never* emphasized, saw, or *highlighted* the word or concept of "justice." The Black pulpit of today has made the issues of justice and its nuances not an additional, optional extra, but the very essence of accurate hermeneutics crying out to be released from the pages of the text to the people of God—not "putting" us in there, but declaring that we have been there all along!

This revolution is upon us. The generals like Moses and Elijah and Paul must connect with young lieutenants like Joshua, Elisha, and Timothy. The revolutionary, powerful pulpit, the life-changing pulpit, must be unapologetically theocentric, bibliocentric, and Christocentric, committed to sound exegesis of the Word of God, proclaiming the salvation offered by the Christ who *still* is "*the* way and *the* truth and *the* life" (John 14:6, italics added). The revolutionary pulpit does not back down, does not shrink back, and does not stutter with the proclamation of these truths. This revolution will not be televised. It must be realized.

FIVE

THE LGBTQ+ MOVEMENT: HISTORY, INFLUENCE, AND CHURCH RESPONSE

SARITA T. LYONS

There are very few topics intersecting today's church and culture as complex and contentious as homosexuality. People's lives, ministries, careers, and families have been attacked or applauded, canceled or celebrated, and protested or praised simply depending on where they have landed on this issue.

Satan wants to destroy what God has created. The LGBTQ+ movement has systematically fought for legal rights and privileges, but ultimately this is a spiritual battle against our enemy, the devil, who wants to influence the culture to pervert, undermine, and dismantle God's gifts of gender, sex, and marriage. What seems like a simple battle for human rights is really an ancient battle between God and Satan, with humanity caught in the middle.

Understanding homosexuality and the various gender ideologies is very complicated, but now, more than ever, the church must be better informed to strengthen our apologetic approach. In this chapter we will look at the history of queer activism to help us discern how the enemy is influencing the culture. In the following chapter we will look at some paths forward for the church as well as some ways to better equip the church to defend the truth and engage the culture with faith, hope, and love.

LGBTQ+ TERMS

There are a multitude of terms and ever-evolving acronyms used in the LGBTQ+[1] community. Even with the best intentions, this can be confusing. We'll begin with an introduction to some basic terms and a brief history of where they originated. People tend to feel better loved and are more open for dialogue when you have some knowledge of their history and try to communicate respectfully.

Same-sex practices, desires, and intimacies, as well as gender variance, can be found in nearly every culture in recorded history.[2] The first recorded use of the term "homosexual" appears in 1869 and is credited to social and legal reformer Karl-Maria Kertbeny, an Austrian-born Hungarian.[3] Kertbeny needed a term to help him define someone based on his or her same-sex sexual desires and actions. But homosexual behavior has been around since ancient times. In 1964, when Egyptologists discovered a tomb at Saqqara, Egypt, they believed it contained the remains of Khnumhotep and Niankhkhnum, now considered by many as history's first documented gay couple.[4] This finding has not been without criticism, as some have argued that the two men had families, and being buried together could mean they were brothers not lovers. Others point to several factors that seem to indicate a same-sex relationship: Khnumhotep is depicted offering Niankhkhnum a lotus flower, which would have been symbolic of femininity in Ancient Egypt and only something a wife would offer her husband.[5] We need not rely solely on Egyptian tomb depictions of possible same-sex relationships or sexual practices to find evidence of homosexuality throughout the ancient world. The book of Genesis in the Bible also records the practice of homosexuality in the city of Sodom (Gen. 19), where the term "sodomy"[6] originates.

Most "gay men and lesbians often cite the ancient Greeks as their historical forbearers."[7] Homer's *Iliad* depicts love between a man and a boy (Achilles and Patroclus), as does Plato's *Symposium*, and the Greeks typically did not favor same-sex relationships between men of similar age. These attachments did not preclude heterosexual marriage.[8] For the most part, however, Greek same-sex depictions were reserved for men; women in the classical world were mainly portrayed as "goddesses, whores, wives, and slaves."[9] One popular exception was the poet Sappho, who lived in the seventh century BC on the island of Lesbos, which is the origin of the word "lesbian." Her surviving sensuous love lyrics were read and studied by young wealthy Greek women who were sent to the island of Lesbos to study the arts with Sappho. The term "lesbian" was first used by sexologist Havelock Ellis in 1897.[10] In the 1970s it was appropriated by feminists who were sexually attracted to other women and wanted to distinguish themselves from gay men.[11] In the early twentieth century, the term "gay" became the underground synonym for "homosexual" and referred inclusively to men who were attracted to men, lesbians, bisexuals, and people who would today be called "transgender." Anatomist Robert Bently Todd first used the term "bisexuality" in 1859 to refer to people having male and female physical characteristics in the same body, but today that condition is called intersex.[12] "Bisexual" today is another widely accepted term referring to those who are attracted to more than one gender. Those who identify as bisexual have often felt like they are not welcome in either gay or lesbian communities, as those groups historically viewed bisexuality as a phase individuals went through on their way to their "true gayness or lesbianism."[13] Mid-twentieth-century gay civil rights organizations, wanting to remove the emphasis of "sexual" in homosexual, coined the term "homophile."[14] The term "transgender," which is the most accepted term to date, generally describes an individual who believes their gender identity does not align with their anatomical sex and challenges gender norms in their behavior and presentation.[15] Throughout the 1960s and 1970s, the words "transgenderism," "transgendered," "transsexual," and "transvestite" were used to describe people who were transitioning as well as those undergoing sex change.[16] The letter "Q" in the LGBTQ acronym can have two meanings, referring both to those who are "questioning"[17] as well as those who prefer the term "queer" to describe their sexual identities or affinities."[18] "Queer," once used as a stigmatizing slur towards members of the LGBT community, has since become a catchall term for LGBTQ and was proudly reclaimed by individuals defiantly asserting that one's sexualities, sexual practices, and erotic and affectional investments lay outside of normative heterosexuality.[19] Some recent iterations of the LGBTQ acronym also include the letters I and A (LGBTQIA). The "I" represents "intersex,"[20] and the "A" can represent both "ally" and "asexual." An ally is defined as someone, typically outside of the LGBTQ+ community, who supports activism efforts and individuals who identify as a part of the LGBTQ+ community. "Asexual" refers to individuals who have no sexual attraction for men or women.

LGBTQ+ GOALS AND STRATEGIES

Unlike a religion with specific tenets of faith, the LGBTQ+ community is rooted in an assortment of premises including diversity, self-identification, and nonconformity. Yet not everyone agrees on what these values mean, and various movements throughout history have had different aims and goals. However, we can discern some overarching positions and aims for the movement. Some of the more obvious goals of the movement are sexual freedom, autonomy (the right to be whomever you want to be), gender and heterosexual nonconformity, equal rights for same-sex couples (the same as married heterosexual couples), and equal protection under the law. From a Christian perspective, there has been a deliberate effort to push a renaming, reordering, and reimagining of God's creation and design for gender, sex, and marriage. At each moment in history, whether spurred by the community's defiance of traditional norms, their outright rejection of biblical teaching, or the unfortunate persecution that the LGBTQ+ community has endured from the church and society, several factors have worked to propel what we now see in the culture as queer "Pride."

I have extrapolated four categories of emphasis from LGBTQ+ history that have shaped and advanced these cultural shifts regarding gender, sex, and marriage. Each category has a "territory to target" that represents a powerful societal entity that was lobbied and influenced to bring about the desired "cultural change." I have also included "worldview change" and "spiritual agenda" categories to spur the church to think more deeply about the larger spiritual impact of LGBTQ+ activism. The four categories or goals of the movement are normality, legality, visibility, and religiosity.

I often hear people in the church lamenting, "Every time I turn on the television or watch a movie, homosexuality is everywhere." We need to understand that what we see happening is not an accident. The Bible is clear that "we wrestle not against flesh and blood" (Eph. 6:12 KJV), and we know that our enemy the devil is both a liar and crafty in his strategies. Every issue an apologist encounters is, at the core, a spiritual issue. This is why it is imperative for us to discern how the devil has systematically developed schemes, core beliefs, and attitudes that have shaped the worldviews and systems of power and influence in our culture today. To be clear, our focus is not on fighting individual people, but fighting against the principalities, powers, and rulers of darkness of this world, those who encourage spiritual wickedness in

LGBTQ+ Goal	Territory to Conquer	Cultural Change
Normal	Psychiatry	Homosexuality can't be a sickness
Legal	Politics	Homosexuality can't be a crime
Religious	The church	Homosexuality can't be a sin
Visible	The media	Homosexuality can't be hidden

high places. Knowing the history, activism, and influence of the movement better equips the church to discern the spiritual worldviews that underlie it. In response, we can prayerfully develop a biblical apologetic that informs our

Worldview Change	Spiritual Agenda
Homosexuality and heterosexuality are both equally valuable and normal variations to sexual expression. Gender is fluid. People's sexual orientation and self-perception do not need to be cured or changed.	Reject God's design for gender, sex, and marriage as described in Scripture. God's design is not good.
Same-sex couples should be afforded equal privileges and protections as heterosexual individuals.	God did not say marriage had to be between a man and a woman.
The Bible's view on homosexuality must be revised or rejected. Flawed men, not a perfect God, wrote the Bible. The Bible affirms homosexuality. God made people same-sex attracted. God is love. Love is love. Love wins. You can define love based on feelings, not the Bible. The church is not a loving or safe place.	"Did God really say?" Don't read or follow the Bible. True freedom and happiness are found in disobeying God. Your desires are more important than obedience to God. Your thoughts and feelings should be trusted more than God's Word. A loving God would not deny you your wants. God made you queer. It isn't wrong to live out how you were made. Love and acceptance can be found outside of God and his church.
Everyone's lives and choices deserve equal attention and representation. The more you see something, the more acceptance you will have. You are an oppressor, homophobic, transphobic, heterosexist, etc. if you reject homosexuality or try to suppress its visibility.	Self-acceptance and Pride are the goals of life. What God thinks doesn't matter. The devil has nothing to do with it.

response and evangelism and encourages relationship building with those in the LGBTQ+ community. We'll spend most of the next chapter focusing on how to develop this apologetic.

AMERICAN HOMOSEXUALITY:
THE 1950S AND 60S

Our first step is to gain some familiarity with the movement itself. What are the historic moments? What is celebrated and remembered in this community? There are far too many activists, events, and subcultures to do this subject justice, but in what follows I have included a brief summary of some of the focal people, ideologies, and transformative moments in the history of this movement in the United States, beginning in the 1950s and continuing to the present day. Based on these, I end the chapter with some instrumental themes that the church needs to grapple with as we seek to be better equipped to engage the LGBTQ+ community.

THE LAVENDER SCARE

In the 1950s, there was a growing fear within some segments of the United States government that homosexuals were a threat to national security and needed to be systematically removed from the federal government. This became known as "the lavender scare."[21] The fear increased in 1953 when President Eisenhower issued a new national security order, Executive Order 10450, which stated that people are disqualified from federal employment by engaging in "any behavior which suggests the individual is not reliable or trustworthy." One specific example given was "sexual perversion," a code word for homosexuality.[22] This was the first time the federal government had officially identified homosexuality as a threat to national security.

THE HOMOPHILE MOVEMENT

In the decades that followed, a movement known as the homophile movement arose. This was "resistant thinking" to the prevailing belief in the culture at that time that homosexuals were errors of nature, pathologically sick, and a danger to society. Two of the major groups that developed at this time were the Daughters of Bilits (DOB), founded by Del Martin and Phyllis Lyon, and the Mattachine Society, founded by Harry Hay, who is often considered the father of the gay rights movement. The group's main goals were to gain acceptance and rights for gays and lesbians through "assimilation" by arguing their similarity with the heterosexual mainstream.[23]

BAYARD RUSTIN AND THE CIVIL RIGHTS MOVEMENT

Bayard Rustin was a key Black civil rights leader, and although he was often "behind the scenes," he served as a mentor to Dr. Martin L. King Jr. Despite Rustin being a principal organizer of the landmark 1963 March on Washington for Jobs and Freedom, little is known about him in comparison with some of the other civil rights leaders of that time. Many assert this is because Rustin was gay and quite open about it. Because gay marriage was not legal at the time, in 1982 Bayard adopted his adult partner Walter Naegle as his son to protect their legal interests. Before there were no marital rights for same-sex couples, adoption was one of the few ways the LGBTQ+ community could secure each other's legal rights.[24] Some have criticized Martin L. King Jr. for capitulating to homophobia within the civil rights movement by not keeping Rustin on staff.[25]

THE STONEWALL INN UPRISING

Today, many LGBTQ people consider the Stonewall riots to be the beginning of the highly visible gay rights movement in the United States. On June 28, 1969, at the Stonewall Inn in New York's Greenwich Village, riots erupted in response to continued police harassment of patrons at the well-known gay bar. Marsha Johnson, an African American transvestite woman (this was the term used at that time) and activist, is mythologically credited for throwing the first brick at police that set off the protests. The Stonewall riots represented a more "spontaneous form of direct action and civil unrest, initiated by primarily working-class individuals and represented an important symbol of the fight for greater queer visibility and political power."[26]

GAY LIBERATION FRONT (GLF)

Less than a month after the Stonewall riots, homosexuals in New York formed the Gay Liberation Front (GLF). This group advocated for gay rights, specifically calling for employment protection, an end to police brutality and harassment, and the decriminalization of sodomy. This group is said to have had a "hatred of capitalism and the traditional family."[27] The GLF believed "social institutions like the heteronormative nuclear family and persistent sexism were responsible for the oppression of gays and lesbians and that these institutions should be actively challenged and overthrown."[28]

AN EMERGING GAY IDENTITY: THE 1970S AND 80S

LESBIAN FEMINISM

The growing gay liberation and women's liberation movements of the 1970s created the conditions for lesbian liberation politics to emerge. Betty Friedan, one of the founders of the National Organization for Women (NOW), warned that a "lavender menace" of lesbians might try and take over with their own agenda and undermine the feminist movement. The Furies Collective and Radicalesbians wanted a separate lesbian nation, exclaiming in "The Woman-Identified Woman" manifesto: "Lesbian, lesbian, any woman can be lesbian."[29] Lesbian feminists believed that all men, including gay men, were sexist and should be avoided. Not all lesbians, however, were separatist. The Combahee River Collective[30] was made up of Black feminist lesbians who rejected separatism for Black lesbians, arguing, "Our situation as black people necessitates that we have solidarity around the fact of race, which white women of course do not need to have with white men. . . . We struggle with black men against racism, while we also struggle with black men about sexism."[31] The Combahee River Collective mission reads, "Our politics at the present time would be that we are actively committed to struggling against racial, sexual, heterosexual, and class oppression."[32]

AMERICAN PSYCHIATRY AND THE DSM CHANGE

The American Psychiatric Association (APA) was founded in 1844 and is the world's largest professional organization for psychiatrists. The APA publishes the Diagnostic and Statistical Manual of Mental Disorders (DSM), used by psychiatrists and mental health professionals for determining a diagnosis. When the DSM-I was published in 1952, homosexuality was classified as sociopathic personality disorder, an abnormality resulting from developmental or familial disturbances and needing treatment.[33] The APA's position caused serious consequences for gays and lesbians throughout the 1950s and 60s, providing justification for employers to discriminate against gays and lesbians in hiring or even firing people on the grounds that they were mentally ill and presented a clear and present danger.[34] In 1973, after months of negotiations with gay activists, the board of trustees of the APA voted to remove homosexuality from the DSM.[35] Out of 10,000 voting members, nearly 40 percent opposed the board's decision to normalize homosexuality. One writer and therapist notes that "the most significant catalyst for the diagnostic change was gay activism, not scientific evidence."[36] While that was a monumental change, it did not immediately end psychiatry's pathologizing of some presentations of homosexuality.[37]

EX-GAY MOVEMENTS AND EXODUS INTERNATIONAL

Exodus International was the largest ex-gay movement, founded in 1976 by Frank Worthen. In 1973, Worthen, a gay man, was making plans to visit a new gay bath house in San Francisco when he says that God spoke to him, saying, "Today I want you back."[38] The premise of this organization and similar ex-gay movements is the belief that God could change you from gay to straight and that gay people should seek to try and become straight. "Ex-gay leaders traveled to churches and appeared on television news programs showing off happily married 'former homosexuals' to prove that sexual orientation is a choice, and that change is possible."[39] This spurred the development and practice of many of the highly criticized conversion therapies[40] that claimed to have developed a way to "cure homosexuality." Exodus International's downfall began when many "ex-gay" leaders left both the movement and their wives to pursue same-sex relationships, saying, "I never saw one of our members or other Exodus leaders or other Exodus members become heterosexual, so deep down I knew that it wasn't true."[41] In 2013, Alan Chambers, who was hired in 2001 as the president of Exodus International, publicly apologized to the LGBT community for the "pain and hurt" Exodus had caused and announced that the organization was permanently shutting down.[42] In reflecting on the harm of the ex-gay movement, Greg Johnson writes,

What made the ex-gay movement's focus on orientation change so problematic [is that] . . . it obscured the gospel from gay people. . . . The emphasis on sexual orientation change redefined spiritual growth as the absence of temptation. To be mature was to no longer experience sexual temptation. That was a standard no straight person was ever put under.[43]

THE ASSASSINATION OF HARVEY MILK

In 1978, Harvey Milk, an openly gay man, was assassinated by former San Francisco city supervisor Dan White. White also killed San Francisco mayor George Moscone.[44] The year before his assassination, Milk was elected to the San Francisco board of supervisors and was well known for defeating Senator John Briggs's Proposition 6 Initiative, which would have prohibited public school teachers from any words or actions that could be considered an advocacy of homosexuality. Milk's death was largely viewed as a martyrdom for the gay rights movement, and Milk became a symbol of the aspirations of gay individuals to participate openly in politics and fight for legal change.[45]

NATIONAL MARCH ON WASHINGTON FOR LESBIAN AND GAY RIGHTS

On October 14, 1979, nearly 100,000 people came to Washington, DC, for the first National March on Washington for Lesbian and Gay Rights. This march also celebrated the tenth anniversary of the Stonewall uprising. Notable speakers included Allen Ginsberg, Audre Lorde, DC mayor Marion Barry, and ousted gay US army sergeant Leonard Matlovich. Angela Davis was also invited to speak but declined because the Communist Party, of which she was a member, did not want to appear to support homosexual rights.[46] The march ushered in the falling away of the assimilationist gay activists[47] of the 1950s and 1960s and the emergence of the new liberationists, who were focused on more of an "in-your-face" approach to sexual freedom.[48]

THE AIDS EPIDEMIC

In the 1980s, doctors in some large urban areas of the United States began reporting a syndrome that affected people's ability to fight disease. This syndrome appeared viral and largely affected gay men, prompting doctors and health officials to call it gay-related immune deficiency (GRID) or gay cancer.[49] In 1984, the virus (HIV) causing acquired immune deficiency syndrome (AIDS) was identified and began a movement of testing, diagnosis, and advocacy. AIDS advocacy groups were very successful at promoting public awareness and raising money for services and research, however, widespread publicity increased visibility of the disease and led to antigay backlash against gay men who were seen as the cause of AIDS. Unfortunately, some Christian groups contributed to this antigay backlash: "As an extreme example, the God Hates Fags crusade . . . claimed that [gay men were] being punished by a higher power to make The United States suffer for becoming a 'fag nation.'"[50] Many have argued that the church was late in responding to the AIDS epidemic and largely failed to do so in a helpful way. Kelly Brown Douglas criticizes the Black church in particular for this, saying, "Black churches gained a well-deserved reputation for being slow in constructively responding to the AIDS crisis. Though AIDS was devastating the Black community, Black churches have been reticent to become involved in HIV/AIDS education and outreach."[51] She and many others attribute the lack of engagement or help with the AIDS crisis by the Black church to their homophobia.[52] While many in the LGBTQ community were scared and dying daily, the church's voice was primarily one of condemnation—a missed opportunity to minister to and care for other image bearers. This condemnation created a deeper wedge between the church and the LGBTQ+ community, highlighting how the church at times has had the right orthodoxy but the wrong orthopraxy, preaching the truth without love and compassion.

GAY PRIDE: THE 1990S TO TODAY

LGBTQ+ PRIDE CELEBRATIONS

For the LGBTQ+ community, the last thirty years have been characterized by the development of unapologetic gay Pride, the open defiance of sexual norms, and a strategy of retaliation against anyone who dares to critique or challenge "their truth." A group that once lived in great fear of persecution now openly celebrates their sexual freedom. There is increased scholarship, additional legal rights, and the fruits of gay activism are seen everywhere today, from genderless bathrooms to requirements that one's pronouns are displayed on profiles in corporate America and in the academic world. The early 1990s were a continuation of the so-called Gayby Boom where children were increasingly born into two-parent same-sex households.[53] More youth "came out" during this time and began defining sexuality and gender identity on their own terms. LGBTQ+ visibility increased in the news, in media, and in popular culture: "Representations of LGBT people in film, on television, and on the Internet have proliferated so rapidly that they have become central to how Americans conceptualize popular culture."[54] In 1991, the first Black Pride celebration was organized in Washington, DC. What started as an 800-person gathering now draws more than 300,000 people to "DC Black Pride" and is now credited as the catalyst for inspiring more than thirty Black Pride celebrations across the country.[55]

MARRIAGE EQUALITY

The Defense of Marriage Act (DOMA) was passed in 1996, defining marriage as the union of one man and one woman. This allowed states to refuse to recognize same-sex marriages granted under the law of other states. It wasn't until Massachusetts became the first state to legally sanction same-sex marriage in 2004 that other states followed by enacting similar legislation for marriage. In 2011, the Obama administration chose to not uphold DOMA, and in 2013 the supreme court struck DOMA down in deciding the case of *US v. Windsor*, ruling that the federal government cannot discriminate against married lesbian and gay couples for the purpose of determining federal benefits and protections.[56] In June 2015, the supreme court further ruled in *Obergefell v. Hodges* that same-sex couples have a fundamental right to marry.[57] This LGBTQ+ victory was celebrated by many as a major win for the gay Pride movement. Many used the hashtag #lovewins to share their celebration. Interestingly, not all LGBTQ+ activists saw this as a win for the community, arguing that it distracted from the more laudable goal of fundamentally questioning (and ultimately eliminating) the institution of marriage, an institution that honors "sexual expression in monogamous, sexist, and heterosexist forms."[58]

WOMANIST THEORY AND THEOLOGY

A related movement of relevance for Black women is the womanist movement. "Womanist" (or womanism) is a term coined by Alice Walker to refer to a person or movement that critically analyzes the intersections of Black women. Womanist theory and theology have contributed to a growing amount of scholarship dedicated to rethinking gender and sexuality beyond the scope of a traditional reading of Scripture. Monique Moultrie, assistant professor of religious studies at Georgia State University, has said that "those who choose celibacy and a black Christian sexuality over fulfilling their same-sex desires can be helped by a womanist sexual ethics . . . (by a) concept of *sexual hospitality* and welcome a full range of sexual expressions and identities."[59] She suggests that a womanist model of sexual fluidity or sexual hospitality is a necessary corrective, largely agreeing with Alice Walker that "a womanist is a woman who loves other women, sexually and/or non-sexually"[60] and that the goal of the movement is to "widen the understanding of fluid sexual categories to recognize nonfixed identities."[61]

NORMAL IS NOT THE GOAL

As we saw in this brief history of the LGBTQ+ movement in America, there were several related efforts that intersected to change our cultural understanding of homosexuality. The community fought the APA and convinced it to change its DSM from labeling homosexuality a sickness because they wanted their behavior to be seen as "normal." As Christians, we know that normal is a low bar compared to what God wants for us and offers us in Christ. Normal is not our goal. The DSM declassified homosexuality as a sickness, but as followers of Christ we know that the real sickness—a sickness all humanity suffers from, gay or straight—is our sin. We all need the cure for sin. Being "normal" in a fallen world means we are still a slave to our sin, but the hope of the gospel of Jesus Christ is that it's not necessary for us to stay that way. The atonement of Jesus Christ gives us the ability to transition from our sinful sickness into healthy sexuality. In a fallen world, acting out on one's same-sex attraction or doing anything that God calls sinful can seem quite normal. In this sense, all of us are "born this way," with a tendency to sin. We are born governed by the flesh, and apart from Christ our thoughts, desires, affections, proclivities, longings, and mind are hostile to God (Rom. 8:7–8). But God doesn't want us to stay as we were born; God wants us to be *reborn*. Through this rebirth we are changed and transformed into the life God intended. This is about far more than a pronoun, how we dress, our gender identity, or genitalia change. It is a heart change, a change at the level of our fundamental desires and our allegiance. Do we live for ourselves or for the one who made us and has redeemed us from our sin? We are born again by killing the old person with the only thing poisonous to sin, the blood of Jesus.

Jesus didn't die for us to be normal, he died to make us new.

LEGAL BUT STILL SINFUL

A major push of the LGBTQ+ community's activism was the systematic overhaul of the laws in the United States (as well as around the world) that discriminated against the human rights of gay individuals. Much of this was in response to police brutality, employment discrimination, criminalization, military exclusion, and hate crimes, as well as efforts to secure marital and family privileges. In all of this the LGBTQ+ community has fought to be treated equally as citizens and to be given the same legal rights as everyone else. And where the law has brought dignity and protection to men and women who were formerly persecuted, Christians should be glad. Our objective is not to persecute those who do not follow God's ways—it is to love them and invite them to experience the real freedom found in Jesus Christ. The laws of the land may change, but that doesn't mean God's law changes. Daniel and his three friends serve as examples of what it means to live in the world but not be of the world (Dan. 3:8–25; 6:1–28). They sought to live out their faith in God boldly, even when it conflicted with the law of the land. But they did so without violence and with respect for others. In light of their example, here are a few considerations for the church as we see the legal pendulum today swinging in favor of the LGBTQ+ community.

First, we need to remember that we are first and foremost citizens of God's kingdom, and God is our King. We should have sober expectations for success in this world. The laws of the land do not supersede the laws of our God, and they may often be in conflict with God's kingdom. Regardless, we can still be a light and conscience for the world. While we should utilize every opportunity we have to vote and engage politically, we cannot forget that our battleground is not primarily legislative but spiritual in nature.

Second, we must honestly come to terms with the history of the Christian church and how we have treated people with same-sex attraction and members of the LGBTQ+ community. Every legal change in favor of the LGBTQ+ community is not something the church should lament or protest. In fact, the church should be in favor of many of the laws and even government funding that protect this community, particularly those most vulnerable to hate crimes like queer youth[62] and transgendered individuals.[63] Instead of contesting every law that benefits the LGBTQ+ community, we should look for ways to be at the forefront of protecting the human dignity and justice of all image bearers, even those with whom we disagree. This does not mean we approve of homosexual behavior or embrace an affirming view, but it does suggest that we reevaluate our default approach if it is largely negative and combative.

This leads us to the question: What battle are we trying to win? If we decide to protest and lobby against unbiblical laws, how can we do this in a way that doesn't compromise our greater goal of pointing people to Jesus? Where our aims may be at odds with one another, we need to ask: Are we trying to win legal battles or heart battles? Is there a responsible way to do both?

GOD DEFINES SIN

Within the Christian church, the LGBTQ+ movement and its allies continue to push the errant belief that "the practice of homosexuality" is not sinful. To resolve this issue we need to define sin. But who has the right to define sin? Only God.

God is God. He existed before everything was created, he alone made everything, and anything that was made was made through him (Gen. 1:1; John 1:3). God alone is qualified as the authority on what has been made because he made it. He is absolute truth. Despite our culture's fascination with relativism, where "your truth, my truth, and their truth" can coexist without a greater authority and submits to nothing other than one's own dynamic thoughts and feelings, there still remains "the truth," and it belongs to God. It stands over and above our faulty imaginations. God is *the* truth (John 14:6, 17; 15:6; 16:13), not *a* truth in a matrix of truth options. Everything God has said can be trusted because God cannot lie (Heb. 6:18), and everything he has commanded should be obeyed (Luke. 6:46). This is true, regardless of our culture or the time we live in because God is immutable (he does not change), and truth is a reflection of his nature and character (1 Pet. 1:24–25). If anyone seeks his own desires and does not obey the truth, they obey unrighteousness and the consequence is God's wrath and fury (Rom. 2:8) because God is holy (Lev. 19:2). God's truth, as a reflection of his nature, is tied to his holiness—his moral purity and otherness. We come to know God and what he desires for his creation through the Bible, the revealed Word of God. The Bible is true because it is God's breathed Word. The Bible is written by men, but it is also inspired. This is not "inspired" in the way a beautiful scene in nature can inspire a poet or a painter who then creates something of their own will. Rather, the Scriptures are inspired because they are the actual words of God written by men who were under the leading of the Holy Spirit (whether they were fully aware of it at the time or not), the Spirit who is God. While much can be said about this, a few relevant Scriptures summarize this point:

All Scripture is inspired by God and is profitable for teaching, for rebuking, for correcting, for training in righteousness, so that the man of God may be complete, equipped for every good work. (2 Tim. 3:16–17 CSB)

Above all, you know this: No prophecy of Scripture comes from the prophet's own interpretation, because no prophecy ever came by the will of man; instead, men spoke from God as they were carried along by the Holy Spirit. (2 Pet. 1:20–22 CSB)

Throughout the Bible, sin is defined as transgression of the law of God (1 John 3:4) and rebellion against God (Deut. 9:7; Josh. 1:18). Again, here are a few Scriptures that summarize this teaching:

- Everyone has inherited sin from the fall of mankind (Rom. 5:12).
- Everyone was born sinful (Ps. 51:5).
- Everyone has sinned (Rom. 3:23; 1 John 1:8).
- There is a penalty and remedy for sin (John 3:16–17; Rom. 6:23).
- Jesus took our sins on himself and paid our sin penalty (2 Cor. 5:21; 1 Pet. 2:24).
- When Jesus saves us from the penalty of our sin, we become new (2 Cor. 5:17).
- Christians should not sin deliberately (Heb. 10:26).
- Christians should not keep on sinning (1 John 3:6–8).
- Christians will be tempted to sin, but we don't have to sin (1 Cor. 10:13).
- We must confess our sins to receive forgiveness (1 John 1:9).
- We must repent of our sins (Prov. 28:13).

Some will argue that the commands given in the Old Testament no longer have any bearing on our conduct today because they are under the old covenant. This is a complex matter worthy of more study, and it is true that there are some elements of the old covenant that no longer apply to Christian followers of Jesus today (such as the Jewish dietary laws, religious practices for worship, etc.). However, a majority of the moral commands of God in the old covenant are repeated or reaffirmed in the New Testament teaching of Jesus and the apostles, including the affirmation of marriage as between one man and one woman and the condemnation of homosexual practices. This is consistent throughout the entire Bible in both the Old and New Testaments.

In the Old Testament writings, we find clear prohibitions against homosexual behavior:

> You are not to sleep with a man as with a woman; it is detestable. (Lev. 18:22 CSB)

> If a man sleeps with a man as with a woman, they have both committed a detestable act. They must be put to death; their death is their own fault. (Lev. 20:13 CSB)

One of the most well-known examples of homosexuality is found in Genesis 19:1–29, the story of Sodom and Gomorrah. Some have argued that the sins of these cities were not primarily homosexuality (if at all), but that "inhospitality" or "rape" were the likely offenses.[64] However, perceptions of Sodom in Jewish literature found in Ezekiel and Jude's mention of unnatural desires makes it clear that Sodom had a reputation for sexual and homosexual sin.[65]

And when we turn to the New Testament, the apostle Paul is very clear in his negative assessment of homosexuality:

> For this reason God delivered them over to disgraceful passions. Their women exchanged natural sexual relations for unnatural ones. The men in the same way also left natural relations with women and were inflamed in their lust for one another. Men committed shameless acts with men and received in their own persons the appropriate penalty of their error. (Rom. 1:26–27 CSB)

> Do not be deceived: No sexually immoral people, idolaters, adulterers, or males who have sex with males, no thieves, greedy people, drunkards, verbally abusive people, or swindlers will inherit God's kingdom. (1 Cor. 6:9–10 CSB)

> But we know that the law is good, provided one uses it legitimately. We know that the law is not meant for a righteous person, but for the lawless and rebellious, for the ungodly and sinful, for the unholy and irreverent,

for those who kill their fathers and mothers, for murderers, for the sexually
immoral and males who have sex with males, for slave traders, liars, perjur-
ers, and for whatever else is contrary to the sound teaching that conforms
to the gospel concerning the glory of the blessed God, which was entrusted
to me. (1 Tim. 1:8–11 CSB)

Despite the clear prohibitions through the Bible, many people will still
object, pointing out that Jesus never says anything specifically about homosexuality. This is a common defense for many of those who are same-sex
affirming. They reason that because Jesus doesn't *specifically* condemn homosexuality, the New Testament examples quoted above are merely "Paul's sexual
ethic"[66] and Jesus himself does not prohibit homosexual behavior. There are
several problems with this reasoning. First, it presumes that the Gospels are,
for some unexplained reason, more authoritative and comprehensive than the
rest of Scripture. Yet the apostles and the early church taught that *all* Scripture
is given by inspiration of God and profitable—not just some parts of it (2 Tim.
3:16). Some of the Bible's most important teachings are found throughout the
Old and New Testaments and are not limited to the Gospels alone. It is wrong
to conclude that any doctrines and teachings not mentioned by Jesus are therefore unimportant. Additionally, that Jesus never specifically says something
about homosexuality does not then imply that he approves of it. We should
look more closely at what Jesus does say, and he says something very clearly
about heterosexuality. He references it as God's standard for humanity (Mark
10:5–9), affirming that sexual expression was created for one man and one
woman in the context of a marriage.

COMMENDING TRUTH DESPITE THE ERROR WE SEE

One of the major goals of LGBTQ+ activism was to ensure that the LGBTQ+
community came out of the shadows of shame and secrecy to proudly live
"their truth" regardless of what anyone thought or believed. For the past
several decades they have pursued the goal of increased cultural visibility and
acceptance. This was made far easier by convincing the psychiatric world that
homosexuality was not to be considered an illness; it continued by the decriminalization of homosexuality and through revisionist affirming theologies that

rejected the Bible as authoritative for the Christian life, declaring that homosexuality is not a sin. With greater political, religious, and cultural visibility, the LGBTQ+ community began to enjoy greater representation in the world of arts and entertainment, and major corporations, universities, and schools began to celebrate Pride month, opening doors for LGBTQ+ persons to hold positions of political power and influence, make scholarly contributions, and exercise leadership in religious circles. However, as we discern the spiritual agenda behind this movement, we understand that LGBTQ+ visibility is the fruit of invisible ideologies and powers. Even as we love gay and transgender people, the church must not underestimate the demonic system at work behind the larger movement of societal transformation. With the increased visibility and celebration of homosexuality in our culture, there is still much that the church can do to help better equip Christians to engage with their neighbors.

First, the church should remain committed to God's Word by teaching that the world does not reflect God's standard. We can't wait for the culture to submit to God so our children can finally have school or entertainment options or social experiences that we feel comfortable with as Christians. Instead of consistently being outraged whenever we see a gay or lesbian character in a movie or cartoon, we should prepare our children to enter the world as it is—a world that does not love God and does not honor his commands. Unless your strategy is to live isolated in your house and never go outside or turn on the television, encounters with the culture are unavoidable, and the Bible doesn't say that God has called us to hide in the safety of our sanitized Christian homes, constantly talking about how mortified we are by the decline of society. Scripture tells us that "in the last days" things will get worse and worse (2 Tim. 3:1–5 CSB; cf. 1 Tim. 4:1; 2 Pet. 3:3). So instead of being surprised or angered that the world is acting on brand, let's roll up our sleeves and equip the church on what we should expect, give them tools that help them respond and know what to avoid, and model how to be a light in the darkness. Now more than ever, the church must be equipped to stand in a culture of scoffers, not scurrying away from the threat of ungodly culture.

To put it simply, the church must become more visible. The LGBTQ+ movement started as an underground community with a few dozen protesters, grew to a marching throng in Washington with a worldwide Pride celebration, and now boasts major influencers throughout the secular world, including

Hollywood. There is space for others to have a powerful influence on the culture, and the church needs to step into that space. We must learn how to navigate and excel in the domains of art, entertainment, social media, politics, mental health, and education, to name just a few, and ensure that truth is just as accessible and visible as the lies we see and hear promoted every day. How successful are you and your church at creating, curating, promoting, producing, and writing in a way that is countercultural? This can be as simple as how you use your private social media or as grand as your church community producing films and television shows. I've heard Christians lament, "Homosexuality is everywhere." My response for the church is, "But let's not forget, Christ and his ambassadors are everywhere too!"

In the next chapter, we'll continue by looking at some practical ways churches and individuals can apologetically engage the LGBTQ+ movement today.

SIX

A BIBLICAL APOLOGETIC FOR GENDER, SEX, AND MARRIAGE

SARITA T. LYONS

Indulge me in a short exercise. Close your eyes for seven seconds and picture anything you believe ranks as "the most beautiful."

What's my point? This isn't scientific, but I suspect everyone who did this pictured something that only God made. It might have been the beaches of Hawaii or the rain forests of Costa Rica or the snowcapped Rocky Mountains of Colorado. Depending on how fortunate you've been to travel or how many travel sites you follow on Instagram, I'm sure you have your own catalogue of beauty to consider. I'm almost certain no one pictured a skyscraper, a massive bridge, a gorgeous mansion, or a car or jet. Even though those things are impressive and beautiful in their own way, few of us think of man-made creations when we first envision beauty because despite our best attempts, no one creates beauty like God. When humankind creates beauty, whether couture fashion or a towering steel building, we are using the raw materials, resources, and intelligence that come from our Creator. We know in our hearts that nothing people create is ever better than what God creates.

My friend Dr. Tiffany Gill once traveled to Dubai in the United Arab

Emirates, and when she returned we talked about her trip, and I was struck by her impressions of the UAE. She remarked that it was "absolutely beautiful, like nothing you've ever seen or experienced, but something about it just felt artificial because I know this place used to just be a desert." She went on to explain how everything she found amazing about Dubai felt somewhat "off" to her, and her guess was that deep down she knew it was not real—the beauty was man-made.

I have noticed this way of thinking even in my children. One day we were driving down a familiar path near our home lined with huge trees that create a canopy of green foliage over the winding road. On this particular morning, to our dismay, we found that all the trees had been cut down, like a thief had come in the night and removed them. The once beautiful trees were now lying where they'd fallen, creating a wasteland of rotting wood. We saw a shiny new billboard hammered into the ground, like a piece of candy offered to a crying baby in church to hold them over to dinner. This sign announced a new "community golf course," and it had a mockup drawing of the future greens that would replace the sea of trees we'd passed for years. Seeing this, one of my kids asked the question we were all thinking: "Do they think this will be better? It's okay, but it's not better than what was already here."

I find myself pondering this whenever I think about gender, sex, and marriage. Though humankind has intelligence, desire, and ingenuity, and we are able to tinker with, chop down, rename, reimagine, and repurpose what God has created in many diverse and creative ways (some of which are okay), in the end many people find themselves thinking, "It's not better than what was already here."

I want to begin from a simple premise provided by theologian Michael Bird: "The Christian view is that human identity is not entirely constructed; it is given, bestowed, revealed."[1] Or to put it even more simply, God created us and therefore God has the right and the perfect wisdom to tell us who we are. Let's begin by looking at what God says about gender.

GENDER

Gender is defined as "the social construction and meaning a given culture associates with a person's attitudes, behaviors, feelings, and their assigned biological sex."[2] A person's sex is defined as the biological and physiological characteristics that determine whether a person is male or female.[3] The Bible tells us that in the beginning, God designed our sex to inform gender, but after the fall, they are dramatically disconnected.[4]

One of the most profound impacts of LGBTQ+ activism has been its ability to influence and change the way the world, including many in the scientific community, now thinks about gender. One need look no further than Facebook, which recently listed over seventy-two gender options to choose from when filling out a personal profile.[5] My children were attempting to "school me" on cultural LGBTQ+ issues and informed me, "Mom, you are not considered a woman anymore. You are called a *cis woman*." "Cisgender," or "cis" for short, was a term popularized in the 1990s and is used to refer to a person who is not transgender. Our understanding of what it means to be a man or woman has been entirely deconstructed and reconstructed today to accommodate the increased acceptance and visibility of the transgender experience.[6]

Gender is no longer viewed as an expression of God's design of male and female. Instead, it is seen through the lens of LGBTQ+ culture as something malleable, able to be defined by the individual regardless of the body God has gifted to them. Please note what I'm not saying. We should never deny the existence of social constructs born out of stereotypes and changing culture. A quick survey of history reveals how men and women have manifested their manhood or womanhood in various ways across cultures. These social constructs change over time. Christians around the world and throughout time who have embraced a variety of God-honoring ways to express what their maleness and femaleness can look like, all falling within the freedom we have in Christ. This is not my focus in this chapter. Our focus more narrowly is on the reframing of gender encouraged by LGBTQ+ activism and those who believe, as theologian Michael Bird summarizes, that

> all people are created as a blank slate, that all differences between men and
> women are a heteronormative patriarchal ploy to oppress women, and that
> governments should promote gender sameness in all things. . . . [Bird disagrees and asserts,] Men and women really are different, that difference is
> coded into every cell of our bodies, even down to the wiring of our brains,
> and that difference is socially manifested.[7]

The Bible takes a rather simple approach with gender. It does not disengage gender from sex in the way the world has come to define and experience gender. Rather, a Christian conceptualization of gender "should be understood as the cultural reality resulting from God making men and women biologically sexed and distinct. . . . Christians should abide by the gender norms set by their culture insofar as what the culture dictates does not transgress God's moral law for upholding the sex distinctions between male and female (Deut. 22:5, 1 Cor. 11:3–16)."[8] We have some measure of liberty regarding how we individually express our maleness and femaleness. However, we should also note that the Bible does not teach gender sameness. There are gender distinctions, and we should be aware of how they are culturally expressed because they are a "common grace mechanism for acknowledging the innate differences of males from females."[9]

Genesis 1 makes it clear that humanity was made in the image of God. We were made male and female in God's image (Gen. 1:27). In Genesis 1–3, the Bible lays the foundation for how and why God created man and woman and the consequence for their identity and relationship after the fall. This section of Scripture is cited by both Jesus and Paul and provides the foundational biblical teaching (the "law of first mention") on men's and women's identities and roles.

- In Matthew 19:4, when the Pharisees question Jesus about divorce, Jesus responds by referring to Genesis 1–3, saying, "He who created them in the beginning made them male and female" (CSB).
- In Romans 1, Paul unfolds one of the clearest defenses of the gospel's implications. The immediate context of Romans 1:18–32 is focused on the idolatry of the pagan world resulting from their suppression of God's revelation in creation. Paul uses Genesis 1–3 to explain three exchanges pagans make in response to God's revelation of himself in creation. Pagans exchange the truth about creation, spirituality, and sexuality for what he calls "a lie" (CSB).[10]
- After man and woman's rebellion against God, there are several consequences. They experience a broken identity that affects how they see themselves (Gen. 3:7, 10–11), broken communion with one another (Gen. 3:12, 16), broken physical functions (Gen. 3:16–19), and broken communion with God (Gen. 3:23–24). The fall significantly undermines God's original design for man and woman. Though subverted,

God's design is not eradicated. It persists as his ideal today and is ultimately redeemed by Christ.

Genesis 2 also indicates that men and women have different roles or functions in the fulfillment of God's creation mandate to humanity. These different functions or roles don't convey superiority or inferiority, since both men and women together are created in the image of God. Our contemporary culture may attempt to deny the distinctions between male and female, but the New Testament reaffirms the Old Testament's teaching on this topic and brings the male-female distinction to its culmination in the Christ-church relationship (Eph. 5:22–33).

THE METAPHOR OF MARRIAGE

Marriage can be a beautiful picture of love and long-term commitment. The most beautiful marriage and the only *eternal* marriage is not between a man and a woman but between Christ and his church. Because every human marriage is affected by sin, if we don't see all marriages through the lens of God's ultimate purposes, we miss the greater purpose, passion, and promise that marriage points to. Marriage stands as a visual representation of the union between God and his people—a metaphor that reveals a miracle. Marriage joins two sinners together in a holy union, which is itself a miracle, but as a metaphor it points to an even more significant miracle, a union only made possible by a perfect suitor's (Jesus's) death to join sinners to a holy God. No internet proposal video can rival what Jesus did for sinful people. He did not get down on one knee, he allowed himself to be nailed to a tree, dying for our sin. There were no violins playing, just the sound of jeering. There was no trail of roses, just a crown of thorns that left a trail of blood. As Jesus cried out "It is finished," the hearts of sinners from Calvary until consummation will all be forced to respond to the Savior's question, "Will you marry me?" That is a picture of committed pursuit, the ultimate example of sacrificial love. This is a picture of the passion of Christ, the promise of Christ, and the purpose of marriage displayed at the cross. When Paul writes in Ephesians 5:22–33 about a wife's submission and a husband's sacrificial love, he offers us instruction for earthly marriages but then speaks of something even greater, explicitly pointing our attention to the relationship between Christ and the church. If the example and created purpose of marriage starts with God, then it must be defined by God and modeled after God's intentions. What God tells us about marriage can then practically apply as the divine example for our everyday lives.

MARRIAGE IS A MONOGAMOUS UNION BETWEEN A MAN AND WOMAN

God created mankind male and female (Gen. 1:27), and when discussing marriage (Matt. 19:4–5), Jesus connected the union of marriage to Genesis 2:24–25, which says, "That's why a man will leave his own father and mother. He marries a woman, and the two of them become like one person [or in some translations 'one flesh']. Although the man and his wife were both naked, they were not ashamed" (CEV). If we revisit the Ephesians 5:22–33 passage mentioned earlier, there is no coincidence that the church, *ecclesia* in the Greek, is put in feminine and called a bride, while Christ, fully God and fully man, is the groom. This picture emphasizes God's intention for marriage, reinforcing what Genesis initially teaches, that it is a union between a man and a woman.

God's paradigm for marriage is also seen in Genesis 1–2 as a *monogamous* or exclusive union between a man and woman. It is significant that the Genesis narrator describes the first marriage using singular nouns and pronouns (Gen. 2:18–23). God intentionally made for "the man" a "helper" (v. 18) corresponding to "him" (CSB). God took "one of his ribs" and made "a woman" and brought her to "the man" (v. 21–22), the man announced, "this one . . ." will be called "woman" for "she" was taken from "man" (v. 23 CSB). There is a clear implication that God envisioned the sexual relationship to be shared between two marriage partners and only two as a monogamous relationship. One man and one woman become one flesh.

MARRIAGE PRODUCES IMAGE BEARERS

God commanded the man and woman in Genesis to "be fruitful and multiply" (Gen. 1:28 ESV). Whether biologically, through adoption, or through discipleship, one of the ministries of marriage is to produce, nurture, and fill the earth with those who love, follow, and obey God. Today, this means raising children as disciples of Jesus. The church, the bride of Christ, fulfills its own marriage vows to Christ by joining with his Spirit in the work of the Great Commission mandate, going into all the world and making disciples.

There is fruit produced by the union of Christ and his church, both corporately and individually, the evidence of our intimate union with Christ. When we are "known" by Christ spiritually—a metaphor for how "Adam knew his wife" and together they produced a son—our own union with Christ is an opportunity for us to spiritually reproduce and raise more Christ followers.

SEX

When speaking of sex, we are discussing how what we do with our bodies fits into the larger framework of sexuality. As Andrew Walker notes, "Sexuality refers to God's anthropological design and pattern for the procreative relationship between male and female and to the experience of erotic desire within that design."[11] We should begin with the obvious: God created sex. And because everything God created is good, sex is good and is designed, given, and blessed by God as a gift to be enjoyed within the boundary of the covenant of marriage between a man and a woman. God intended sex to be shame-free, pleasure-drenched, deeply unifying, and honored by all. Sex within marriage has several purposes, including but not limited to:

- Procreation (Gen. 1:28)
- Pleasure (Prov. 5:18–19)
- Protection (1 Cor. 7:2, 5)[12]
- Physical unity (Gen. 2:24)
- Peace and comfort (2 Sam. 12:24)[13]

Even though you can have sex and it "feels good," feeling good does not make it good sex. God requires holy sex, and sex is only holy when it happens on God's terms. Despite the church's preoccupation with homosexuality today, homosexuality is not the only sexual sin that displeases God. Other unholy sexual acts listed in the Bible are fornication (1 Cor. 6:18), premarital sex (Deut. 22:13–21), prostitution (Lev. 19:29; Prov. 7:4–27), bestiality (Ex. 22:19), adultery (Deut. 5:18), rape (Deut. 22:25–29), and incest (Lev. 18:6–18).[14] When married couples have sex in accordance with God's commands, they express their love for one another and God in an atmosphere of holiness, and there is nakedness and no shame. Only in this context is sex an act of worship reflecting God's image and very good design. While there are multiple ways to have sinful heterosexual sex (see above), it is important to note that while the Bible talks positively about heterosexual sex when it's not condemning unholy heterosexual practices, the Bible never talks about homosexuality in positive terms.[15]

We see from Genesis 3 that man and woman's fall into sin damaged our beautiful, powerful, God-given sexuality. Sin caused us to see things God never intended us to see, revealed our nakedness and caused vulnerability, brought on shame, gave us a propensity to hide from God, and led us to isolate from one another. Sin caused us to foolishly try and fix what we don't understand without consulting God. We cover our gender differences with things like fig leaves that will eventually die. We are lost and disoriented and don't know the answer to God's question when he asks us, "Where are you?" We just know that we are afraid. We point the finger and blame others for our discomfort with ourselves. We even get mad at God instead of taking responsibility for our sin (Gen. 3:7–12). We are born into this, slaves to our sin, and struggle to realize that the serpent who deceived us long ago is still asking us the same question: "Did God really say?" (Gen. 3:1). Our sexual lives have been dominated by sin, and our powerful God-given sexual desires are now called "lusts" of the "flesh" (Rom. 13:14 NASB; Gal. 5:16). As a result, what was created as good and for good is often expressed in perverse and wicked ways. Marriage doesn't cure sexual brokenness; it just makes it much harder to hide. We all have sexual brokenness—the single, the married, the transgendered, those attracted to the same sex, and those who are heterosexual. We all need the power of God to heal us, teach us, and keep us so that we can honor God through our sexuality. The saddest part of our postfall reality is that we often miss the God-made provision for our sin—not dying fig leaves, but animal skins that he made after he killed an animal to cover us (Gen. 3:21). It was this first bloodshed for sin that pointed to the death of his son Jesus. Jesus's death on the cross would be the only way to redeem and fix all that was broken from the beginning.

JESUS WAS A SEXUAL BEING BUT DID NOT SIN

The church rarely, if ever, talks about Jesus as a man who had a sexuality because so many of our views of sexuality and the human body are a product of our own brokenness. Jesus had a body with a brain, eyes, skin, nerve endings—and I am not trying to be crass—but it is fair to assume he had genitals as well. We can also infer that he, like all humans, experienced sexual temptation. The Bible tells us that "we do not have a high priest who is unable to sympathize with our weaknesses, but one who has been tempted in every way as we are, yet without sin" (Heb. 4:15 CSB). Rachel Joy Welcher says that during his time on earth, Jesus had to "figure out his body and control its reactions as a young boy and later as an adult, even as women knelt at his feet or tugged on his robes."[16] Why is the church uncomfortable discussing Jesus and his sexuality? Welcher shares her thoughts on this: "I believe it is because we struggle to separate sexuality from sexual sin, and therefore it is hard for us to imagine that Jesus could be both sexual and sinless."[17] But this should be good news to us because Jesus is our great high priest and our great hope! While he was on earth, he was a man, a sexual being, and yet he did not sin. He did what the Scripture tells us to do: "For this is God's will, your sanctification: that you keep away from sexual immorality, that each of you knows how to control his own body in holiness and honor, not with lustful passions, like the Gentiles, who don't know God" (1 Thess. 4:3–5 CSB). Christians are not God incarnate, but we have God's person and power in us through the Holy Spirit. We are called to "flee sexual immorality! Every other sin a person commits is outside the body, but the person who is sexually immoral sins against his own body. Don't you know that your body is a temple of the Holy Spirit who is in you, whom you have from God? You are not your own, for you were bought at a price. So glorify God with your body" (1 Cor. 6:18–20 CSB). Like Jesus, we can be sexual beings and not sin sexually. We can have desires, but they don't have to control us. Someone needs to say this out loud, "No matter what I desire, I don't have to sin." If you are a Christian, your desires are not your master. Jesus is! Is it easy? No! We all will struggle in this earthen vessel, this temple made of clay, but we will not struggle forever. This body that was promised to return to the dust will one day be resurrected. Then we will receive the promise of a new body and for the first time experience what it feels like to have a body not corrupted by sin. There will be no lust, no shame, no confusion, no temptation, no insecurity, no loneliness, no lack of pleasure or sinful desires. Everything will be perfect and new. We will be in the presence of God, worshiping with the saints, forever unburdened by the weight of corruptibility. That is the day we groan for with joyful expectation.

A SPECTRUM OF POSTURES TOWARD THE LGBTQ+ COMMUNITY

In the church, we may discuss the issue of sin and agree that it is wrong. We may even talk about how we can love the LGBTQ+ community. But rarely do we interrogate and locate the problem in our own hearts, thinking, and behaviors. Might there be something in us that possibly hinders us in representing Christ well? In what way are we stumbling blocks to God being glorified? Below are several categories I've created to help Christians locate themselves on a spectrum of common dispositions and responses to the LGBTQ+ community. As you read through these, see if you can locate yourself in one of these categories. Is this close to how you respond to the LGBTQ+ community? This is not meant to be easy, but rather a sobering and humbling assignment.[18] While some may contend that certain categories are better than others, finding yourself among the eight options listed below is difficult because all of them are in some way problematic for a Christian.

1. ALLY

The "ally Christian" may or may not be a member of the LGBTQ+ community. They are a strong supporter of LGBTQ+ people and queer agendas. They advocate for their equal treatment and civil rights, and they see no problem with the practice of homosexuality. Allies don't see homosexuality as unbiblical or sinful and may even believe the Bible affirms this lifestyle and behavior.

2. AMBIVALENT

The "ambivalent Christian" is someone who does not have a clear or discernable position about homosexuality, same-sex attraction (SSA), or LGBTQ+ activism. They may say they can see good things on "both sides" of the issue: the affirming and non-affirming position. They tend to be more apathetic or disinterested in being involved or articulating a response to this topic, believing that "people can do whatever they want to do. It's none of my business how people live their lives."

3. ACTOR

The "actor Christian" is a believer who, like a secret agent, leads a double life. They portray Christian values and affirm Christian beliefs in their

Christian circles, but in environments where Christ or biblical truth is not welcomed, they "turn off" and cover up their faith (Matt. 5:15–16). The actor may cosign queer-affirming lifestyles in affirming circles or silently sit back and not say anything to disrupt the comfort of friendships. They may be sensitive to the assumptions made about them if they were to identify as a Christian. To both nonbelievers and other Christians, there is little evidence to convict this person of being a strong disciple of Jesus, although they may attend and even serve in their church.

4. AMENABLE AVOIDER

The "amenable avoider" is the Christian that focuses on being friends with someone from the LGBTQ+ community but never engages their friend with the gospel or any matters of faith that might make the LGBTQ+ person uncomfortable. These individuals believe their witness for God should primarily be relational, and they focus exclusively on showing grace through friendship. Some amenable avoiders recognize and lament the harm Christians have caused the LGBTQ+ community over the years and value being a corrective experience for that person. The amenable avoider may have hope that a genuine relationship without the pressure of discussing homosexuality or other uncomfortable faith topics will make a person from the LGBTQ+ community feel safe and perhaps see them as "a different type of Christian." They may believe that God will open a door to share the gospel or in some way represent a biblical perspective on sexuality and spiritual matters; however, the amenable avoider sometimes takes this passive posture for so long that they "get friend zoned," making it more difficult to be transparent about faith or their convictions. They tend to miss or ignore opportunities to share the gospel or withhold truth when it would be plausible to share. The amenable avoider may also feel guilt for engaging in conversations about same-sex relationships with a friend in a way that made them seem like a supportive ally and now fears looking like a backtracking hypocrite. The amenable avoider may fear retribution or the loss of the friendship if they made their faith an important aspect of their friendship.

5. AMENABLE MISSIONARY

The "amenable missionary" is a Christian who intentionally attempts to befriend someone from the LGBTQ+ community, but their true agenda is only to address their same-sex attraction. They see members of the LGBTQ+ community as "projects not people"[19] needing to be saved from their SSA. Their focus is fixing, not friendship. Their goal or agenda is to call out sin, diagnose the problem, and point people to a solution. This person quickly shares Bible verses and God's sexual ethic, couched with platitudes of how much God loves the sinner but hates the sin. This person may share recommended books and send YouTube videos about someone becoming "ex-gay." The amenable missionary does not spend time with members of the LGBTQ+ community out of genuine curiosity about their life (except to use it as data to piece together the puzzle for "curing" their homosexuality).

6. ALARMIST

The "alarmist" is the Christian who is always responding to the LGBTQ+ community and their increasing visibility with shock and disdain. These individuals find memes, articles, and disturbing pictures or videos to share about the LGBTQ+ lifestyle as if the world has been invaded by some new alien monster that threatens their kids and offends their fragile sensibilities. These people set off alarms of concern and encourage others to clutch their Christian pearls, but they are totally disengaged from people, do not have conversations with members of this community, and never take time to think through how the church can get equipped to respond and lovingly build relationships. They know the latest same-sex couples, the latest queer movie characters, and the most recently discovered transgendered person. They sound the alarm, but they have no solutions. They have OMG and SMH tattooed on their proverbial forehead, full of judgment but paralyzed by their apathy. They sound the alarm, yelling "fire," but they don't help anyone get out of the burning building.

7. ALOOF DISSENTER

The "aloof dissenter" is the Christian that may share a disapproving position regarding the LGBTQ+ community among their friends, family, or circle of influence. They may have a clear and accurate biblical position that they preach or post on social media, but they never move toward LGBTQ+ people relationally. Their lack of engagement with actual people from this community causes their truth to feel vacant of love and empathy. They have a platform but no presence in the lives of the community on which they comment. The aloof dissenter likely cares about pleasing God and is willing to be disliked for the sake of the truth, but they may have a blind spot regarding their ineffectiveness at pointing people to Jesus and loving the LGBTQ+ community well. Unlike the amenable avoider, they are more willing to sacrifice relationship for truth. The aloof dissenter would likely be shocked or sad to hear that their words and ignorance of the LGBTQ+ or SSA experience could be discouraging for them. The aloof dissenter is not as aggressive or mean-spirited as the antagonist, but their greatest weakness is seeing issues to debate or defend vs. seeing people to love and win.

8. ANTAGONIST

The "antagonist" is the Christian who values the sword of truth over the Spirit. They are clear about biblical truth on the issue of homosexuality, but grace and love are absent. In fact, they are not just graceless and merciless, they are intentionally injurious. The antagonist believes they are not only truth tellers but dispensers of God's wrath. They don't just speak biblical truth without compassion, they also serve punishment. This punishment can come in the form of tasteless jokes about the LGBTQ+ community, name calling, stereotypical gay behavior imitation, encouraging others to laugh and poke fun at the LGBTQ+ community, and in extreme cases it might escalate into physical violence. They say that the LGBTQ+ community needs Jesus while failing to look like Jesus in their personal or online presence. The antagonist is unloving and Pharisaical, verbally callous, and intentionally injurious to other image bearers. This person may consider homosexuality to be a greater sin than other sins, but even if they don't believe that is true, they are blind to their own sins of pride, self-righteousness, and hatred.

WE MUST NOT MISUSE BIBLICAL TRUTH

The spectrum of different characters listed above represent various ways in which believers wrongly seek to interact with those in the LGBTQ+ community. Some of these approaches are commendable at times, but they all have a weakness of one kind or another.

The Black church has inferentially been accused of playing the part of the actor. The Greek word for actor, *hypokrites*, rightly describes the hypocrisy often experienced in the Black church by members of the LGBTQ+ community. Preaching that uses Scripture to sarcastically joke that "God created Adam and Eve not Adam and Steve" while also giving queer people positions of leadership and esteem for their musical talent is hypocritical. Dade notes, "While many black pastors condemn gays and lesbians from the pulpit, the choir lofts behind them often are filled with gay singers and musicians. Some male pastors themselves have been entangled in scandals involving alleged affairs with men."[20]

Luke, one of the disciples of Jesus, provides us with a helpful account in his Gospel, a warning against allowing our own anger and desire for justice to overwhelm the grace of God in reaching out to sinful men and women. It is helpful for the church in discerning how to represent Jesus in a hostile world and offers a caution by way of application about misusing our sword of truth. Luke shares how Peter, in wanting to defend Jesus, takes up his sword and causes an untimely injury. Luke 22:48–51 says,

> Jesus said to him, "Judas, are you betraying the Son of Man with a kiss?" When those around him saw what was going to happen, they asked, "Lord, should we strike with the sword?" Then one of them struck the high priest's servant and cut off his right ear. But Jesus responded, "No more of this!" And touching his ear, he healed him. (CSB)

Peter's problem in this narrative is that he rushes ahead of Jesus. The disciples ask Jesus, "Lord, should we strike with the sword?" But Peter (as we learn elsewhere) strikes the soldier on his own, being guided by his emotions instead of Jesus. When we "fight the good fight of faith" and "contend for the faith," let's be sure we are doing it when and how the Lord wills. It is clear in Luke that obedience to Jesus, not defending Jesus, is the goal. We can't promise that people won't get offended or hurt by truth, because the gospel itself is offensive to our sinful desires (Matt. 10:34; 1 Cor. 1:18), but we can be sure that if we are swinging the sword out of uncontrolled emotion or outside of God's will, we will always cause a cut that God will have to rebuke and heal.

How should we respond instead? The Bible suggests three categories: faith, hope, and love. Each of these are distinct, yet they all have some things in common.[21] Instead of responding with anger or frustration or hatred, we should have *faith* in the testimony of God, *hope* in the gospel of God, and show *love* for others in the way God models it for us. We need faith to stand on biblical truth and maintain our convictions in a shifting, secular culture. We need the hope of the gospel to remind people that they are loved and accepted by God, and in Christ, not only do they have eternal life, but they can experience abundant life in the present. Lastly, we need the love of Jesus to help us love God, love his Word, love ourselves, and love people. We need the love of Jesus to see ourselves rightly and to see others the way Jesus sees them.

When some Christians advocate for the church to change and embrace homosexuality or celebrate queerness because it's the twenty-first century, that is not progressive, it's regressive. There is no *faith*, *hope*, and *love* in offering people an option for life where Christ is not at the center as Savior and Lord. To abuse, abandon, and abhor people is not showing faith, hope, and love; but to accommodate, acquiesce, and retreat from the culture is not a demonstration of faith, hope, and love either. What would it look like if the church—both inwardly and in its outward witness to the world—was marked by faith, hope, and love toward the LGBTQ+ community?

COUNSEL FOR THE CHURCH: LET'S TALK ABOUT SEX

As new parents, my husband and I learned an important lesson—don't just settle for the "sex talk" with your children. Have multiple talks. We knew that if we didn't teach our kids about sex, they would learn about it from the world. The Black church has been critiqued for not talking enough about sex. Some theologians assert that faith-based sexuality ministries, if a church has them at all, often avoid discussions about self-pleasure, sexuality among seniors, what it means to be a sexual being, and teach a sexual ethic that limits the possibilities individuals have to express sexual desire.[22] While there may be divergent theological positions, the reality is that the church needs comprehensive biblical discipleship on gender, sex, and marriage to strengthen our Christian worldview and doctrine. The church must seek to find a way to bridge the gap between knowledge and application. Churches may have good, biblical teaching, but they still produce immature Christians who struggle to discern truth from error and know how to *practically apply* truth to daily decision-making. We must learn to lead with the gospel, and this means focusing on five key goals with regard to the LGBTQ+ community: conversion to Christ, conforming to the likeness of Christ, becoming convinced of the Bible's authority, being consecrated or set apart for God's purposes, and finally, providing a community of love and care for those struggling with same-sex attraction.

CONVERSION

If the focus of our efforts becomes converting people's sexuality and not the eternal security of their souls, we are missing our unique purpose and overstepping the power of the gospel. The mission of the church cannot be reduced to making queer people straight or getting same-sex-attracted people married to the opposite sex. The mission of the church is not to promote a "heterosexual gospel"[23] as Jackie Hill Perry has noted, but rather to share the one true gospel of Jesus Christ. I don't know who said it first, but there is truth in the saying that "you can't clean fish you haven't caught." The church is often guilty of trying to clean people who aren't even caught (converted) by focusing on changing their sexual orientation before they have experienced heart transformation. As Greg Johnson has noted, without a relationship with Jesus, "there is no point speaking of a biblical sexual ethic [because] no gay person is going to embrace such an ethic unless they fall in love with Jesus [whereas] a heart smitten by grace is not only willing but eager to follow the one who died for us."[24]

CONFORMED

Sometimes we try to clean fish that aren't caught. But there are other times when we are trying to clean fish too quickly—seeking to push change on those who are resistant or slow to give up their old way of life. Have you ever seen a caught fish, before it is dead, flapping around on the boat and doing everything it can to squirm its way back into the water? Outside of its natural habitat, a fish will die. New Christians can be like this caught fish. Someone may have confessed their sin and made a profession of faith in Christ, but they are still struggling to die to self and live a consecrated life for the Lord. Only the Holy Spirit can help them lay down their life completely and be conformed into the image of Christ. God supplies the fish (election), we fish (evangelism), converts die daily (submission), the Holy Spirit cleans (sanctification), and the church community helps people get acclimated to their new life in Christ (discipleship). Justification is instantaneous, but progressive sanctification is a lifetime process in the faith. Many people who are babes in Christ feel like fish out of water, and the church is called to walk in humble patience with them—not compromising truth, but being longsuffering and enduring with people's process of change the way God and others have done with us.

CONVINCED

Part of sanctification is being convinced that God's Word is true and that it is the authoritative, inerrant, and infallible rubric with which we align our lives. I heard a professed gay Christian man say on a podcast that his relationship with the Bible was like a friend who can make suggestions and give good advice, but it was not his parent: "The Bible is not my authority." One of Satan's agendas is to get Christians to either revise what the Bible says or reduce and minimize the Bible's authority. When people have not been convinced of its authority or they just outright reject that the Bible is God's Word, this opens the door for them to sin. They reject God's good design for humanity because the devil is constantly asking them, "Did God really say?" just as he did to Eve in the garden. The church should help believers understand what the Bible is, why we can trust it, and how to respond to opponents of Scripture. "Faith comes by hearing, and hearing by the word of God" (Rom. 10:17 NKJV). As people have regular exposure to biblical truth, know the history of the Bible, and then gain the tools to understand it themselves, their convictions are stabilized.

CONSECRATED

"Then Joshua said to the people, 'Consecrate yourselves, for tomorrow the LORD will do wonders among you'" (Josh. 3:5 ESV). In the Bible the word "consecration" means "separation of oneself from things that are unclean, especially anything that would contaminate one's relationship with a perfect God."[25] The instructions Joshua gave to the people before entering the promised land symbolize that sin is a defilement (Ps. 51:2, 7), and we must be cleansed before we can truly follow the Lord with our whole heart. We also see a call to consecration in the New Testament (Eph. 4:26–27; Col. 3:15–14). As believers we are called to be separate from the world (2 Cor. 6:17) and to offer ourselves as living sacrifices to the Lord as an act of worship (Rom. 12:1–2). Joshua's instruction under this new dispensation of grace reminds us that we have already been washed and made acceptable to God through the shed blood of Jesus, however, we still are called to cooperate and be a willing participant in our consecration. Joshua said, "Consecrate yourselves." There is human responsibility in our walk of holiness. There are things we will have to sacrifice, separate from, and be cleansed from in our new lives with Christ, but the Holy Spirit will help us since we can't do this in our own strength. When our minds have changed but our desires have not, we trust God and do the right thing (James 4:17). As our minds are continuously renewed, we will more clearly be able to see that there is no greater longing, desire, or fulfilment that we can have other than what we have in Christ. It may take time for people to see and experience that reality, but Joshua's words remind us that no matter the cost, the blessed hope is that "tomorrow the LORD will do wonders."

CARE

One of the downfalls of the ex-gay movements is that they focused almost exclusively on curing sexual orientation instead of caring for those with SSA. There are some with SSA who may never stop having those internal leanings. We must consider what experience of care is being offered in our local congregations for SSA individuals. We should have great empathy and pray for believers who may be in a variety of different situations on the spectrum of singleness and same-sex attraction. Some may never have their sexual or marital longing fulfilled. They may never have their own biological children. And yet they can choose daily to live for God by refusing to act on desires that do not comport with God's standards of holiness. Yes, the Holy Spirit will help all of us to live for God, but God has said from the beginning, "It is not good for the man to be alone" (Gen. 2:18). We all have a need for connection, help, companionship, and community. Marriage is not the only way these needs are satisfied. Even more than praying for SSA individuals, the family of God must become a real family for those in our congregations who have SSA. If we only give SSA individuals biblical truth but not a place in our hearts and homes, we have failed. One of the major obstacles SSA Christians struggle to overcome is loneliness—wanting to be known and invited to know others more intimately and personally, being welcomed into the lives of other believers. One SSA man confessed that what he needed most was a pastor who cared for him: "Even if he offers no cure, might [he] at least offer care."[26]

The church's biggest obstacle is not figuring out how to love people who struggle with sin. We all struggle with sin. What the church has failed to confront is that we have difficulty coming alongside those who don't struggle with sin *like us*—with sins that we might not understand or feel comfortable with. For example, if a man attends a men's ministry and asks for prayer because he is struggling with watching pornography or lusting after his girl-friend, we can easily picture other men giving him bear hugs, saying "We got you, man," starting prayer circles and offering accountability calls, making offers to do a book study, and affirming how they can relate to his struggle. He would receive encouragement, invitations to lunch outings, pickup basket-ball games, or Topgolf hangouts for support. Now imagine in that same men's ministry what would happen if a man said, "Hey fellas, I need your help. There is a queer guy at my job that I am really sexually attracted to, and I'm struggling with lust and the desire to have sex with him." How would the men in your church respond? Do you hear the Scooby Doo "Ruh Roh" inside a paralyzed men's group? Obviously, not all churches would react poorly, but we must admit that the church hasn't done a great job of fostering an environment where SSA is talked about as a real and regular struggle for people. And this, more than anything else, will keep fellow image bearers and colaborers living in shame, isolation, and depression, remaining in the closet and possibly in secret sin. As an act of love and care, the church must initiate these conver-sations and offer SSA individuals care and community and the hope, love, friendship, and acceptance that is found in Christ and his local church. The culture of the church must shift. We must be biblically sound yet gospel driven in our behavior and relationships with others.

CONCLUSION: TAKE YOUR STAND

"Take up the full armor of God, so that you may be able to resist in the evil day, and having prepared everything, to take your stand. Stand, therefore" (Eph. 6:13-14 CSB). The history and activism of the LGBTQ+ community has undoubtedly had an influence on how the culture thinks about gender, sex, and marriage. Targeting psychiatry, politics, religion, and media, the LGBTQ+ movement has found great success in promoting to the culture that homosexuality and gender nonconformity is a variation of the human experi-ence that is normal, legal, nonsinful, and even praiseworthy.

The devil has masqueraded within our culture to confuse and condition people to revise or reject God's Word to rob God of worship. However, God's design for his human creation was very good from the beginning and remains the standard for how we are to understand the identity that God bestowed.

In times past, and in some cases today, members of the LGBTQ community have suffered harassment, criminalization, discrimination, and even death, all of which are detestable ways to treat people created in the image of God. The church must own our part in these evils, apologize for how we have caused harm, and correct our missteps to pave a better way forward that dignifies and loves God's image bearers.

And yet, while the church has certainly failed at times, we must also acknowledge that we live in a cultural climate that quickly labels any disagreement as trauma. Christians and other dissenters are now considered homophobic, transphobic, heterosexual-normative oppressors, and binary bullies. Those who subscribe to anti-Christian worldviews have marketed the defense of Scripture against LGBTQ lifestyles as "violence" no matter how loving or patient one's approach or apologetic may be.

However, the Christian is to never forget that the Word of God is a weapon. It's a sword (Eph. 6:17), and swords have no earthly or spiritual purpose but to cut. The sword of the spirit is the Word of God, and it is "living and effective and sharper than any double-edged sword, penetrating as far as the separation of the soul and spirit, joints and marrow. It is able to judge the thoughts and intentions of the heart" (Heb. 4:12 CSB). The sword cuts the one it targets, even as it cuts the one who wields it. No one is immune to its conviction, no one can hide, and everyone must give an account to God for their choices and actions.

However, the beauty of God's Word is that when it cuts us, its purpose is to heal us: "He sent out his word and healed them, and delivered them from their destruction" (Ps. 107:20 ESV). The hope of the gospel is the only thing that doesn't crush us when the Word condemns our sin, "For the letter kills, but the Spirit gives life" (2 Cor. 3:6). Even when the sword of truth is swung in our direction, it illuminates not decapitates. The Holy Spirit does not desire to disconnect us from our minds but renew them (Rom. 12:2). Like a scalpel in the hands of a skilled surgeon, the Spirit of God cuts and convicts us to repair us.

Can encountering the Word of God feel like violence even if it is on a rescue mission motivated by love? Certainly, it can. The church has always been persecuted for speaking truth. Christians feel tension in being called to address these difficult cultural issues, but this awareness reminds us that our fight is not with individuals but with the unseen realm. Spiritual warfare in the culture should increase our awareness of our need for God, cause us to pray without ceasing, stabilize our convictions, and push us to seek God's wisdom on how to engage the culture. Christians are called to be humbly introspective and corrective regarding our own actions and dispositions toward the LGBTQ+ community, revealing any that are sinful or might be stumbling blocks to others. My exhortation to fellow Christians, leaders, preachers, teachers, and apologists everywhere is to take up your cross, follow Jesus, and stand!

SEVEN

FAITH DECONSTRUCTION

ERIC MASON

Today we are experiencing a growing openness to pick-and-choose-your-own spirituality, selecting the spiritual expression that best fits and matches you as an individual. This has led to a growing syncretism where people are adding to or equating their Christian faith to other forms of spirituality. In the Black urban context, this is often some form of African spirituality or a variant of new thought or new age ideologies that they find inclusive and informing to their Christian faith. This syncretism is dangerous because it parades itself as welcoming and inclusive of traditional Christian beliefs, encompassing things God teaches, and leads people to think it has its origins in his truth. Consider the words of one syncretistic blogger:

> Crystals and Christianity may not be best friends now nor ever, but working with healing crystals when you're a Christian isn't a Fastpass to hell. Beyond the bible mentioning crystals being used in structures and Aaron's breastplate, the key here is that you're not worshipping a crystal when you do crystal healing.
>
> God created everything on Earth and He didn't create anything evil. If you'd want to believe that those of us who use healing crystals are being

deceived by demons, then please remove your diamond ring or pearl necklace today.

Did you know that crystals in the Bible are mentioned many, many times? Yes! That same Holy Bible that many a thumper uses to denounce working with crystals. If they cracked open that thing that they thump on, they might have to stop and do some research for themselves.[1]

This blogger goes on to talk about how crystals are imbued with powers and how they are mentioned throughout the Bible, everywhere from the construction of the high priest's breastplate, to the imagery of Ezekiel's vision, to the new heavens and new earth in Revelation. Writings like this reflect how, in reaction to Western imperialistic Christianity, many believe that Christianity has been altered and that we must now uncover where there have been alterations and reengage where the "true" content has been corrupted.

Syncretism is problematic, but an even bigger issue is when there is a full-on abandonment of the Christian faith. Over the last few years there has been a parade of public figures—artists in Christian rap, CCM artists, and pastors and ministers—who have publicly renounced their profession of faith in Jesus. And this apostasy isn't limited to leaders and artists but extends to everyday parishioners—possibly even some of your own friends or family. Many believers have been left in a fog, wondering what to make of all this.

The postpandemic church is feeling the effects of silent apostasy. I have seen people who haven't gathered with the saints in a while drift, as the writer of Hebrews warns, away from the faith (Heb. 10:25). Some verbalize their reasons for drifting; others simply rant about it on social media. But where is this influx of false teaching originating? And why are we seeing this apostasy now?

The apostle Paul warned of a growing crisis of faith that will happen as end times draw near. The kingdom of darkness will ramp up its efforts to oppose the making of redeemed, image-bearing disciples by spreading the doctrines of demons throughout the world. Paul states, "Now the Spirit explicitly says that in later times some will depart from the faith, paying attention to deceitful spirits and the teachings of demons, through the hypocrisy of liars whose consciences are seared" (1 Tim. 4:1–2 CSB).

Alarmingly, these doctrines may not seem overtly demonic. In fact, they will be rather palatable: "For the time will come when people will not tolerate sound doctrine, but according to their own desires, will multiply teachers for themselves because they have an itch to hear what they want to hear. They will turn away from hearing the truth and will turn aside to myths" (2 Tim. 4:3–4 CSB). These teachings scratch the itch of proclaiming what you want to hear. In Gordon Fee's words, the origin of these false doctrines is "'spirits' from the other side, Satan's own demonic forces. . . . They are not merely those who 'teach different doctrines,' who 'promote speculations' and love 'controversies'; they are dupes of Satan, and their teaching is inspired by 'deceiving spirits.'"[2]

People will see these teachings as something that meets a need. It's what they have been looking for and wanting. This is because their conscience has been seared, no longer functioning as it was designed by God to function, and consequently they have lost any sense of discernment. They are unable to recognize truth from error. When I'm engaged in evangelism, I see this and begin to better understand what Paul was talking about when he describes people "whose consciences are seared." Clinton E. Arnold draws our attention to the significance of Paul's description:

> This arresting analogy . . . was particularly vivid in antiquity where penal branding took place. An inscription found in the vicinity of Ephesus threatens branding (possibly on the foot) as punishment for seditious bakers who had been instigating local riots (*IvE* 2015). Closer to Paul's image, runaway slaves who were recaptured might have their foreheads branded by harsh masters.[3]

The searing of the conscience is a spiritual signet by the spirits done on people. They are staking claim to them as those who belong to another kingdom; they are their slaves. Today, we're seeing more and more people who are in the process of deconstructing their faith. Yet many who are deconstructing and falling away aren't freeing themselves from Western captivity. They are chaining themselves to demonic influence. And one of the key tools the devil is using to draw people away from the faith is the cultural trend of deconstruction.

WHAT IS FAITH DECONSTRUCTION?

Faith deconstruction is the process of reevaluating your core beliefs or evaluating whether the religious belief system you were nurtured in is worthy of embrace. Jamin Hübner describes faith deconstruction as "the process of questioning one's own beliefs (that were once considered unquestionable) due to new experiences, reading widely, engaging in conversations with 'the other,' and interacting in a world that is now more connected and exposed to religious diversity than ever before."[4]

Deconstruction is not new, but it has become more complex and common today. Brandon Briscoe traces the concept of deconstruction to Jacque Derrida, a mid-twentieth-century philosopher and post-structuralist. Briscoe explains,

> Derrida coined the term "deconstruction" in response to what he thought was the imposition of Western philosophical bias on culture, thought, politics, and writing. Derrida believed that the written word holds too much ambiguity to be understood from one perspective. Deconstruction was intended to challenge the relationship between text and meaning, exposing the complexity, instability, and failure of written symbols to consistently produce a singular interpretation.[5]

As time went on Derrida's work evolved and took on a life of its own, transitioning from other academic and scholarly traditions into a cultural phenomenon; by the late twentieth century, "*deconstruction* was sometimes used pejoratively to suggest nihilism and frivolous skepticism."[6] Deconstruction became the mainstay tool for evaluating historical values that have been held for generations. And like most tools that have this level of momentum in the public square, it eventually made its way into Christian circles. Hübner writes,

> The phenomenon of "deconstruction" . . . is now more or less synonymous with intellectual, spiritual, and social change after modernity. The term has gained considerable currency amongst post/non-evangelical groups dedicated to it—such as The Deconstructionists and The Liturgists, as well as among social media venues of "progressive Christianity" and "progressive evangelicalism."[7]

A tool in and of itself isn't bad. The question is, Does the user of the deconstructing process have a clear aim, a goal in mind, before they begin wielding it?

GOOD DECONSTRUCTION

Faith deconstruction is not inherently bad. In fact, it can be good and helpful if it is done in a healthy way in community with others. Deconstructing done in this healthy way is really just a part of the process of sanctification and spiritual formation, something that is vital to our journey toward maturity as believers. Healthy deconstruction can enable believers to:

- **Own the faith for themselves.** This is especially true for people who grow up in church. They may believe the truth and want to follow Christ, but they've never been challenged to defend what they believe or think through what it means for their own life.
- **Find out what you really believe.** Harmful ideologies like legalism, licentiousness, tribalism, nationalism, patriarchy, ethnocentrism, and sexism may have been discipled into us in ways that we don't quite understand or even know. Deconstruction can help us identify those ideologies and move beyond them.
- **Realize you may not be a Christian.** Some individuals may have grown up in a church or a Christian family but have never heard or understood the gospel message. Often they may be rejecting elements of tradition or church, but not the gospel or the core tenets of the Christian faith.
- **Start moving forward on the journey to an authentic faith.** Other individuals have started the journey of following Christ but have stalled soon after and never really grew beyond that initial first step. Healthy deconstruction can get them back on track.

When I was younger, I remember someone telling me that Christianity was a copy of Egyptian spirituality. They even showed me books and pictures that suggested some scary similarities between the two, and I began to doubt my faith. I thought my faith journey was over. However, the Spirit of God alive in me gave me the courage to investigate further, and as I began to research, I found that those peddling this belief had no original sources and that much of what was being propagated was a knock-off of a two-hundred-year-old argument that had been refuted many times before. By working through a process of investigating and testing my doubts, my faith was actually strengthened in the end.

Christians do not need to fear challenges to their faith. Deconstruction can sometimes be a healthy process of questioning wrong assumptions or more deeply investigating truths that we've just accepted at face value. Digging deeper can lead us to a deeper, more authentic faith, and this practice is nothing new. The writings of Frederick Douglass show us that slaves needed to deconstruct the difference between the slave master's Christianity and biblical and historic Christianity. Douglass writes:

> Between the Christianity of this land, and the Christianity of Christ, I recognize the widest possible difference—so wide, that to receive the one as good, pure, and holy, is of necessity to reject the other as bad, corrupt, and wicked. To be the friend of the one, is of necessity to be the enemy of the other. I love the pure, peaceable, and impartial Christianity of Christ: I therefore hate the corrupt, slaveholding, women-whipping, cradle-plundering, partial and hypocritical Christianity of this land. Indeed, I can see no reason, but the most deceitful one, for calling the religion of this land Christianity.[8]

Deconstruction, when done well—under the guidance of the Holy Spirit, in a community, and by turning to the original sources—can be rewarding. Yet when it is done poorly and in isolation, it can lead away from Jesus.

BAD DECONSTRUCTION

Deconstruction is harmful when it leads believers away from God. Those who follow this path of deconstruction have abandoned the pursuit of truth and are walking in the footsteps of the first deconstructionist: Satan himself. In Genesis 3:1, the serpent Satan is described as "the most cunning" (CSB)—so we know he is clever, crafty, and tricky, with a focus on evil treachery. When he speaks, we see that he has a mastery of deluding people into not following God. "He said to the woman, 'Did God really say, "You can't eat from any tree in the garden"'?" (Gen. 3:1 CSB). With a simple question, he convinces Eve and Adam—who spoke with God face to face—to question their values and their most intimate experiences with God. Satan hoodwinks them into believing that God isn't enough, that God is keeping them from experiencing their greatest potential for advancement.

Between 2020 and 2022, there has been a major shift in the American church. As people isolated and avoided contact with others, there was a steep rise in the consumption of media online. Coupled with widespread biblical illiteracy in the church, people were being regularly discipled in everything but a Christian worldview, whether from exposure to videos, memes, blogs, or television shows. Our worldview is constructed from the things we take into our minds, and the rise of social media shows a staggering change in our consumption:

> Last year, driven in no small part by the pandemic, Americans spent more than an average 1,300 hours on social media according to a new study from Uswitch. Facebook led the way, where Americans spent an average 58 minutes a day on the app—or 325 hours a year. However, the social network has been on the decline among younger users, who are increasingly gravitating towards apps including Instagram and TikTok—which allow them to be more creative and express themselves, the study's authors noted.
>
> Instagram was the second most used service, and it remained most popular among Gen-Z users, who spent almost 53 minutes per day, or 297 hours year; while Snapchat was also popular with the younger crowd, who racked up 50 minutes per day on the app or still 277 hours a year.[9]

The growing consumption of media that reflects an unbiblical worldview is just one of the contributors to deconstruction. There are several other factors that are leading people to deconstruct out of Christianity. Another challenge is that people today view the form or culture or tribe from which they are deconstructing as the authentic representation of the faith. In deconstructing from Western Christianity, many are signaling that they are done with the way it has been wedded to unhealthy patriotism—what some are referring to as "Christian nationalism." This isn't a new problem, but in recent years it has become a *glaring* problem. Because of the association of evangelical Christianity with particular political beliefs, evangelicalism and the Christian faith are also being deconstructed. Evangelicalism isn't monolithic, of course, but for many people it is difficult to separate the core tenets of evangelicalism from the actions and rhetoric of those calling themselves evangelicals.

Another related factor is the deconstructing of self-identity. This is a massive issue facing the church right now. It includes ethnic minorities who don't want their cultural identity to become part of the melting pot of America, as well as those who want to embrace alternative gender identities. Theological tribes, camps, and denominations are splintering into pieces, and this is particularly true among some of the more conservative groups. Many who were raised in Christian homes and are now coming into adulthood have begun to reevaluate whether or not they really embrace the faith they were raised in.

Most of the deconstructing that I have dealt with as a pastor to my people has been in these categories. There are also some in the Black church who view our deconstructing as a way of decolonizing from bad forms of Western evangelicalism, not deconstructing out of the Christian faith altogether. Here, the goal isn't to find the faith I want or resonate with, but the real essence of what it means to be a disciple of Jesus.

Deconstruction doesn't just happen. There are many reasons why people deconstruct. We turn now to consider some triggers that can lead an individual to question their faith and consider leaving it.

TRIGGERS FOR DECONSTRUCTION

- **The problem of evil and suffering.** Many people have suffered painful experiences that lead them to question God's love and goodness. While we cannot always answer the question "Why?" to the reality of evil, we can affirm that God is greater than the suffering we experience. We point them to the cross of Jesus as evidence of God's faithful love and compassion.
- **Church hurt and spiritual abuse.** The church is not a perfect place. It's messy, and people hurt each other. Leaders sin and betray trust. Some are even abusive. And this leads many to question the truth of the Christian faith. Hypocrisy breeds distrust.
- **College.** Life changes often mean changes in our social groups and friendships. And when people leave to go to college, they are often in a

new place building new relationships. In addition, many college campuses are hostile to the Christian faith. Professors and fellow students may raise questions about the faith that have never been asked before, leading some to question their childhood faith.

- **Family upbringing.** Some families attend church and claim to follow Christ, but it is never a real part of their family life. As they grow older, they realize it was just something they did and was never a core part of their identity.

- **Hypocrisy and moral failures in leadership.** Similar to church hurt, when people see evidence of hypocrisy in the media or among their relationships with Christians, they may begin to feel that it is all a show and have doubts.

- **Legalism.** Some churches do not teach or practice the gospel of grace. They are more concerned with conformity to rules or obedience to certain moral teachings. Those raised in these environments may reject what they think is Christianity, having never been exposed to the real gospel message.

- **Illegitimate or misplaced hurt.** We often carry pain from past hurt into other relationships. A person may have been hurt through a failed marriage, a bad family situation, or other relational pain, and they transfer that to the church.

Remember, this is not just about having answers to intellectual objections or questions about the Bible. We have to exegete the text, but we must also exegete the culture and our congregations. In addition, we have to create new ways for our people to dialogue about what they are thinking through and what beliefs and values are directly affecting them and their families.

DECONSTRUCTION AMONG BLACK CHRISTIANS

One of the pastors at our church was doing a devotional for the children in our tutoring program when, suddenly, a six-year-old blurted out, "God is real, but Jesus isn't because he was created by the white man." The class erupted into chaos. I was bewildered. Somehow this six-year-old was being discipled into believing folklore. I've found that one of the primary ideologies Black Christians need to navigate today is the idea that Christianity is the white man's religion.

This idea is nothing new. But what is new is how the idea is being branded among Blacks in the Gen X, Millennial, and Gen Z generations. And this is one of the primary reasons we see deconstruction happening among Black Christians today. For those of African descent, deconstruction can be helpful, leading them to a deeper and more robust faith. But it can also lead them away from the faith. Jerome Gay, in his landmark work on this issue, brings clarity, precision, and good scholarship:

> There's a growing sentiment amongst people of African descent as well as people across the globe that Christianity is a Western created, European influenced, white-owned religion of oppression. While this is historically inaccurate, there are legitimate reasons why many have adopted this assertion. Dr. Vince Bantu says, "Christianity has been perverted into a mechanism of tyranny by many Western nations." The main reason for this growing sentiment is historical and cultural whitewashing as well as the under-emphasized reality that the gospel took firm root in Africa, the Middle East, and Asia long before even an idea of it traveled to the West. In order to properly present the gospel and the Christian faith accurately, it must be understood that Christianity is not the cultural property of any single racial or ethnic group.[10]

In a previous volume (*Urban Apologetics: Restoring Black Dignity with the Gospel*) we addressed some of these concerns, and we'd encourage anyone who is wrestling with these issues to consult that volume for further insight.

RECONSTRUCTION: COUNTERING DECONSTRUCTION

What is the answer to deconstruction? Reconstruction. Reconstruction is the process of solidifying your core beliefs. And it begins by prioritizing and emphasizing discipleship. We need to teach people what it means to follow Christ.

PRIORITIZE DISCIPLESHIP

Sadly, many professing Christians have never been discipled. They've never had a season of intense discipleship when someone has intentionally modeled for them and taught them what it means to follow Jesus. I define a disciple of Jesus Christ as one who has renounced him or herself and pledged one's life to being in a lifetime apprenticeship under the Lord Jesus Christ (Matt. 10:39). When I think of discipleship, I'm thinking of multiple streams of discipleship within the local church. This isn't about that one super Christian who knows everything, but about being taught how to plug into all of the varied means of ongoing renewal that root and grow us in Jesus.

Churches have to make their growth paths clear. What does discipleship look like in and through the church? In our church, everything is a mechanism for discipleship. From personal spiritual formation, to life-on-life connections, small groups, retreats, men's and women's ministry, premarital, Equip U Bible study, Sunday mornings, serving—it all is centered around the goal of conforming people into the image and likeness of Christ. Ultimately the Holy Spirit has to make this happen, but these mechanisms develop solid connections and form Jesus in people. They provide a context for the Spirit to work and transform people. It begins with the basics—the milk of the gospel—and as people grow it continues into what the writer of Hebrews 5:12–14 refers to as solid food:

> Although by this time you ought to be teachers, you need someone to teach you the basic principles of God's revelation again. You need milk, not solid food. Now everyone who lives on milk is inexperienced with the message about righteousness, because he is an infant. But solid food is for the mature—for those whose senses have been trained to distinguish between good and evil. (CSB)

Our expectation is that everyone will participate in strengthening the journey of other believers. These actions in and of themselves don't keep us, yet as a reborn person they are essential to our journey.

WELCOME DOUBT

One the most telling verses in the Bible on doubt is Mark 9:23–24, where Jesus is asked if he can heal a man's son: "Jesus said to him, "'If you can'"?

Everything is possible for the one who believes.' Immediately the father of the boy cried out, 'I do believe; help my unbelief!'" (CSB). Jesus welcomed the man's doubt as it coextended with the man's unbelief. Jesus didn't run him off—he engaged him.

We can't give people cheap answers. As Jerome Gay says, we must not run from challenges, and we do not use faith as an excuse to avoid difficult questions: we do not answer fact-based questions with "faith-based" answers. And while we address historical concerns, make no mistake about it, we're passionate about our faith, which is why we study the Scriptures and history in order to address the core concerns of those who have legitimate questions about Christianity.[11]

We must not shrink back from lovingly and boldly engaging people's questions. At the same time, we never trust that their salvation is found *in* answering their questions. I have answered and refuted claims, but that in itself does not (in many cases) lead to immediate transformation. It has a role, though. For many, it is part of the process of investigating and testing Christianity. And for those who already believe, it helps strengthen them in the faith they have in Jesus.

ADMIT WHERE THE CHURCH HAS FAILED

We must also pursue emotional health. We need to be honest with our hurts and failures and acknowledge the trauma the church has caused for some people. Sometimes our work is excavating and healing wounds that weren't intellectual but emotional. And we need to understand that "church hurt" can also play a significant role in people deconstructing out of the faith. The doctrine of the Trinity, the person of Jesus, or the historicity and validity of the Bible might not be their problem—it may be people and bad relationships. Truly bad experiences need to be dealt with and repented of by the church and its leadership. I have had to work through unintentionally hurting people, meeting with them and repenting for any harm I might have caused. In many instances this has led to great reconciliation.

SHEPHERD DIFFICULT PEOPLE

We have a culture of what I call "associative church issues." What I mean is that people have issues with the church without having ever experienced the church in any real way. These are people who use the church as an easy scapegoat for their hurts, frustrations, and traumas. Today's generation has language for these experiences—particularly bad experiences with the church. Sometimes, people will even weaponize their experiences to throw shade at the church.

Some of the hardest cases I've dealt with are those who have come to us with unresolved conflict—either in the home, past relationships, or past experiences with other churches. I've had people say that my preaching was constantly traumatic and triggering for them. I've asked, "In what way?" and they shared some examples. To some I've admitted, "Maybe I could use more tact in what I said." Other examples were very strange and subjective. Sometimes, as I've better understood their family and church history, it becomes clear that they failed to process their pain in a healthy way. And all of their current relationships are now unknowingly being viewed through these past hurts. I've had to shepherd people through what most would consider normal, everyday conflict, but for them it was experienced as an enormous trauma. I try not to tell people how to feel, and instead we work to lovingly help people through these experiences—if they allow us.

As Scripture says, "And we exhort you, brothers and sisters: warn those who are idle, comfort the discouraged, help the weak, be patient with everyone" (1 Thess. 5:14 CSB). With those who are discouraged and weak, we have to make time. Those who are struggling need help, and we cannot treat them as a problem to solve, but as people to shepherd and love. Again, this only works when the person is open to it. I have found that when a person doesn't want to talk and they walk away, it is difficult to do much for them. But if they are on the fence and open to meeting with you, there is a chance for God to work.

GET AHEAD OF THE CURVE

Local churches and leaders must be students of the Bible, history, *and* culture. And being aware of what is happening in the broader culture means getting ahead of the curve—having a healthy, and perhaps prophetic, anticipation of what you will be dealing with. This means preparing believers accordingly, and if done correctly, it will have a tremendous impact. Jesus told his disciples that he was sending them out as sheep in the midst of wolves, preparing them for what was coming in order that they would be able to endure it (Matt. 10:16–20).

Contrary to popular belief, the younger generations haven't left the church. There is a bleed, but there has always been something similar in the past. What's different is that today the internet allows the testimonies of those aborting the faith to be seen and heard widely. Countering the normal doom and gloom message, Barna shares a bit of encouraging news from their research:

> When it comes to Scripture, practicing Christian Millennials—self-identified Christians who attend church at least once a month and who describe their religious faith as very important to their life—are quite orthodox and continue to hold the Bible in very high regard. In fact, nearly all of them believe the Bible contains everything a person needs to know to live a meaningful life (96%). The same proportion claim the Bible is the actual or inspired word of God (96%). Among these young adults, a plurality say, "The Bible is the actual word of God and should be taken literally, word for word" (46%); an additional four in 10 agree it is divinely inspired and has no errors, though "some verses are meant to be symbolic rather than literal" (39%); and 11% say the Bible is the inspired word of God, "but has some factual or historical errors."[12]

In my own experience, many of the Gen Z and millennials in the church I pastor say to me, "Pastor, it's many of us who are here and committed to Jesus, holiness, and standing firm in the faith." As a shepherd, these are your people. Disciple them and teach them how to make disciples of others.

CONCLUSION

Every person that walks away from Jesus stings—I know. We tend to take it personally and see it as a personal failure. But the more I grow as a believer and as a pastor, the more I realize that while I have responsibilities as a pastor, even my fulfilling responsibilities fully isn't enough to keep someone in the faith. Only the Spirit of God can do that, and their greatest need is not more answers but the Spirit. They need to encounter God in and through the gospel if we are to have any hope of them enduring until the end.

I believe there is a cleansing going on in the church. In saying this, I'm not trying to throw people away, but simply understanding that this is the biblical reality (1 Tim. 4). As the time for the return of the Lord draws nearer, there will be differing ways in which people are removed—leaving the faith—while others are revived. All in all, our work to love, serve, and challenge people must be done in reliance upon the Holy Spirit. Ultimately, no one really comes to God or remains in him without the guidance of the Holy Spirit (1 Cor. 12:3). We do the work God gives us in faith, walking each day with the Spirit, ready to proclaim God's truth where he leads.

TEN PRINCIPLES FOR CREATING ONLINE CONTENT

LISA FIELDS

’ve always had a strong conviction that in order to reach the lost, we must go where they are. This conviction has sent me on more than a few adventures. In my undergrad years, it sent me to some of the most dangerous neighborhoods in Jacksonville, knocking on doors and sharing the gospel on Saturday mornings to whomever would listen. It once brought me to a nightclub parking lot on Saturday nights to share my faith. But today, it frequently takes me online. Much of the content I create today has the goal of reaching people through various online platforms.

According to Indeed.com, "Content creation is the process of brainstorming and writing relevant content pieces and publishing them in different content forms, like blog posts, infographics, white papers and eBooks."[1] Creating online content includes writing posts for a blog, creating visual memes, and developing digital media, like podcasts or short- and long-form videos for social media. In our current landscape, content creation is one of the most effective ways to reach people with the good news about Jesus.

Our worldview is constantly being shaped by digital media. Fewer and fewer people today, especially among younger generations, are turning to books or newspapers for information. Instead, they are turning to social media. This means that our core beliefs are being shaped by content creators who use 280 characters, memes, status updates, and cleverly curated long- and short-form videos. I find it is not uncommon for people to cite memes, viral videos, and other social media posts as they give reasons for why they do not believe the truth claims of Christianity.

With so many competing narratives in the public square of social media, how do Christians break through all this noise? How can we raise the belief bar when it has sunk so low? This may seem like an insurmountable task, but it's not impossible. Here are ten principles that I believe will help us cut through the noise.

1. BE CREDIBLE

In order to cut through the noise, we need to establish credibility. No one can be an expert on all things. It strengthens our platforms when we are able to highlight trusted voices in various fields. In some of the content I've developed, I've invited scholars and pastors to discuss their expertise. If we want to cut through the noise of virality, we have to establish ourselves as credible voices with our intended audience. We can't just be *another* voice; we have to show why *our* voice should be trusted above other voices. Trusted voices vary based on what audience you want to reach. This is why you must also study your target audience.

2. REEVALUATE SUCCESS

When considering how to reach an audience, we must not measure success based solely on virality—those media pieces (videos, posts, etc.) that garner thousands and millions of views or likes. Chasing virality is like chasing the wind. It's a fruitless endeavor. Since virality is simply based on how fast and quickly content is shared online, it is not always a reliable metric for intended impact. Additionally, if we define success based on virality, we may be tempted to compromise to get it. This compromise can take place through misleading titles, overuse of click bait in our content, or hostile polemics. When we are in a rush to go viral, compromise is inevitable.

This is why we must make sure our definition of success is not shaped by the culture of virality, but by the Word of God. The goal for content creation in Christian apologetics is to curate content that unfogs the lenses of hearts so that the skeptic can see the gospel clearly and to help Christians better engage skeptics.

3. ANALYZE THE DATA

A content creator's best friend is social media analytics, which gives us the ability to listen to our audience through their interaction with the content. Our audience speaks without talking to us by how long they watch our content and whether they like or share it. There is no greater ego deflator than metrics. But it also allows us to see under the hood to pinpoint issues. For instance, a video could have one thousand views on Facebook, and the analytics reveal that most of the views were only three seconds long. From this we see that it's not that our content is bad, but it's just too long. When we recognize that most people are looking on their phones in between various tasks, so they rarely have the time to dedicate longer than two minutes to a video, we can create our content accordingly. Another aspect of analyzing data is studying how your audience receives information. Methods of communication should always be flexible based on the needs of the intended audience. Data helps us make these adjustments.

4. BE CREATIVE

Content must be engaging. Content creation requires a level of creativity. Even if creativity is not your strength, it doesn't mean you can't produce creative content. This is where community comes in. In the body of Christ, we all have different gifts and talents. When we open up our deficiencies to the body of Christ, we give them an opportunity to be strong where we are weak, which will help foster stronger communities. For example, older pastors who are struggling to curate relevant and creative content can lean on younger, more creative people in the church to help assist them. Their knowledge and wisdom of Scripture coupled with a younger, more creative member can blossom into relevant, robust, and creative content. This not only helps produce helpful content, but it also helps build intergenerational relationships and becomes a tool of discipleship.

5. PRODUCE QUALITY

Quality adds another layer of credibility to the content we produce. High-quality content is more likely to be trusted than low-quality content. This does not mean that you need to purchase a DSLR camera, studio lights, Premiere Pro, and Photoshop. But it does mean that you need to produce content with a spirit of excellence. All work, even content creation, should be done as unto the Lord.

6. BE INCARNATIONAL

The content we create as Christian apologists should be both informational and incarnational. Authors Hindson and Caner explain, "Informational apologetics represents the explanation of essential biblical tenets to the Christian faith. Incarnational apologetics represents the actualization of those same biblical belief systems into the authentic expressions of a believer's life."[2] I like to think of these tenets as wings on a plane. You need both wings to take flight; likewise, you need both informational and incarnational apologetics for the gospel message to take flight. Many of our apologetics never get off the runway because we haven't given enough attention to both wings.

What good is it to be able to give a thorough defense of the resurrection if you don't live under Christ's lordship? What good is it to be able to give a defense for the authority of Scripture if you don't love like Christ? What good is it to dispel the myth that Christianity is a white man's religion if you don't do it with gentleness and respect? It is not just about the content we create. It's about how we embody that message of the gospel online and offline.

7. LISTEN WELL

Too many apologists answer questions that aren't being asked because they haven't taken the time to listen first. Listening is an act of love, and you can't give a good defense for the faith if you haven't first listened well.

Listening can be challenging for people who have researched and studied a lot. It can be difficult to listen when you feel like you have enough knowledge to refute a claim. However, I've discovered over time that most people's *initial* objection to Christianity is not their *real* objection. Whether it takes ten minutes or four hours, listening helps us uncover the real problem.

8. BE LIGHT

One of the ways we embody the message is through shining light in darkness. Social media has become an increasingly hostile place. The comments section on social media alone can be a dark pit of insults, assumptions, and dehumanization. While this darkness is discouraging, it has also created a unique opportunity for Christians to be light in the darkness. Anywhere we see darkness, it's our job to bring light.

9. LET CONVICTIONS GUIDE

As we engage in content creation, it is crucial to have the courage to hold onto your convictions. Our convictions are our guideposts. They are shaped and rooted in the word of God. They should never be at the mercy of public opinion, they should only be at the mercy of a holy God. If our convictions change based on people's opinions of us, we will never be courageous. Courage is simply the ability to do what scares us. That means that fear is actually a prerequisite for courage. Ironically, you can't have courage without it. Fear isn't the enemy of courage, it's a partner. Therefore, it's important to know that when we are creating content around sensitive topics, fear will come. You will be tempted to change your stance on matters like sexuality, the exclusivity of Jesus, the authority of Scripture, etc. The fear of the online mob could seemingly cripple you, but stand fast. Fear may enter, but that doesn't mean your courage isn't holding its hand. Stand firm and hold onto your convictions. Truth will always win in the end.

10. REMEMBER DISCIPLESHIP

One of the important things to remember about content creation is that it is a tool of discipleship. The way we curate content will be duplicated by those who follow our platforms. My mother never sat down to teach me how to pray, but she constantly demonstrated it in front of me. As a result, I know how to pray. Similarly, how we interact online will frame how our followers interact online. If our content is laced with hostility, snarky comments, and insulting rhetoric, it begins to disciple our followers in a particular way.

Everything we do or say online has an audience, and that audience is taking notes on how we behave. We never want to misrepresent opposing perspectives for views. We aren't looking to win arguments, we are trying to win people to Christ and equip the body of Christ. We want to dignify those who think differently than us by presenting their perspective the same way we would want our perspectives and beliefs represented. The way we give answers is just as important as the answers we give. When we give an apologetic with gentleness and respect, we equip onlookers to do the same.

I pray that these principles are like "a lamp for [your] feet, a light on [your] path" as you curate and create content for your target audiences (Ps. 119:105). I pray that you remember the goal is not to build a platform for yourself but to glorify God through your gifts and talents. I pray that your life embodies the gospel message and that you always give an apologetic with grace and truth, no matter what medium you use.

PART TWO

CHRISTIAN SECTS AND CULTS

EIGHT

WHAT IS A CULT?

ERIC MASON

One night, we received a call from a newer family in our church. They had belonged to a cult for many years and had recently left. But they were reaching out to us because their teenage son had been taken in again after talking with several members of the cult. They had convinced him that he needed to make his own decisions, telling him: "Because your parents left us, they are being disobedient to God. You don't have to listen to them anymore. Listen to us." The cult members were making plans to bring the child out of the country and away from his family's reach.

I realize this may not be a typical experience in many churches. But in new church startups like ours, you tend to attract all different types of people. Our church is located in the heart of Philadelphia in what is called North Central. We are connected to Temple University's campus and attract a wide variety of people. Some are attracted to the area because of gentrification. There are working-class residents, those on public assistance, those struggling with crime, drugs, and violence, as well as those trying to renew the area through entrepreneurial efforts.

Several months earlier, a new group of families had started coming to our church. Immediately I knew they had a story to tell. There was something different about them—a seriousness that others didn't have. Over time, I began meeting with several of them and working through some different topics with them, both theologically and practically. Then came the night of that call, and it became clear to me that although the family had walked away from a legalistic cult, their teenage son was still deeply indoctrinated. Fortunately, we were able to help the family contact the authorities, and they were able to return the child to his family.

But that was just the beginning of the battle for his heart and mind.

At first, their son was very hostile toward us and extremely verbally disrespectful. But we didn't give up. Eventually, through the love of the community in the church, consistent Bible teaching, and the outreach of many people, that teenage boy was detoxed from an unhealthy community. Today he is an extraordinary young adult. He is being actively discipled at our church and has himself become a stout disciple maker within our church's college ministry.

I'd like to say this was the only challenging experience I've had with people being influenced by or coming out of a cult, but sadly, that's not the case. Whenever I encounter people who are being drawn into a cult or leaving one, I'm reminded of my duty as a shepherd to protect the flock of God. I have fresh appreciation for these words from Titus 1: "[Hold] to the faithful message as taught, so that he will be able both to encourage with sound teaching and to refute those who contradict it" (Titus 1:9 CSB).

One of my favorite superheroes is Spiderman. He has enhanced strength, speed, agility, and the ability to crawl up walls, but the superpower I appreciate most is his "Spidey sense." Whenever there is looming danger, Spiderman gets a tingling sensation, enabling him to respond to it quickly. As believers, we need a spiritual "Spidey sense" rooted in biblical discernment. So many believers are easily duped into doctrinal fallacies and false ideologies. As followers of the way of Jesus, we need to develop our discernment. And this is especially true for anyone who is a leader or making disciples in the church.

THE DEFINITION OF A CULT

Some people may wonder what we mean when we use the word "cult" to describe a community or group of people. More specifically, what do Christians mean by the word "cult"?

There are a myriad of different cult types: sociopolitical, religious/spiritual, entrepreneurial/business, military, and self-improvement cults. Sometimes these categories will overlap one another, but there is usually a mission distinction that defines the primary aim of the group. From a religious perspective, a cult is often seen as a group that acts *deceptively*. They present themselves as one thing (familiar or desired), but the truth is hidden and is often very different from their outward presentation. In presenting themselves and what they believe, the members of the cult may try to convince others that what they believe about the meaning or purpose of life, an idea or teaching, or a Bible doctrine or religious practice is normal and familiar, when in reality they have a different definition or understanding of that idea, term, or practice. Cults come in many forms, as we will see in the chapters that follow, but not all cults are created equal.

I have sometimes heard people call a group a cult because it was an unhealthy community or they had a bad experience, but in truth it should not have been categorized as a cult. I've found it helpful to view groups according to a discernment grid, which portrays visually each group's leadership structure, doctrine, treatment of outsiders, connection to the outside world, and other matters to determine where along the spectrum they belong. I have developed three categories to give us a working framework for categorizing beliefs on this spectrum: (1) cultic tendencies, (2) cultic, and (3) cult.

CULTIC TENDENCIES

The first category is what I would describe as a group with "cultic tendencies." This includes churches that tend to overly "cover" their members, meaning they are overly protective or even controlling. This might include telling members not to listen to other churches or requiring members to seek permission to visit another church. Churches that have cultic tendencies sometimes encourage members to cut off communication with those who leave the congregation. I had someone once tell me about a church they belonged to where, whenever they were not at church, they had to tell the pastor and leaders where they were going. The only way to leave the church was to move to another part of the country (possibly for work) or die.

Churches with cultic tendencies often ignore sin patterns in leadership because of the gifting of the leader or the place the leader occupies in keeping the organization rolling. These churches will ignore apparent leadership marital issues, promiscuity, racism, sexism, and other sinful behaviors. Often these types of churches exhibit some degree of spiritual abuse toward their members.

CULTIC

A church can be categorized as "cultic" when it has several of the same characteristics as those communities and churches with "cultic tendencies," but they go even further by *teaching members that leaving the group is the same as leaving God.* They present themselves as the exclusive and only way to have a relationship with God. This differs from an established religious belief that holds to exclusive beliefs about salvation in that they are teaching that it is their particular, local community or group that holds the keys to salvation. Some groups will tell members they will lose their salvation if they leave that community.

Cultic groups also have doctrines that either contain additions to the gospel, are characterized by heterodoxy (clear deviations from historic orthodox doctrines or beliefs), or are heretical (a formal rejection of a belief articulated by one of the ecumenical Christian councils). Some of these ministries will exalt the sign gifts (like prophecy and tongues) above the revealed Word in the Bible.[1] Some believe that you aren't saved by grace through faith in Jesus Christ, but you are only saved when you are physically baptized and come up out of the water speaking in tongues.

Cultic churches tend to have an extremely high view of the pastor or founder, sometimes even venerating that individual. After the death of the founder, these ministries have an extremely hard time moving on because they are intimately connected to the leader and have no succession plan. The founder or leader is often more important than the gospel mission, and they refuse to let new healthy leaders lead. Cultic churches also view the leader or group of leaders as a channel for the blessing of God.

I remember hearing one cultic leader say, "I was able to buy a Bentley, but the Lord spoke to me and said, 'How do you have a Bentley and your covering doesn't?' So I took my car back and didn't get one until they had a car of that level." These churches may also teach that the pastor, bishop, or apostle is a means of blessing, so when individuals sow money into the man or woman of God, God causes that individual to reap a financial blessing. This is very common in churches that teach a version of the prosperity gospel.

Money is often a commonly discussed topic in cultic churches. So much of the church or community is dedicated to increasing finances, and often this involves giving to the leader or man and woman of God as a means of comprehensive blessing. I remember going to a large church start-up where the pastor taught that God made everything as a seed to reproduce, and the only way to keep what God had begun going was to take the seed from what was in the fruit and replant it. He then opened an apple, took the seed out, and told people to sow $1,000 into that seed and then pass the seed to the person behind them and continue sowing down the line. He then made some extravagant promise to those who gave their money. I walked out, deeply saddened and frustrated. I believe in the principles of giving and blessing taught in 2 Corinthians 8–9 and Galatians 6, but manipulating people to give under compulsion is a direct violation of the Scripture.

CULTS

The dictionary defines "cult" as "a religion or religious sect generally considered to be extremist or false, with its followers often living in an unconventional manner under the guidance of an authoritarian, charismatic leader."[2] Dr. Braden defines a cult as "any religious group which differs significantly in one or more respects as to belief or practice from those religious groups which are regarded as the normative expressions of religion in our total culture."[3] These are both helpful definitions that highlight a few key characteristics— namely, that there is a normative expression of a religion, and then there are those that significantly differ, even to the point of describing what they teach (by comparison) as false or extremist.

Walter Martin, another prominent expert on cults, says that "a cult might also be defined as a group of people gathered about a specific person or person's misinterpretation of the Bible." He lists as examples of this the Jehovah's Witnesses, whose interpretations are based on the work of Charles T. Russell and J. F. Rutherford, and the Christian Scientists, who are disciples of Mary Baker Eddy and her interpretations of Scripture.[4] To this list we might add several groups that have made inroads within the Black community, including the Hebrew Israelite movement, the Israelite School of Universal Practical Knowledge (ISUPK) group, and the Nation of Islam. All of these groups can be considered cults because their beliefs differ from normative expressions of established religions to the point that the mainstream expressions have determined they are false or errant.

CULT LEADERS OFTEN HAVE MYTHICAL ORIGINS

Most cults have a charismatic leader who either claims deity or claims to have had some special encounter with God or a spirit being that sets them apart as the only viable conduit for communicating information. For instance, Elijah Muhammed claimed that a man by the name of Wallace Fard Muhammed was God in the flesh and that he revealed his truth to him. Yet Fard's identity is debated, "as he had no less than fifty different aliases."[5] Nobel Drew Ali of the Moorish Science Temple also has a mythical origin story. His followers claim that he was a healer who voyaged to Egypt, where he went through the same "secret rites" they claim Jesus went through.[6]

Many groups create these mythical origins and spiritual experiences for their founders as a way of verifying them as divine or justifying their veneration. This convinces their followers to follow them with absolute devotion. These stories then become the bedrock of whatever doctrinal framework the leader creates to reinforce their image as a figure who has touched or communed with the divine. For instance, Muhammed of Islam claims to have had contact with the angel Jibril/Gabriel and this angel "brought down the Qur'an for recitation."[7]

Stories of mythical encounters add an accent of additional authority to doctrine, which then gives them a special ability to lead. Since this divine event happened (at least in the minds of their followers), the cult leader has a unique connection that needs to be respected and followed at all costs. The mystic nature of these stories can cause followers to set aside their best judgment, even after red flags appear.

CULT LEADERS OFTEN EXHIBIT TOTALITARIAN TENDENCIES

Totalitarianism is a concept often used to refer to governments that impose "a form of government in which the political authority exercises absolute and centralized control over all aspects of life, the individual is subordinated to the state, and opposing political and cultural expression is suppressed."[8]

Totalitarian governments are often synonymous with authoritarian leadership. And oddly enough, these two terms are also regularly used to describe cults and cult leaders.

In fact, one of the most prominent characteristics of a cult is the presence of an absolute, authoritarian leader who defines and controls the members of the community. A single leader is most often the sole authority, but at times there may be an elite "ruling coterie" (a small group of leaders) who also function in that pivotal position of power. The group is primarily personality driven and functionally defined by its living leader or leaders.[9] For instance, the Nation of Islam has always had national spokesmen. Malcolm X would always make sure that he overcommunicated his loyalty and made it clear that the origins of what he taught and believe came from the honorable Elijah Muhammed. To this day, Louis Farrakhan, who continues the teaching of the Nation of Islam, sources his own position and teaching in the teachings and leadership of the honorable Elijah Muhammed.

As another example, a group out of Australia called "The Family" led by Anne Hamilton-Byrne provides a frightening example of totalitarian leadership. Burn was believed by her followers to be Jesus Christ. She and the other leaders of the cult were somehow able to seduce middle- and upper-class people so that as their children were born, they would take them to a camp or compound run by the cult. The children were delivered over to this group and raised by a group of "Aunties." They were harshly abused and malnourished. Anne was viewed by everyone in the cult as their mother, and everyone followed her teaching without question.

Most of these leaders, however, don't come off as evil and harsh. They often tend to be charismatic and winsome, which makes for effective recruitment. People are willing to follow a leader who is clear and articulate, reads people well, and is knowledgeable of the human condition. Cults and their charismatic leaders prey on those longing for something legitimate that is missing from their lives. They use a person's longing as a gateway to winning them into the cult. For instance, most Black Religious Identity Cults (BRICS) use the broken ethnic identity and the "mystery of our past" as a way to recruit people and draw them in. The Nation of Islam, the Hebrew Israelites, the Nuwaubians, Kemetics, and many other groups in the Black "conscious community" begin a conversation by asking, "Do you know who you are?" Non-BRIC groups may find other entry points into the lives of Black men and women.

CULT LEADERS UTILIZE THOUGHT REFORM

In a cult, members are taught *what* to think, not how to think. Psychiatrist Robert Jay Lifton coined this practice "thought reform" and speaks of its use by the military, prison system, and universities. He explains,

> Whatever its setting, thought reform consists of two basic elements: *confession*, the exposure and renunciation of past and present "evil"; and *re-education*, the remaking of a man in the Communist image. These elements are closely related and overlapping, since they both bring into play a series of pressures and appeals—intellectual, emotional, and physical—aimed at social control and individual change.[10]

Thought reform is presented as a beneficial and good thing—a way of escaping the common and wrong way of thinking. But in reality, the individual is manipulated and coerced into the cult's hive thinking. In this process, the participant is assimilated into the cult and kept captive in it by ongoing thought reform. This is where the stronghold lies, the effective means of keeping people locked into the cult. Paul describes these "strongholds" as a mindset in 2 Corinthians 10:3–7:

> For although we live in the flesh, we do not wage war according to the flesh, since the weapons of our warfare are not of the flesh, but are powerful through God for the demolition of strongholds. We demolish arguments and every proud thing that is raised up against the knowledge of God, and we take every thought captive to obey Christ. And we are ready to punish any disobedience, once your obedience is complete. Look at what is obvious. If anyone is confident that he belongs to Christ, let him remind himself of this: Just as he belongs to Christ, so do we. (CSB)

My working definition of a stronghold is a mindset, value system, or thought process that hinders your growth and prevents you from exalting Jesus above everything in your life. Another way of saying this is that we must reject "stubborn ways of thinking that refuse God-driven change"![11] Ed Silvoso states that a stronghold "is a mind-set impregnated with hopelessness that causes us to accept as unchangeable, situations that we know are contrary to the will of God."[12]

Thought reform indoctrinates people into the cult and normalizes ways of thinking for those in the group. Often, these ways of thinking are kept secret from outsiders, and members keep them under wraps because they know the outside world will not understand or will react negatively if they were ever to be publicized (we will see this in the next chapter on the Seventh-day Adventists). Thought reform is a way of maintaining absolute control over the members of the cult. "Coercive persuasion" (another term for thought reform) leads to the breakdown of critical and independent thinking. It also causes those affected to become increasingly dependent on the group and its leadership, to the point where leaders make value judgments for members, provide analysis, and in some situations determine the parameters of reality.[13] Soon, we have an environment in which every doctrine and belief of the group is *essential*. Having a different view of things leads to shaming, demonization, or shunning. Followers are even discouraged from asking questions. Leaders of these groups have an inordinate fear of losing their control over people's minds and allowing their followers to think for themselves. Thought reform itself becomes part of the hive thinking of the community, becoming so ingrained in members that everyone sounds the same and uses all of the same phrases to communicate.

I realize that anyone reading this can easily look at Christianity and point out some similarities. In Christianity we have our share of clichés and Christianese—to the point where those who are not Christian may think we are speaking another language. Even in comparing different Christian pulpits, there will be rhetoric or cadence that feels similar to many subcultural and ethnic groups within the Christian faith. Yet one of the hallmarks of orthodox Christian faith is that while there are commonalities around core doctrines, there is diversity of expression. In Nation of Islam mosques and Hebrew Israelite (HI) camps, for example, you will find consistency and similarity. Cult groups emphasize consistency of the brand—even better than your local Chick-fil-A! From clothing, to decorum, to speech patterns, to rigidness on both essentials and nonessentials, most cults want everyone to conform to the approved standards. Anything different is rejected and shunned.

In many Black Religious Identity Cults (BRICS), thought reform begins with a question: "Do you know who you are as a Black man or woman?" For Blacks this is a jarring question. It strikes a chord for many because it is not easy to have a clear view of who you are as a Black person ethnically. The history of our ancestors and our ethnic heritage has largely been stripped from us. And while there is nothing wrong with learning one's ethnic heritage, these groups exploit that pain by connecting spirituality to unlocking deeper truth about one's heritage. Some groups teach that all Blacks in America are Moors, others say Egyptians, Nubians, Asiatic, Hebrews, aboriginal to the Americas, or even African diaspora Jews.

In many cases, the next step is to decapitate the Western narrative by making it fully illegitimate. In its place, they create another narrative of ethnic history, one coupled with a spiritual system that is presented as older or more authentic than Christianity. From this point, an individual begins a journey of destruction from which few find their way back. Only the powerful truth of the gospel can reverse this one-way ticket to the ethnic netherworld.

INTERACTING WITH CULT MEMBERS

When I went to seminary, I met several African, European, and Caribbean brothers, and they started talking with me about football. I started off naming several teams I had seen, and they were clearly confused. I, too, was shocked that they'd never heard of the Cowboys or the Eagles or 49ers. Then they all started laughing and said to me, "Not *that* football!" and explained that football where they live is entirely different. I said, "Oh, you are talking about soccer," and a goodhearted argument commenced. We had the same name for two vastly different sports.

In interacting with cults, this happens all the time. As you will see in several of the chapters in this first section, biblical terms are frequently twisted into a different meaning within the cult. Of course, the cults will say that while the term means something different, it's close enough that we're all on the same page. Whether it is the eternality of Christ, the nature of God, or the way of salvation by faith—core beliefs in orthodox Christianity—these concepts and doctrines have very different meanings in cults.

SALVATION

Pretty much every cult has highjacked the term "salvation" and infused it with their own meaning. Salvation for Christians refers to being delivered from the wrath of God, sin, death, and Satan's tyranny (1 Cor. 15). Yet in other groups, even groups that try to apply the label "Christian" to themselves, the meaning is either entirely different or the same but with unorthodox additions.

The Nation of Islam (as discussed in the previous *Urban Apologetics* volume) pioneered this way of using Christian terms in an effort to make Black Christians pluralistic (accepting of other religious views as a means of salvation). Consider carefully how the Nation of Islam defines salvation: "*This alone is salvation, just to be brought out of the darkness of ignorance into the light of the truth. Who is in more need of the truth than the American so-called Negroes who do not have the knowledge of self nor of anyone else, and who love those who hate them and spitefully use them?*"[14] The Nation of Islam and other BRICs often list knowledge of self as central to what it means to be saved. And many of the groups that we'll discuss in the coming chapters of this volume often couple their view of justification by faith with other items that undermine the work of Jesus on the cross as sufficient to save.

WHO IS JESUS?

Every cult also seems to have its own take on Jesus's identity. For instance, the Family's Anne Hamilton-Byrne claimed to be the return of Jesus Christ. Orthodox Islam says that Jesus is a prophet. Jehovah's Witnesses describe Jesus in terms that are christologically Arian (an ancient heresy), and Five Percenters say that Jesus was an example showing us how to be gods ourselves. You can't just ask people, "Do you believe in Jesus?" You have to ask, "*What* Jesus do you believe in, and *who* do you believe him to be?"

LIMITED AVAILABILITY OF TEACHINGS

A leader and member of a cult group I have been connecting with asked me to do a public "dialogue" with him on several theological topics in the Bible. I told him, "I will agree to this when you and your leaders make your beliefs and philosophies publicly available in written form. You have videos, but I've seen nuance and changes that you make to these based on the situation." To dialogue with these leaders, I need to be able to hold them to what they believe in a written format. Not surprisingly, they declined!

Seventh-day Adventists, the Nation of Islam, Jehovah's Witnesses, and most cults will limit access to parts of their teachings to only members. For instance, Seventh-day Adventists limit access to their doctrines on the person of Christ, salvation, the role of the Sabbath, and other core teachings. They know that you have to go through a process of thought reform in order to stomach their deeper teachings on these matters.

Israel United in Christ is the only formal HI group I know that has made some basic info available in writing for the public (available in their Welcome Home packet). But this is an introductory pamphlet not a real book or commentary. The Jehovah's Witnesses have the Watchtower and something called *Reasoning from the Scriptures*, which is a verse-by-verse response to Christian groups. But even these resources do not cover the full range of doctrines and beliefs they teach.

TARGETING CHRISTIANS

Many of the cults, especially those we'll discuss in this book, see Christians and the Christian church as their primary mission field. It is rare to find someone in the cult who didn't grow up in the church or have a connection to a Judeo-Christian tradition. So how do they convince Christian believers to join their group?

One of the most common tactics is sometimes called "love bombing." This describes "the seemingly unconditional affection . . . members direct toward them."[15] Many groups use this strategy to clear conflict from the runway and bring the person into the cult. Once the person is hooked, they can then begin the thought-reform process. Ross talks about this in relation to the Unification Church: "This 'love' is actually highly conditional and based on their growing acceptance of Unification Church principles and corresponding progress in the group. This contrived but intense experience in the context of a controlled group environment can produce the desired commitment."[16] In this phase the potential inductee can do no wrong. Everything is taken care of for them.

> I remember one time a group offered me a free trip "for pastors." They gave me all the info, and it seemed like a dream come true. I asked, "What are the requirements?" They said, "Every morning, you have to come to a 1–3 hour seminar on our organization." I did some research and found out it was a Unification Church sponsored trip. They were providing free trips for pastors to get them converted. Now that's love bombing!

The tactic reverses, however, once you are in the cult as a member. I had several family members who were in a cultic church for many years. Many of us were wary of their involvement because of the tone of the leadership in worship services and what looked like financial mismanagement and manipulation. Many of the offerings they took were dedicated for the leadership, not for mission or ministry. When someone would call this out, they were rebuked. If they left, they were shunned and demonized in a damage-control meeting.

LOOKING AHEAD

In college, I almost joined the Nation of Islam. I was in a very vulnerable place, looking for identity and guidance. I went to the mosque and was blown away by the discipline, respect, identity affirmation, self-love, dedication to protecting Black women, and fearlessness to speak truth to power. Yet, as I learned more of the teaching, something didn't feel right. I couldn't accept the mythical origins behind their creation story and their clear misinterpretations of the Bible. Using basic context clues, I found obvious fallacies in their Bible interpretation. Although I wasn't a believer at the time, the Lord began setting off massive alarms in my soul. One of the things I try to tell people is if you feel uneasy about something, never ignore what you are feeling. While our feelings aren't always a reliable guide to truth, feelings can often be the beginning of a process of deeper examination. Maybe that feeling you have is your conscience and soul being pricked by the Holy Spirit when knowledge is absent.

Thankfully, I didn't drink the Kool Aid, but a dear friend who was with me already had.

I saw firsthand how cults master those whom they target to bring them into their fold. I saw how they gravitate toward those who have experienced some form of trauma—people who have experienced loss, have identity issues of some kind, are lonely, or desire meaning. Cults usually market themselves as the absolute answer to our deepest issues and longings. Because cults are frauds, this retraumatizes those dealing with pain and loss and many times ends up turning people away from faith communities altogether. The manipulative nature of cults can injure a person's ability to see authentic faith as helpful. Because they have made themselves vulnerable and that trust was betrayed, they are less likely to trust again.

The truth is that cults take advantage of legitimate needs and longings. And as we think about how to reach people, we need to acknowledge those needs and longings as legitimate. Even after coming to Jesus, I still felt some longings that I didn't feel my church was addressing. And there were still questions I had that weren't being answered. But I didn't blame Christianity, I blamed those who were leading.

In the following chapters, we will focus exclusively on groups that might be defined as religious cults—groups that have a cultic ideology. Why these particular cults? Because in our work with Black communities and Black churches, these are several of the groups that we most commonly encounter and that were not previously covered in the first *Urban Apologetics* volume. Our goal here is to aid the reader so you have a better awareness of what these groups believe, how they originated, and then how to utilize an accurate biblical and historical worldview to lovingly engage people in these groups, as well as anyone who might be headed in that direction.

NINE

SEVENTH-DAY ADVENTISTS

ELCE-JUNIOR LAURISTON

The Seventh-day Adventist Church is a sect that has respected organizations, universities, schools, hospitals, charities, parachurch and independent ministries all over the world. The global membership is estimated to be eighteen to twenty million. Adventists are represented in perhaps every sector of society. Some Seventh-day Adventists (SDAs) have risen to high leadership positions: US Senate chaplain Dr. Barry Black; renowned neurosurgeon, former US presidential candidate, and former Secretary of the Department of Housing and Urban Development Dr. Ben Carson; the governor general of Jamaica, Sir Patrick Allen; and Jamaica's prime minister, Andrew Holness. Adventists have television and radio stations, social media pages, websites, and electronic mass communication channels that reach far and wide. They are generally known for their Saturday churchgoing, their abstinence from pork, shellfish, and alcohol, and for not wearing jewelry.

From the 1840s to the 1950s many evangelical denominations considered the Seventh-day Adventist Church to be a non-Christian cult. However, since the 1950s several factions within the SDA church have tried to align themselves with evangelical Christians, attempting to present Adventism in such a way that minimizes the ways it is distinct from orthodox Christianity. In the 1950s, dialogue between evangelical Christians and several SDA scholars and apologists led some evangelicals to reconsider labelling the SDA Church as a cult.[1] In 1957, the SDA church also published a book called *Questions on Doctrine*, which convinced many orthodox Christians that there was a movement toward orthodoxy growing within Adventism.[2] Yet not everyone in the SDA church agreed with the book or its positions, and it was considered by many to be a watering down of traditional teaching. The book soon went out of print, though it was republished in 2003.[3] Today, even if some in the SDA church have moved toward orthodoxy, there remain large parts of the global SDA church that hold tenaciously to the heritage of Ellen G. White and her teachings, while some SDA churches and members fall somewhere in between. Yet those who continue to hold to the teachings of White are clearly unorthodox in their beliefs and practices.

Thus, despite its global successes and efforts at reform, Adventists are still considered heterodox by many orthodox Christians today. They deviate in significant ways on a number of Christian teachings regarding scriptural authority, the person and work of Jesus Christ, salvation, justification, the Sabbath, Sunday worship, the atonement, race issues, and the nature of humankind. Their views on many key topics distinguish them from both mainline Protestant Christianity and Roman Catholicism. Adventists also hold unique teachings around jewelry, cosmetics, and dietary laws that further set them apart.

Why have we chosen to include a detailed examination of Seventh-day Adventism in this volume? Adventism is prevalent around the world, yet the bulk of its global membership today is in predominantly Black nations and communities. And even in predominantly white countries, SDA tends to have a strong presence in Black communities. For this reason, Seventh-day Adventist theology and cultural ideologies frequently steer the lives of persons in such countries and communities. While Adventism in some cases has ameliorated the lives of people in Black countries and communities, a fair assessment of SDA's impact shows that it has also had serious negative effects on Black nations and communities.

HISTORICAL DEVELOPMENT OF THE SEVENTH-DAY ADVENTISTS

Seventh-day Adventism was born during the Second Great Awakening of the nineteenth century in North America. This time was marked by religious fanaticism, and many pseudo-Christian cults and sects arose, each with their own authoritative prophet who either started or guided their church. Many of these groups believed that Christianity was apostate from the death of the apostles to the time their church was born and that God had specifically raised up their church to be "the true church" to "restore" Christianity.

Adventism traces its roots to William Miller. After reading Daniel 8:14, "Unto two thousand and three hundred days; then shall the sanctuary be cleansed" (KJV) and using the popular but spurious "one day for a year" interpretation of Bible prophecy, William Miller was convinced that Jesus was returning in 1843. The "day for a year" method of interpreting Bible prophecy is proof-texted from Numbers 14:34, in which God punishes Israel with forty years wandering the wilderness because they had spent forty days spying out Canaan. Ezekiel 4:4–6 is also referenced, in which the prophet is instructed by God to lie on his side to bear the iniquity of the house of Israel and Judea respectively. He has to lie on his side 390 days for the house of Israel and 40 days for the house of Judea, with each day representing one year of their punishments from God. Miller reached the conclusion that Jesus was returning in 1843 by counting 2,300 years from 457 BC (which he determined was the year that King Darius issued the decree to rebuild Jerusalem found in Dan. 9:25). Miller believed that the cleansing of the sanctuary described in this verse referred to the earth's destruction by fire.

Miller's preaching snowballed and became popular in many US states. Thousands left their churches to join what was then coined the "Millerite Movement." When ministers attempted to point out to Millerites, as Miller's followers came to be called, that date-setting the Second Coming was wrong according to Jesus's own words in Matthew 24:36, they were accused of not loving Jesus's return. The Millerites expected Jesus to return between March 21, 1843, and March 21, 1844. March 1843 left them disappointed. And the spring of 1844 left them disappointed for a second time.

When Miller's initial calculations were proven incorrect, his most dedicated followers attempted to calculate for themselves the day of Jesus's return. Most prominent was Samuel S. Snow, who determined that October 22, 1844, was the specific day Jesus would return. He based his calculations on the fact that the Jewish Day of Atonement occurs on the tenth day of the seventh month and his interpretation that Jesus was the antitypical fulfillment of the Day of Atonement. As the Millerites anticipated the second advent just a few months away, countless of them neglected their fields, sold their homes, farms, and possessions. Ripe crops were left to rot in the fields. Some quit their jobs, and others rejected job offers.[4]

Christian pastors refuted the date-setting of the Millerites and admonished their members against the fervor of Millerism. The Millerites ignored these warnings; instead, they accused such pastors of being indifferent false shepherds who did not love Jesus and did not want him to return.[5] Some of these pastors had to disfellowship some of their members for disorderly conduct, insubordination, and untamable fanaticism. Ellen G. Harmon (later White), who would eventually become the founder of the Adventist movement, and her family also suffered that fate.[6]

As October 22 approached, the Millerites eagerly prepared themselves. They made white "ascension robes" for their families.[7] Many climbed high rocks, hills, and rooftops, waiting. Yet on the morning of October 22, 1844, nothing happened. Through the night hours, nothing happened. When the clock struck twelve a.m. October 23, 1844, the Millerites were bitterly disappointed for the third time. Seventh-day Adventists still celebrate October 22 every year as "Great Disappointment Day."

The Millerites were in a state of pandemonium. Confusion, panic, and despair was rampant. Some husbands killed their families and then themselves. Some mothers committed murder-suicide. Some teens and young adults attempted suicide; some even succeeded.[8] Many became impoverished or mentally unstable, filling insane asylums. Millerite-induced insanity was considered to be "more of a public health threat than yellow fever and cholera"[9] in those states overrun with Millerism.

Whereas some Millerites recanted and went back to their churches, others reasoned that something significant did happen that day—just not the event they had anticipated. On October 23, 1844, one such Millerite, Hiram Edson, announced that he had a vision while walking through a cornfield. In the vision he saw Jesus move from the Holy Place of the heavenly sanctuary to the Most Holy Place to begin a work of "investigative judgment" and "cleansing" of the sins of believers. Many devoted Millerites quickly embraced this "vision," viewing it as an important event and becoming convinced that their disappointment was divinely orchestrated.[10]

Roughly two months after Edson's vision, in December of 1844, a seventeen-year-old girl named Ellen G. Harmon claimed to have had her own vision.[11] From that point on, she became the central figure of a small section of Millerites who would later form the Seventh-day Adventist Church. She, along with her husband James White and a man named Joseph Bates, went on to officially found the SDA Church in May 1863. Ellen White served as the key figure and authority of the SDA Church as well as its prophetess.

Ellen White adopted the "vision" of Hiram Edson when prophetic status was finally conferred upon her. She later confessed that Miller's failed prophecy, date-setting, and the proof text of Daniel 8:14 was the foundation of Adventism.[12] Ellen White stated that God had directed Miller's false date-settings and speculative chart. She claimed that God had purposefully hid a number in their calculations and caused the ghastly disappointments they had experienced.[13] From the very beginning of her prophetic career, Ellen White was grossly ignorant of Scripture,[14] rejected its clear statements, and had twisted views about the nature and character of God.

BELIEFS AND CORE VALUES OF SEVENTH-DAY ADVENTISTS

Seventh-day Adventists see themselves as a special movement[15] to whom God has given "special light." Their claims are based on their interpretation of Revelation 14:6–12, called the "Three Angels' Messages," which they believe they must take to the world, especially to Christians. The Three Angels' Messages is the Adventist gospel.[16] They interpret these messages to mean that they ought to call people to keep the Ten Commandments, announce the Investigative Judgment, urge and defend Sabbath, warn against embracing the Roman Catholic Church and Protestant Christianity, and warn against worshiping God on Sunday, as that is the mark of the beast.

Adventists emphasize family, community, education, evangelism, behavior modification and deportment, and health. The official voices of the SDA Church follow a hierarchical structure that starts with the local church. Several churches combined together make up a district. All churches in a particular locale make up a conference. Several conferences combined make up a union. Several unions in a section of the globe makes up a division. Those divisions make up the General Conference of SDAs, which has its headquarters in Silver Spring, Maryland. The highest organizational authority of the SDA Church is the General Conference. And this is so because Ellen White said so. She states that the General Conference is "the voice of God,"[17] God's "highest authority" on earth, and "when the judgment of the General Conference, which is the highest authority that God has upon the earth, is exercised, private independence and private judgment must not be maintained, but surrendered."[18]

In the following paragraphs, we will explore in greater depth the core tenets of SDA teachings and demonstrate how these teachings deviate from widely accepted Christian doctrine.

THE DIVINE AUTHORITY OF ELLEN G. WHITE

Although Joseph Bates and James White were instrumental in the establishment and organization of the SDA Church, only Ellen White is held as a prophet and as the supreme authoritative voice. To this day, through her writings, her role remains the same. Seventh-day Adventism cannot exist without Ellen G. White. Adventism revolves around her. Adventists embrace her, and only her, as God's end-time prophet for the last-day church (which is the SDA church).

Ellen White was born November 26, 1827. She was educated until the age of nine, when she was hit in the face with a stone that incapacitated her and she was unable to continue with schooling. This greatly affected her physically, emotionally, psychologically, and spiritually. When she began to experience visions at age seventeen, Ellen White claimed for herself direct inspiration from God. Adventists believe and affirm this as true.

Ellen G. White's position was cemented at the very beginning of Adventism. When the SDA Church was studying a topic and were stuck on the matter, she'd be taken off into a vision where clear explanations of passages were given to her as well as instructions about how to labor and teach. Through these visions they would understand Scripture and teachings about Jesus. Everything was revealed to her—spanning from that time in history to the time at the end when they would enter into the Holy City.[19]

A large majority of SDA doctrines, views, beliefs, interpretations of Scripture, and practices are based on White's writings. Her writings are at the heart of Adventist church life, culture, diet, practices, theology, organization, church disciplinary actions and procedures, and evangelism. Adventists today will deny that her writings are on par with Scripture, but subconsciously, in practice and in official documents, her writings are still equated with Scripture and at times are considered superior to it. Her writings remain the primary guide for the SDA Church, as they utilize her writings alongside Scripture in sermons, Sabbath School Study Guides, Bible classes, lectures, university courses and classes, and church guidelines and practices. They preach and do studies from her books in the same way Christians engage the Bible. Her writings are used to clarify, to interpret, to justify, to expand, or to strengthen anything in their official Twenty-Eight Fundamental Beliefs, their Church Manual, or in Scripture. What White has said is the ultimate arbiter of any matter in dispute in the SDA. Departing from her writings can greatly jeopardize one's career or standing in the SDA Church. Ellen White "surrounded" Scripture with her writings as the present guide for life, and her followers themselves neglected to read the Bible, preferring her writings.[20] Her writings are the lens through which Adventists filter, interpret, revise, and understand Scripture and Christian church history.

Before anyone is baptized into the SDA Church, they must pledge to submit to a set of thirteen vows in the form of questions. Anyone who does not agree with the vows cannot be baptized. Vow number eight asks, "Do you believe the Biblical teaching of spiritual gifts, and do you believe that the gift of prophecy is one of the identifying marks of the remnant church?"[21] The "gift of prophecy" is understood to refer to Ellen White and her writings, which the SDA Church says speaks with "prophetic authority" and provides "comfort, guidance, instruction, and correction to the church."[22]

In fact, Ellen White makes it clear that SDA doctrines are the standard by which all teachings and biblical interpretations must be tested. Any biblical interpretation or application of Scripture that threatens SDA doctrines must be rejected.[23] At the 2015 SDA General Conference Session, the delegates reaffirmed their faith and confidence in Ellen White's writings by saying, "We reaffirm our conviction that her writings are divinely inspired, truly Christ-centered, and Bible-based. Rather than replacing the Bible, they uplift the normative character of Scripture and correct inaccurate interpretations of it derived from tradition, human reason, personal experience, and modern culture."[24] Though some might argue that this differentiates White's writings from Scripture, in fact it puts her writings above Scripture. Her writings are so necessary for practicing SDA faith that they teach that "the last deception of Satan" will be attempts at causing people to lose faith and confidence in her writings.[25] White herself predicted that the final apostasy and ultimate destruction would begin with people losing faith in her writings and SDA doctrines.[26]

The Christian View

Despite the lofty claims that Ellen White made for herself and the height to which the SDA Church has elevated her, from the beginning of the movement, Ellen White made many false predictions and preached and taught a different Jesus, a different gospel, and a different atonement. She believed her inspiration and authority was greater than that of the biblical authors and above Scripture itself. She taught many heterodox and bizarre things, making innocuous things mandatory for salvation. She was also a known plagiarist, and charges of plagiarism dogged her throughout her ministry and continue today. Ellen White contradicted Scripture and herself on many issues, disregarding some of her own visions and counsels but threatening members of the SDA Church with hellfire if they disobeyed them.[27]

THE GREAT CONTROVERSY AND THE TEN COMMANDMENT LAW

Adventists believe in a "great controversy" that is ongoing between God and Satan.[28] The great controversy can be visualized as an arm-wrestling match in which the Ten Commandments are central and God and Satan are wrestling for supremacy, sovereignty, and worship. This conflict, according to Adventists, started when God promoted[29] Jesus to deity status, but Satan became jealous of Jesus because he thought he was better suited for that promotion.[30]

The SDA precreation narrative was formulated by the dreams and visions of Ellen G. White, and it taught that Jesus was not always God, that Jesus was in reality Michael the archangel,[31] one of many archangels[32] and commander of the angelic hosts. Satan is also an archangel and commander of angels.[33] Eventually, God "invited" Jesus into his counsel and exalted Jesus to be equal to himself,[34] a position which Satan had desired.[35] Satan, angered at Jesus's promotion, traveled around heaven and the "unfallen worlds" campaigning and complaining against God and his law. He charged that God was unjust and his laws unfair and impossible to keep. Some angels were convinced by Satan's arguments and joined forces with him.[36] As a result, God is now embroiled in a great controversy with Satan in which he must vindicate his character, prove that his law is just and can be kept, prove that Satan's accusations are wrong, and win the eternal loyalty of his subjects (humans and those in the unfallen worlds).[37] The main point of Jesus becoming a man was to be an example of perfect law keeping to humans, and through his power we can perfectly keep the law too.[38] Jesus's death on the cross was necessary to "vindicate" the law and uphold its eternal binding claims.[39] The climactic event that will end the great controversy just before Jesus returns is when Christians will merge with the unsaved to persecute and kill Adventists over the law.[40]

The Christian View

Christians do not see God or Jesus as being gridlocked in a great controversy with Satan in which God's sovereignty is undermined. God is sovereign (1 Tim. 6:15). He is not wrestling with Satan for supremacy. Even Satan is under his authority (Job 1–2). He does not have to prove that he is just and worthy of worship (Rev. 4:11). The Ten Commandments are not an eternal, irrevocable law at the center of a supernatural conflict. The Ten Commandment law and covenant has been abrogated (2 Cor. 3; Gal. 4:21–31). Jesus Christ eternally exists with the Father as God. He was not promoted to godhood (John 1:1–3; Phil. 2:5–11). He is not Michael the archangel (Heb. 1).

THE INVESTIGATIVE JUDGMENT AND UNCERTAINTY ABOUT SALVATION

The investigative judgment is a doctrine that is unique to the SDA Church and frequently leads to fear and salvific uncertainty for many Adventists. Ellen White expanded the SDA Church's beliefs on this doctrine after she adopted the "vision" of Hiram Edson. This doctrine can only be understood, explained, and defended with Ellen White's writings.

White claims that on October 22, 1844, Jesus entered into the Most Holy Place of the heavenly sanctuary to appear in God's presence to engage in "the last acts of His ministration" for man: to investigate them. This "ministration" is "an atonement" that will reveal all who are "entitled to its benefits." This investigative judgment is a "final atonement" that considers the cases of God's professed people. The wicked aren't being investigated in this investigative judgment, only alleged believers. The wicked will be investigated at a later (unknown) period.[41]

According to this doctrine, Jesus is investigating the lives of all who believed in him, beginning with Adam's generation and moving on to every successive generation. He will then investigate those living. The names of every believer will be mentioned and their lives "closely investigated." Some believers will be accepted for salvation and some will be rejected. Any unrepentant and unforgiven sin will cause the names of those believers who committed them to be blotted out of the book of life, with all their good deeds erased.[42]

Ellen White claims that every sin is recorded with "terrible exactness" against believers.[43] In order for the sins of believers to be blotted out they "must pass its searching scrutiny."[44] Ellen White said that this scrutiny is so intensely meticulous that it will be as though there were no other being on earth.[45] A single, forgotten, unrepentant sin is enough to condemn a believer.[46]

One of the most frightening things about the investigative judgment is that no SDA knows when God has finished investigating the lives of dead saints and has moved on to the living.[47] One might have failed to pass the investigation but continues with religious activities not knowing that it is all in vain. The purpose of the investigative judgment is to ensure that believers have achieved sinless perfection and are "prepared" for heaven.[48] When the investigative judgment is over, every believer's destiny will be decided for eternal life or death.[49] Having assurance of salvation in this doctrine is impossible. Dead saints will only know they did enough to pass the investigative judgment when they shockingly wake up to the resurrection of life.

The Christian View

The investigative judgment is an egregiously false doctrine. For the more than two millennia of Judeo-Christianity, no one who read Scripture ever concluded that it teaches an investigative judgment that will begin in 1844. This doctrine is unorthodox because it distorts the biblical gospel, rejects Jesus's complete atonement on the cross, and undermines the omniscience of God. Jesus did not enter the Most Holy Place on October 22, 1844. Scripture teaches that he did so at his ascension (Heb. 6:19–20; 9:11–13). God is not poring over books, investigating the lives of believers before determining if they are safe to save. God already knows those who are his (John 10:25–30; 2 Tim. 2:19). He has forgiven us, blotted out our sins, and does not hold them against us (Rom. 4:7–8; Col. 1:13–14; Heb. 8:12). Believers will not face an investigative judgment, in which we could possibly be condemned by God. Jesus has redeemed us from condemnatory judgment and death and given us eternal life (John 5:24). There is no condemnation for those who are in Jesus Christ (Rom. 8:1). Salvation is solely by grace through faith in Jesus (Eph. 2:8–10). We currently possess eternal life (John 3:16) and can be sure of our salvation (1 John 5:13).

SATAN IS THE SCAPEGOAT AND ULTIMATE SIN BEARER

Adventists at every level of Adventism teach that Satan is the scapegoat and sin bearer referenced in Leviticus 16. Their official doctrinal statement of faith, *Seventh-day Adventists Believe*, states, "A careful examination of Leviticus 16 reveals that Azazel represents Satan, not Christ, as some have thought."[50] This doctrine is closely tied to the investigative judgment and is another unorthodox doctrine held by the SDA Church. Adventists have tortured Scripture to make Satan the scapegoat because Ellen White has said "the scapegoat typified Satan, the author of sin, upon whom the sins of the truly penitent will finally be placed."[51] She repeats, "Christ will place all these sins upon Satan, the originator and instigator of sin. The scapegoat, bearing the sins of Israel, was sent away 'unto a land not inhabited' so Satan, bearing the guilt of all the sins which he has caused God's people to commit, will be for a thousand years confined to the earth."[52]

The Christian View

Whereas Satan is the scapegoat and ultimate sin-bearer in SDA theology, this is not true for Christians. The Day of Atonement and the animals involved are a shadow of Christ's atoning work (Col. 2:16–17). The goat that died and the scapegoat in Leviticus 16 represented *one sin offering* depicting both the sacrificial and expiatory aspects of Jesus's single sacrifice (Lev. 16:5). Jesus is the one who died for our sins and also the one who bears them away (Isa. 53:4–12; John 1:29; 1 Pet. 2:24). He is the perfect, guiltless one who bore the guilt and sins of others (2 Cor. 5:21; 1 John 2:2).

THE SABBATH, SUNDAY WORSHIP, AND THE MARK OF THE BEAST

At the center of their law-centered "great controversy between God and Satan" is the Sabbath of the Ten Commandments. Adventists believe that the Sabbath is universal, mandatory, and salvific. It is the "golden clasp" that unites them with God.[53] They believe that it is the only command by which God, the Lawgiver, can be known and accurately worshiped.[54] According to their teachings, the Sabbath is the "test of our loyalty to God";[55] it is the "seal of God," the seal of salvation.[56] SDA members tend to be legalistic and judgmental toward non-Sabbatarian Christians despite their own hypocrisy and inability to keep the Sabbath in accordance with the biblical rules and the several hundred rules added by Ellen White.

In their eschatology, the Sabbath is the ultimate determiner of salvation.[57] It will be "the separating wall" between the saved and unsaved and will demarcate "the true Israel of God" (SDAs) from unbelievers (Christians and the unsaved masses).[58] Just before Jesus returns, SDAs will experience a great revival in which they will be empowered by the Holy Spirit to "proclaim the Sabbath more fully," and hordes of Christians and unbelievers will be converted to Adventism and the Sabbath.[59] The Sabbath has saving and condemning properties.[60] One's orientation to the Sabbath will be the "determining factor" for eternal salvation or eternal damnation.[61] In this eschatological vein, Sunday stands in opposition to the Sabbath. Sunday is the false papacy Sabbath.

Adventist teaching holds that while Sunday worship is not yet the mark of the beast, if persons continue to keep and worship God on Sunday, it will earn them the mark of the beast and will eternally damn them.[62] They believe Sunday is a pagan and sinful day on which to worship God. It is disobedience to God and his Word. Persons who worship God on Sunday in ignorance are not held accountable, as God only holds people accountable to "the light" that they have. However, when such persons become aware of the Sabbath through Adventist preaching, teaching, and literature and reject it, continuing to worship God on Sunday, they are in sin and preparing themselves to receive the mark of the beast.[63]

In addition to this, Adventists believe that mainstream Protestant Christians will unite with Roman Catholicism and will eventually unite with secular governments to enforce universal Sunday laws, beginning with the United States of America,[64] which will bring about persecution and death to Adventists for worshiping on Saturday.[65] Those who obey this law will receive the mark of the beast and face the judgment of God while SDAs will be sealed and vindicated.[66]

The Christian View

The Bible does not teach Adventist doctrines about the Sabbath, Sunday worship, and the mark of the beast. The Sabbath was an old covenant sign between God and the nation of Israel (Ex. 31:12–17; Ezek. 20:12, 20). It was not automatically binding on gentile nations (Neh. 10:28–31; 13:15–22). God promised to put an end to all of Israel's Sabbaths and festivals (Hos. 2:11), and he did just that when Jesus fulfilled the old covenant (Matt. 5:17–19; John 19:28–30; Heb. 8:8–9:5). The early church worshiped God on Sundays without qualms (Matt. 28:1, 9; Acts 20:7). The New Testament teaches that observance of days is a matter of personal conviction (Rom. 14:5–6). Further, we should not judge each other over Sabbath and feast keeping because these are shadows that pointed to Christ (Col. 2:16–17). Fastidious observance of days for moral, spiritual, and salvific reasons is a sign of retrogression to weak, worthless, enslaving elements (Gal. 4:9–11). Our seal of salvation is not the Sabbath; it is the Holy Spirit (2 Cor. 1:21–22; 5:5; Eph. 1:11–14; 4:30). Our Sabbath in new covenant faith is Jesus Christ, and we enter into the rest of faith when we hear the gospel and believe it. The rest that Jesus gives is permanent (Matt. 11:28–30; Heb. 4:1–11).

THE ADVENTIST HEALTH MESSAGE

Adventists are widely known for their emphasis on health. Their health institutions, hospitals, and programs are generally respected and utilized worldwide. Given their success and respectability, you might assume that Adventists focus on health for humanitarian purposes or out of a desire to see people healthy. But while those aspects are related to Adventist health prowess and expertise, the underlying reason Adventists place so much emphasis on health is because they believe diet affects morality, spirituality, and even salvation.[67]

Adventists believe that adherence to aspects of the old covenant dietary laws are mandatory and salvific for Christians under the new covenant. Adventists reject the plain reading and meaning of every New Testament text that rescinds dietary laws for Christians and reinterpret them so their own distinct beliefs and teachings are upheld. They utilize Isaiah 66:15–17 and 1 Corinthians 3:16–17 as prooftexts to teach that God will destroy Christians at the second advent of Christ for eating pork, shellfish, and consuming other things that their doctrines disavow.

Ellen White calls SDA teachings on diet "the gospel of health."[68] She says that God gave her these teachings about diet for their salvation and the salvation of the world.[69] As a result, Adventists believe that their teachings about diet and health are the "right arm" of the gospel—that is, an integral part of it.[70] Rejecting these teachings on diet is tantamount to rejecting God himself: "God gave the light on health reform, and those who rejected it rejected God."[71]

Adventists are generally vegans or vegetarians because Ellen White demands *total abstinence* from eating meat in preparation for the second advent of Jesus in order to inhabit heaven.[72] Adventists who refuse to become vegetarians or vegans will apostatize from the Adventist Church and will not be saved.[73] Adventist pastors who eat meat set "an evil example."[74] Additionally, Ellen White has written voluminously against the use of tea, coffee, caffeine, cheese and dairy products, condiments, alcoholic beverages, and wine.[75] She teaches that consuming these products is sin.[76] The SDA Church upholds and abides by her teachings and calls them "the Health Message."[77]

The Christian View

The Adventist health message is in error because Christians are not under the old covenant dietary laws. What we eat or drink does not defile our morals, spirituality, or affect our salvation (Mark 7:14–23). Foods will not bring us close to God (1 Cor. 8:8). Mandating vegetarianism for spiritual purposes is a sign of weak faith (Rom. 14:1–3). No food is existentially unclean (Acts 10:9–16; Rom. 14:14, 20; 1 Cor. 10:25–27). Believing that persons are morally or spiritually unclean because of their diet, and therefore are unfit for salvation, is contrary to God's will (Acts 10:28). Whatever we choose to ingest is subjective, cultural, and a personal preference (Rom. 14:14). We should not pass judgment on the diets of others (Col. 2:16–23). Being preoccupied with foods is attempting to establish one's faith on that which does not profit, moving us away from God's grace that does benefit us (Heb. 13:9). Being divisive over foods is hypocritical and walking contrary to the gospel (Gal. 2:11–14).

SINLESS PERFECTIONISM

A major aspect of Adventist Christology is Jesus's human nature. Ellen White contradictorily taught that Jesus had both an unfallen sinless nature[78] and a fallen sinful nature.[79] Despite this, Adventists generally lean toward the view that Jesus had a fallen, sinful human nature because Jesus proves that by obeying the law and cooperating with God, we (like Jesus) can achieve sinless perfection.

In Adventist theology, salvation is a combination of faith plus keeping the law,[80] specifically the Ten Commandments.[81] From this view, Ellen White developed a system of sinless perfectionism whereby Jesus came into the world to empower us to live sinless lives, just as he did.[82] No one can ever be sealed for salvation if they have a single imperfection.[83] One must achieve sinlessness if one is to inherit God's kingdom.[84] Jesus has not returned yet because Adventists are not sinlessly perfect yet. Adventists must have the character of Jesus "perfectly reproduced" in them before he can come to claim them as his own.[85]

Not only are Adventists to achieve sinless perfection before Jesus can return, but they also need it in order to be able to stand before God "without a mediator" when Jesus ceases his intercession in heaven.[86] Many Adventists shudder at the thought of standing before God without Christ interceding for them. This creates much anxiety and salvific hopelessness for untold numbers of SDAs because no SDA has ever achieved sinless perfection—not even Ellen White,[87] their highest authority and the most revered SDA. Some fanatical SDAs, such as Thusia SDAs, even believe they are "sinfree" and sinless.

The Christian View

The Adventist doctrine of sinless perfection is biblically untenable, espousing salvation by works and putting undue stress and uncertainty on its adherents. Achieving flesh perfection is not possible in this life. Our flesh will continue to be what it is and desire things that are opposed to the Spirit of God (Gal. 5:16–26). As a body of believers, we will always have weaker members among us who will fall into sin (Rom. 15:1; Gal. 6:1–2). We all stumble in many ways (James 3:1–2). If anyone claims to be sinlessly perfect in this life, they are only deceiving themselves (1 John 1:8). As we mature in Christ, our behavior and life pattern become more like him (2 Pet. 3:18); we gain victory over weaknesses and temptations (1 Cor. 10:13); and we are better equipped to deny the flesh. Nevertheless, we can never perfect the flesh (Rom. 7:18). It is not expected that we become sinlessly perfect in order to inherit the kingdom of God. Our salvation is secured in Jesus. We are complete and positionally perfect in him (Col. 2:9–10; Heb. 10:14). But we will never be perfectly behaved in this life. We have been delivered from the state and dominion of sin (Rom. 6:12–14; Col. 1:13–14), yet we still occasionally commit acts of sin, which God forgives us for (Col. 2:13; 1 John 1:9).

THE NATURE OF HUMANKIND

Adventists have a strictly materialistic view of the nature of humans. They believe that humankind is purely matter. In their theology, the "breath of life" that God breathed into Adam was only oxygen that merged with the clay, then he became a "living soul" (Gen. 2:7 KJV). Men and women are only physical, material bodies. Nothing else. Fundamental Belief 7 states that man "is an indivisible unity of body, mind, and spirit."[88] They compare the breath of life in man to "streams of electricity" that flow through electrical appliances to make them work.[89] For them, man does not have an immaterial, conscious spirit or soul that survives the death of the body.[90] Because of this, they believe in soul sleep at death and annihilation.[91] For Adventists, soul sleep is a state in which the person is unconscious and does not have a continued conscious existence until the second advent and resurrection. Annihilation is the final punishment that will be executed on the unsaved. After the final judgment, the unsaved will be incinerated until they are totally annihilated and subsequently become nonexistent.

The Christian View

The vast majority of Christians believe in either a bipartite (body and spirit/soul) or a tripartite (body, soul, and spirit; 1 Thess. 5:23; Heb. 4:12) nature of humankind. Scripture consistently makes a distinction between the soul (or spirit) and man's physical body. Jesus stated that persons may be able to kill the body of believers, but they cannot kill the soul (Matt. 10:28). Our souls are conscious and are the part of us that is regenerated at the moment of conversion (Rom. 1:9; 8:16; 1 Cor. 7:34; Eph. 2:1–3; Titus 3:3–7). The soul consciously exists after we die. At death, the souls of believers go to be with Christ in heaven (Luke 23:43; 2 Cor. 5:1–9; Phil. 1:20–25; Heb. 12:23), while the physical body awaits the resurrection (1 Cor. 15:51–55; 1 Thess. 4:13–18). Whereas the souls of believers go to be with Christ at death, the souls of unbelievers go to Hades (Luke 16:22–31) and are kept under punishment until the judgment (2 Pet. 2:9). At the second advent of Christ, their bodies will be resurrected, they will be judged, and then they will suffer eternal conscious punishment (Matt. 25:41, 46; Rev. 14:9–11; 20:10).

SECTARIANISM AND SUPERIORITY COMPLEX

The SDA Church sees itself as being spiritually and theologically superior to Protestant churches. Protestant churches are often taken aback when they become aware of how Adventists classify them in their preaching and teaching. They use 2 Corinthians 6:14–18 as a prooftext to support their view that orthodox Christians are "unbelievers" with whom they should not be "unequally yoked" (KJV).

Ellen White stated that the denominational name not only carried the features of their faith, but that it also had convicting and converting abilities.[92] She said that the name would be a rebuke to Protestants and set Adventists apart as the "true worshipers of God."[93] They believe the name "Seventh-day Adventist" creates a sharp separation between themselves and Protestant churches. From its inception, Adventism has always been very anti-Roman Catholic and anti-Protestant Christianity.

Because of their sectarian bias, Adventists attack and demonize Roman Catholicism and Protestant Christianity.[94] Ellen White taught that all Protestant churches are false, fallen, demon-possessed, in error, and that their prayers, exhortations, and professions are "an abomination" to God.[95] Adventists call the Roman Catholic Church "Babylon," "the whore of Babylon," and call Protestant churches "apostate Protestantism," daughters of the whore of Babylon, and various other malicious names. Adventist doctrine, preaching, and evangelism are very hostile toward the wider body of Christ and are clearly not ecumenical. In recent years, a few Adventist leaders have tried to engage in ecumenical dialogue and programs,[96] but these efforts are generally frowned upon by the broader Adventist community and even decried as "apostasy" among some.

The Christian View

The Adventist Church's belief that the wider body of Christ is Babylon, fallen, and in apostasy is at odds with most Protestant churches, as well as the Roman Catholic Church. Believing that it alone is the "true church" is a sign of sectarianism and it encourages a superiority complex among many SDA members that is cultish in nature. The SDA Church is not God's remnant church, nor is it superior to the larger body of Christ. The body of Christ is one: the faith is one (Eph. 4:1–6). While various denominations in the body of Christ may have different doctrinal emphases, as long as they hold to the essential, orthodox truths of the Christian faith (generally defined as the Apostles' Creed and the doctrines of the major ecumenical church councils), we are all brothers and sisters in Christ and members of one church of God scattered over the world and through time. Adventism claims to be the superior true church, but it distorts several core essentials of the Christian faith. Adventism does not subscribe to *sola scriptura*, and it holds unorthodox views about the Godhead, the law, the Sabbath, the Holy Spirit, faith and works, the nature of humankind, the atonement and scapegoat, the Christian church, worshiping God on Sunday, dietary rules, and hordes of other biblical teachings. In addition, it continues to exhibit several cultish tendencies, including doublespeak, cognitive dissonance, and subterfuge.[97]

RACE ISSUES IN ADVENTISM

It sometimes surprises people to learn that the vast majority of SDA membership is in predominantly Black nations and African countries. And yet racial issues are ongoing problems in the SDA Church and some of its institutions. Ellen White was a conundrum regarding racial issues. She made many positive statements about Blacks, vied for their human and salvific equality,[98] campaigned for their betterment,[99] called for reparations,[100] and even assisted in founding what is now Oakwood University, a historically Black university. Yet despite this, she made several racist statements about Blacks that have led to many of the racial issues we see in Adventism today.

PROBLEMATIC TEACHINGS ON RACE

Ellen White taught that nonwhite races were produced as a result of humans interbreeding with animals (amalgamation).[101] She taught that Blacks were inferior to whites morally,[102] intellectually, spiritually, and socially.[103] She upheld and promoted segregation.[104] She absolutely forbade Black and white interracial marriages.[105] She states, "No one is capable of clearly defining the proper position of the colored people," and argues that social justice issues pertaining to them should not be agitated, studied, nor discussed.[106] She taught that in heaven, segregation will end because Black people will become white like Jesus.[107]

Today, Adventist pastors and apologists do their best to hide the racist teachings of Ellen White from regular members, or they attempt to explain them in a way that is palatable today. Yet because of the teachings of Ellen White, there still exist segregated Black and white SDA churches[108] and conferences in North America today.[109]

The Christian View

Racial tensions and inequalities are always sensitive matters. It is heart-breaking when people mistreat others solely on the basis of race. It is even more disappointing when religious organizations that subscribe to the Judeo-Christian worldview get tangled up in racial tensions, discrimination, and injustice because of false views about race. Adventism finds itself in this mix because of the false teachings of Ellen White. Contrary to what she taught, people of color are not the result of "amalgamation" between humans and animals. People of color, just like everyone else, are made in the image of God (Gen. 1:26–28). All races are one human family, descended from the same ancestor (Acts 17:26). Therefore, one race or culture is not superior to any other. Black music, exuberant worship styles, culture, and idiosyncrasies are not inferior to European ones. And neither do they need to be suppressed or erased while European ones are elevated to replace them. One skin color is not superior to another. We are all God's children by creation. And in God's kingdom, there will be people from every race, tribe, nation, and people group. Jesus will not whiten everyone's skin color in heaven (Rev. 7:9). All races are image bearers, and we will continue to bear God's image throughout eternity.

NEGATIVE EFFECTS OF ADVENTISM ON BLACK CULTURE AND COMMUNITIES

Because of the influence of Adventism among Black communities in North America and around the world, the doctrines and culture of the SDA Church have had many negative effects on Black culture.

Cultural Superiority and Criticism

First, within SDA culture there is a prevailing sense of the superiority of European culture to that of Blacks. Black cultural attire, colloquialisms, customs, hairdos, traditions, etc., are often painted in negative ways in Adventist teaching, preaching, and church gatherings. They are often spoken of as things that ought to be suppressed or divested from, with European ones adopted in · their place.

Because Ellen White prognosticates that the second advent of Christ will be counterfeited by Satan with false revivals and lively music, dance, drums, etc.,[110] in Adventism Black music and exuberant worship styles are demonized.[111] The *SDA Church Manual* rules, "Any melody partaking of the nature of jazz, rock, or related hybrid forms, or any language expressing foolish or trivial sentiments, will be shunned. Let us use only good music in the home, in the social gathering, in the school, and in the church."[112]

Adventist churches generally do not have drums in them. Adventists constantly decry using drums in worship. They occasionally do seminars and presentations on Black music styles (reggae, rap, hip-hop, jazz, R & B, soul, Black gospel music, etc.,) and argue that they were birthed from demonic influences to distract and deceive the world.[113] In contrast to this, they present European music and rhythm as being the godly, good, and acceptable type of music that SDAs should listen to or produce (mainly classical, baroque, and opera).[114]

Stifling Progress

While the SDA Church has elevated many persons in the Black community (myself included) because of its focus on education and health, it has stifled the progress of the Black community in many other ways. There are many Black SDAs in the US, the Caribbean, Africa, and other countries who have forfeited or lost opportunities to better themselves as a result of SDA doctrines. They may have been encouraged to quit jobs or careers that require working on Saturday. They will not engage in or build businesses that are involved with the use of alcoholic beverages, pork, shellfish, or other meats and substances that they deem sinful. Some who become vegans will not involve themselves with businesses related to even clean meats. This has crippled a great deal of progress and prevented wealth creation for many SDAs in the Caribbean, especially in Jamaica, and in contexts in which raising chickens, pigs, and other animals is lucrative.

Many SDAs cannot pursue their dreams and aspirations if they have to work or be engaged in work-related tasks on Saturday. There are some SDA members whom I personally know whose raw talents in sports and athletics have gone to waste because their parents would not allow them to practice or compete on Friday nights or Saturday. Some have quit because Ellen White condemns competitive sports, athletics, ball playing, card playing, checkers, chess, horse racing, and similar activities altogether.[115] There are those who convert to SDA who were talented in sports and athletics but had to eventually give those up because of their adherence to SDA doctrines.

On a personal note, I regrettably have lost my billiards skills because I converted to SDA. I had no choice but to give it up because I was binge reading

Ellen White and discovered that she condemned those things, and because most of the games and competitions were held on Saturday. Coming from a life of teenage truancy, dissolution, and dysfunction, Adventism seemed to have been the answer I was looking for. It brought tremendous change to my life and nothing was too dear to me that I wasn't willing to give it up for the sake of Adventism.

Adventism also negatively affects the Black community by encouraging paranoia and fearmongering through its eschatology. Such fear and paranoia affects careers, businesses, finances, education, and social development. Adventists constantly speculate that Sunday laws will pass every other month, every year, and have been doing this from the 1840s to the present. They expect the United States to enact Sunday laws, and then other countries will follow suit. They constantly watch for news of the pope, the US president, and other global events so they can interpret these as "signs" that the Sunday laws are about to pass. In recent decades, some Adventists have even begun predicting specific dates for the Sunday laws to pass and for Jesus to return. Alarmed by such "signs," some have closed their businesses, sold their property, and quit jobs, and others have refused to go to college, believing that it would be a waste of time to engage with such things. Instead, they form SDA offshoot groups or join existing ones they feel are "finishing the work." I have spoken to many former Adventists from all over the world who pursued this course thirty or forty years ago, but now live with regret.

Sadly, there are Adventists who are making the same mistake today. There is a new SDA offshoot in Jamaica called "Following the Blueprint Ministry" that has separated from the wider society and has established their own commune in St. Mary.[116] An Adventist young woman broke from her family and withdrew from law school[117] to join them to help "finish the work." That group has been spending thousands of dollars putting up billboards in key sections of Jamaica, warning the public about Sunday laws and urging everyone to keep the Sabbath.[118] These stories were local headline news there.

ENGAGING SEVENTH-DAY ADVENTISTS

Seventh-day Adventism has greatly impacted the ministry efforts of Christians in Black communities. Because of the Adventist view that the wider Christian church is Babylon and in apostasy, the SDA Church will not support the work of non-SDA missionaries and churches in their area.

Adventism has convinced its adherents that it is the sole, authentic representation of Christian orthodoxy and expression. Because of this, Adventists are very suspicious about non-SDA Christians. Even those who eventually leave Adventism after discovering that it is a false system have great difficulties becoming Christians in orthodox churches. The majority of former Adventists often drift into agnosticism, atheism, or a more austere legalistic system.

Adventism has also misled people to conflate its errant doctrines and beliefs with orthodox Christianity. This makes it difficult to preach the gospel to Adventists or to discuss Christian doctrines with them. SDAs may have a false sense of security and sufficiency in their doctrines or church attendance. Generally speaking, they will not support any social issue or Christian endeavor if it does not directly relate to the SDA and its doctrines.

Adventism makes ministry difficult in Black communities by its consistent demonization, antagonization, and denunciation of Christians and non-SDA denominations. Even persons who are not Adventists often become unsupportive, unreceptive, and suspicious of ministers and churches that Adventism denounces. Those who are exposed to SDA rhetoric may not become SDA, but they may also reject Christianity because of their exposure to misinformation. They tend to put up strong resistance against the gospel.

Despite the difficulties that Christian churches and ministers often face in communities where SDAs are present or prevalent, there are ways to overcome these challenges. Christians can break through the barriers Adventists erect by knowing how to engage them. I have done this for many years, and I believe the following tips can help Christians and ministers meaningfully engage SDA members.

ENGAGE ADVENTISTS PRAYERFULLY

First, engage Adventists prayerfully. Adventists are extremely stubborn in holding to their beliefs and will regurgitate the punch lines that are constantly hammered into them. If you let them control the conversation, it will be frustrating. Therefore, engage them very prayerfully. James 5 reminds us that the fervent prayers of the righteous avail much (James 5:16). Pray that God would unblind them from the law, which veils them from seeing Christ and the gospel in new covenant faith (2 Cor. 3:12–16).

UPHOLD SCRIPTURE AS THE ONLY RULE OF FAITH

Adventists claim to believe in "the Bible and the Bible alone" and say they can defend their doctrines with Scripture alone, but that is not true. In practice, Adventists believe in the Bible *as interpreted by* Ellen White. Because of this, there are layers of bad assumptions, eisegesis, and theology that determine how they read and understand the Bible. To counter this, you must uplift Scripture as the *only* rule of faith, doctrine, and practice for Christians. Any assumption they express or interpretation they give, ask them to prove it from contextual exposition of Scripture.

LIMIT DISCUSSIONS TO ONE SCRIPTURAL CONTEXT

If you try to have a prooftext battle with an SDA, you will be defeated. Adventists have mastered the art of ripping Scripture out of context in efforts to prove their doctrines. In biblical discussions with them, keep them in the context of texts. Do not take the bait as they hop from one text to another to weave their doctrines together. Focus your discussion on one text and its various contexts (author, genre, audience, covenant, surrounding passages, linguistics, history, culture, purpose, etc.) at a time. By focusing closely on the context of the text, Adventists generally begin to recognize some of the gaps between orthodox Christian beliefs and Adventist theology. This is often the catalyst to many eventually leaving the Adventist Church and embracing the gospel.

DEMONSTRATE THAT ELLEN WHITE IS A FALSE PROPHET

Adventists revere Ellen White. She directs, influences, and controls every aspect of an Adventist's life through her writings. She is an idol for many Adventists. Only a few dare to disagree with, challenge, or demote her from her supreme status within the movement. One of the primary ways to help Adventists break from the Ellen White spell is by showing them how her teachings deviate from orthodox Christian teaching. Some will not be moved, but others will do more research about her and eventually see the truth that she often contradicted Scripture and herself. They also learn that she was a harsh, legalistic person who said many absurd things.

DISTINGUISH OLD COVENANT FROM NEW COVENANT

Ellen White stated that the old covenant is still in force today.[119] Today, Adventist leaders and apologists continue to wildly contort Scripture to make her right. In general, they do not understand the covenants, so when engaging them on matters about the law, help them understand the biblical covenants and show them that believers are no longer under the old covenant, including the Ten Commandments (Ex. 34:28; Deut. 4:13; 5:22; 9:9–11; Heb. 8:13–9:5). Show them that Christians are under the new covenant.

ARM YOURSELF WITH HISTORICAL FACTS

Adventists do a great deal of historical revision. It will behoove you to correct their historical revisionism with historical facts. Do your own research and be ready with facts about the Sabbath, the papacy and Sunday worship, Constantine the Great and the Sunday Law in 321 AD, and other historical issues. You have to arm yourself with the facts to correct the errors they constantly push as a means of justifying their conspiracies and paranoid eschatology.

SHOW THAT CHRISTIANS ARE NOT APOSTATES

Christians need to impress upon the SDA or SDA-influenced person that orthodox Christians are not apostates who are deliberately deceptive and want to harm them because of their beliefs and practices regarding the Sabbath. Explain to them that the Christian church has been in existence from the days of the apostles of Jesus Christ and has continued with many of the beliefs and practices that we hold today. Show them that the peculiar emphases of various denominations are not necessarily evil and certainly do not make these Protestant churches apostate. At the same time, show them that there are essential doctrines that make one an orthodox Christian and there are nonessentials that one can hold to that will not jeopardize one's Christian faith. Doing this may help the Adventist or SDA sympathizer to widen their scope of understanding about the Christian faith and denominations, and they may begin to see Christians and ministers through a different lens.

CONCLUSION: NEXT STEPS

What do I suggest as a next step if you want to learn more? Christians should inform themselves about Adventism and can begin by consulting some of the sources I referenced or quoted in this chapter. All of the SDA sources I utilized are legitimate SDA source materials. Read them for yourself and you will see what they really believe and teach. There are also some helpful works by former SDAs that Christians can read for additional insight. I have also written several recent books that might be of help, including: *Hiding in Plain Sight: The False Doctrines of Seventh-Day Adventism, Volumes I, II, and III*. Other resources to consult are *Cultic Doctrines of Seventh-Day Adventism* by Dale Ratzlaff, *Seventh-Day Adventism Renounced* by D. M. Canright, *Out of Adventism: A Theologian's Journey* by Dr. Jerry Gladson, *Exposing Seventh-Day Adventism* by Dr. Russell Earl Kelly, and *Truth Led Me Out* by Dale Ratzlaff. There are also several great YouTube channels that can provide helpful information about Adventism including *Back to Bible Basics* with CMB the Ambassador; *KerryTerry*; *Academy Apologia*; *Former Adventist Fellowship*; *Christian Scholars Forum; Answering Adventism*; and *Testing the Prophet*.

As I hope you can see, the Seventh-day Adventist Church has had a deleterious effect on Black countries, culture, and communities because of the errant doctrines taught by the SDA Church. Adventist teachings and practices have frustrated the gospel ministry efforts of Christians, stifled the progress of many Blacks around the world, and are frequently antagonistic toward Christians. Yet, with some awareness of their history and their doctrine and a strategy for engagement, it is possible to overcome these barriers and reach those involved in this movement. As we engage with Adventists, it is imperative that we seek to be faithful witnesses and humble Christian apologists (1 Pet. 3:15), trusting the Holy Spirit to water the seeds that are planted. We cannot convert SDAs to Christ—only the Holy Spirit can do that. However, as we witness to what we believe we must know the gospel, know the Word, know what they believe and teach, and learn how to properly respond to them by dispelling misinformation. Trust the Holy Spirit to use your witness to penetrate hearts so they melt under the power of the gospel and eventually submit to Christ and embrace orthodox, biblical Christianity.

DEVELOPING BIBLICAL CONVICTIONS IN DISCIPLES

JEROME GAY

John 16:8 says the Spirit will "convict" (CSB) the world of sin, but what does it actually mean to have convictions, and why are they so important? To convict means "to convince someone of the truth; to reprove; to accuse, refute, or cross-examine a witness." It comes from the Greek word *elencho*. The Holy Spirit acts as an attorney in a courtroom who lovingly exposes our sin and awakens us to our need for a Savior (Eph. 5:14).[1]

H. E. Jacobs says this about conviction:

> It is a decision presumed to be based upon a careful and discriminating consideration of all the proofs offered, and has a legal character, the verdict being rendered either in God's judgment (Romans 3:19), or before men (John 8:46) by an appeal to their consciences in which God's law is written (Romans 2:15). Since such conviction is addressed to the heart of the guilty, as well as concerning him externally, the word "reprove" is sometimes substituted. To "convict . . . in respect of righteousness, and of judgment" (John 16:8),

refers to the conviction of the inadequacy and perversity of the
ordinary, natural standards of righteousness and judgment, and the
approval of those found in Christ, by the agency of the Holy Spirit,
as the great interpreter and applier of the work of Christ.[2]

In other words, convictions aren't merely feelings of guilt about something
you've done wrong or even a deep sense of shame. To be convicted is to feel the
unpleasantness of sin because the Holy Spirit impresses upon you the reality
of God's displeasure with your actions, thoughts, deeds, or inactions. It also
means that there's a transformation of your attitude toward sin.

Conviction is reflected in these words of Joseph, who flees the temptation
of Potiphar's wife: "No one in this house is greater than I am. He has withheld
nothing from me except you, because you are his wife. So how could I do this
immense evil, and how could I sin against God?" (Gen. 39:9 CSB). Conviction
is what Paul calls godly sorrow: "For godly grief produces a repentance that
leads to salvation without regret, but worldly grief produces death" (2 Cor.
7:10 CSB).

WHEN ARE WE CONVICTED?

While convictions involve doctrinal beliefs, they're not strictly cognitive or
merely a matter of assessing right and wrong. It's not enough to say: "The
wages of sin is death" (Rom. 6:23). Many people are aware of this truth, but
without the Spirit to convict us, we won't live like we actually *believe* that sin
warrants or leads to spiritual death.

Conviction happens when we stop delighting in what God hates. Since
the Holy Spirit transforms our desires, conviction occurs when what we want
doesn't match or align with what God wants for us. When we're mindful
of how much our sin dishonors God, we change. A great example of this
is David. He is convicted by the Holy Spirit after being confronted by the
prophet Nathan (2 Sam. 12:1–31). Later he writes in Psalms, "Against you—
you alone—I have sinned and done this evil in your sight. So you are right
when you pass sentence; you are blameless when you judge" (Ps. 51:4 CSB).

THE ROLE OF CONVICTION

David shows us that conviction has two forms: internal and external. Internal conviction happens when the Holy Spirit impresses upon us that what we're about to do or how we're thinking doesn't line up with God's Word. This precedes a decision to sin and is one of the ways the Spirit provides a way of escape from sin (1 Cor. 10:13). External conviction is when God sends someone or uses circumstances to deter or convict you of a decision that dishonors God.

Conviction makes us aware of God's wrath as well. When we become deeply aware of God's wrath, it exposes us to the dire nature of our souls without Christ (Rom. 1:18). When the Philippian jailer falls at the apostles' feet and cries, "Sirs, what must I do to be saved?" (Acts 16:30 CSB), he is under conviction. He is certain that, without a Savior, he will die.

Having conviction protects us from deconstructing our faith to the point of apostasy. Deconstruction is the process of systematically dissecting, doubting, questioning, and possibly rejecting the beliefs you held previously. Sometimes a Christian will deconstruct all the way to atheism. Satan's plan for your deconstruction is demolition. But demolition of what?

- **Devotion**—treating God's standard as antiquated and/or unrealistic
- **Discipleship**—denying relationships that challenge you in favor of echo chambers that affirm all of your ideas
- **Doctrine**—treating God's Word as subjective and in need of additions or ideological edits

We should thank God for the convictions we experience, both internal and external. Without God convicting us of sin, there could be no salvation. No one is saved apart from the Spirit's convicting and renewing work. Scripture is clear that all people are rebellious by nature and that we live in hostility to God. Ephesians 2 lets us know how bad our situation is without conviction. We are:

1. Dead (verse 1)
2. Devilish (verse 2)
3. Disobedient (verse 2)
4. Destructive (verse 3)
5. Doomed (verse 3)

Ephesians 2 goes on to offer these powerful words: "But because of his great love for us, God, who is rich in mercy, made us alive with Christ even when we were dead in transgressions—it is by grace you have been saved" (Eph. 2:4–5). God mercifully chooses and draws us to himself: "No one can come to me unless the Father who sent me draws him" (John 6:44). Part of that "draw" to Jesus is the conviction of sin.

As the Holy Spirit convicts people of their sin, he represents and carries out the righteous judgment of God (Heb. 4:12). There is no appeal of this verdict. The Holy Spirit not only convicts people of sin, but he also brings them to repentance (Acts 17:30). The Holy Spirit brings to light our relationship to God. The convicting power of the Holy Spirit opens our eyes to our sin and opens our hearts to receive his grace (Eph. 2:8).[3]

DEVELOPING BIBLICAL CONVICTIONS

It is imperative that Christians are active in developing convictions through what the Bible calls a "proving" process—rationally examining the evidence (Rom. 12:2; Eph. 5:10; Phil. 1:10; 1 Thess. 5:21).[4] Here are some steps we as believers can follow to uphold biblical convictions:

- Search the Scriptures for direct teaching on the subject and allow the Bible to form your worldview (Matt. 4:4).
- Seek godly counsel that's rooted in Scripture over "good advice" (Prov. 11:14).
- Stay rooted and grounded in a biblically orthodox, gospel-centered local church (Mark 3:34–35; 1 Tim. 3:15).
- Have a disposition that's willing to submit to God's will even if it hurts (Luke 22:42).
- Be led by the Spirit and not your emotions (Eph. 4:26).
- "Let the peace of Christ rule in your hearts" (Col. 3:15)
- Choose faithfulness to God over popularity (Gal. 1:10).
- Remember to "put on" Christ daily by seeking to honor him with your decisions (Eph. 4:24).
- Share the gospel (Mark 16:15–16).
- Teach others to have biblical convictions (2 Tim. 2:2).

As we develop our own convictions, we can also equip others to have convictions. When we do so, we're helping others have the confidence to stand on God's Word without being ashamed or embarrassed of not having enough knowledge to address difficult subjects (2 Tim. 2:15). Here are a few strategies to keep in mind as we help others develop their convictions:

1. **Teach the importance of a biblically based soteriology.** Soteriology refers to our doctrines and beliefs about salvation—how God saves us and what he saves us from. Too often people equate salvation with things like church attendance or proximity to spiritual teaching or objects. But salvation is a gift of God, attained by grace and through faith in Christ and that alone (Eph. 2:8–9). If people are incorrect or incomplete in their understanding of salvation, their convictions will be misguided, and people will be led toward a works-based view of salvation.

2. **Don't separate Christianity from discipleship.** The disciples were called "Christian" at Antioch (Acts 11:26). While most people point out that this term was used pejoratively, it's important to note that the Bible doesn't separate "disciple" from "Christian." They're synonymous. We must be intentional about not allowing people to separate the two because this causes confusion about what it means to follow Christ and what spiritual maturity looks like. When we separate them, people will think that discipleship is an optional level of maturity that they may not be "ready for." It can be helpful to utilize quality discipleship resources and tools, like *Be 1 Make 1*,[5] which provides a how-to guide for discipleship and teaches eight commands of Christ that emphasize the aforementioned and more.

3. **Consistently testify to the beauty and necessity of the church.** The COVID global pandemic revealed a theological and relational hole in the way people see the church and its place in their lives. Not only did people see church as optional, but they were fine substituting physical community with a screen. Ephesians 5 makes it clear that the church is Jesus's bride and cannot be replaced by technology. We need to uphold the beauty of the bride of Christ as a physical, local community of saints and the necessity of belonging to that community for spiritual growth and maturity in the faith.

It's vital that as we help people develop conviction, we conduct ourselves with humility and not with pride (1 Pet. 3:15). God will use you to enlighten others of theological dangers they have not seen when you teach conviction in love. We must teach people how to think critically for themselves in order to determine what they believe and why they believe it. It's important we realize that motivation leads to emulation. As we share with others the blessing that comes from believing and obeying the truth, they will want to emulate our character and conduct. Let us seek to model what we teach in biblical community.[6] *"If only they had such a heart to fear me and keep all my commands always, so that they and their children would prosper forever"* (Deut. 5:29 CSB).

TEN

JEHOVAH'S WITNESSES

DAMON RICHARDSON

Since their organizational inception in the late nineteenth century as Bible Students and later the Watchtower Bible and Tract Society, those who are called "Jehovah's Witnesses" have held to beliefs that deviate from historical Christian orthodoxy. In this chapter we will examine the historical origin, development, and distinctive doctrines of the Jehovah's Witnesses in an effort to understand who they are, what they believe, and how to properly respond to their teaching. We will also consider why their teachings might find resonance with Black image bearers who may be particularly susceptible and receptive to the anti-Christian messages of sub-Christian cults like the Jehovah's Witnesses. This can be particularly true within an urban context where there is already suspicion of Christianity.

The Watchtower (used interchangeably with the Jehovah's Witnesses or JWs) draws most of its membership from among the uneducated and lower socioeconomic classes rather than the affluent. This has led to growth among groups on the margins of society. Not surprisingly, there are also a number of famous Black athletes and entertainers who have been raised in Jehovah's Witness families. Among them are the Jackson family, Prince, rapper Ja Rule, Venus and Serena Williams, baseball legend Lou Whitaker, the Wayans family (Damon, Keenen, Shawn, Marlon, etc.), rapper the Notorious B. I. G., singer

Jill Scott, actress Michelle Rodriguez, model Naomi Campbell, comedian Sherri Shepherd, singer Marques Houston, actor and rapper Donald Glover a.k.a. Childish Gambino, and jazz great George Benson.

As of 2022, the Jehovah's Witnesses boasted an active membership of 8.6 million adherents worldwide with a global presence in 239 countries. In 2021, according to their annual grand totals, they reported over 1.4 billion hours of field witnessing, averaged over 5.9 million hours teaching home Bible studies, and spent over 229 million dollars in financial support of missionaries, circuit overseers, and pioneers. They are by far one of the most aggressive and fastest spreading cults here in the US and are unrivaled in their efforts to propagate their message, publishing, and distributing more literature in one year than all biblically orthodox Protestant Christian denominations combined.

JEHOVAH'S WITNESSES' ORIGINS AND HISTORY

The Jehovah's Witnesses arose at the same time as other restorationist cults such as the Mormons, Seventh-day Adventists, Churches of Christ, and the Christadelphians. Like the Seventh-day Adventists, they trace their origins to the nineteenth-century Adventist Millerite movement (see chapter 9 for more background). Following the "Great Disappointment"—a phrase describing the profound disheartening and despondency felt by many Millerites after the identified dates of Jesus's return passed without Jesus returning—Miller's followers divided into several Adventist factions over differences in their views about what actually happened, what didn't happen, and why. Many who had their hopes dashed abandoned the faith altogether, while others, both embarrassed and disillusioned, returned to the mainstream Christian churches that they had separated themselves from. Still others formed new Adventist splinter groups, like the Seventh-day Adventists.[1]

Some hardline Adventist factions were determined to develop new calculations and set new dates for Christ's return. Among one such group was a Millerite preacher named Nelson Barbour, who was convinced that Christ would return in 1873. He wrote a small booklet in 1871 titled *Evidences for the Coming of the Lord in 1873* or *The Midnight Cry* and began a magazine in 1873 called *The Midnight Cry* to propagate his views. When 1873 had come and gone, Barbour, like Miller, changed his date to 1874. That date also came and went, further disappointing and discouraging the followers of Miller who still held onto end-time date-setting expectations.

Barbour was determined to understand why his prediction had failed, so he turned to an associate, B. W. Keith. Based on his English-Interlinear Bible *Emphatic Diaglott*'s translation of the Greek word *parousia* as "presence" rather than "appearance" or "arrival," Keith formulated a new view of Jesus's invisible return. He convinced Barbour that Christ was coming in two stages: an initial stage that was his invisible presence (which had occurred as expected in 1874) and a second stage that would imminently be made visible in order to rapture believers and judge the world. Barbour then changed the name of his magazine from *The Midnight Cry* to *Herald of the Morning*.

CHARLES TAZE RUSSELL

In 1868, one of Barbour's associates, Jonas Wendell, held a religious meeting where he taught that Christ would return in 1873 and rapture the faithful and that God would destroy the world with fire shortly after. This message caught the attention of a sixteen-year-old man named Charles Taze Russell. Raised as a devout Presbyterian, Russell had for several years been seeking answers to questions he had about the authority of the Bible and Christian doctrines such as eternal hell. He'd left the (evangelical) Presbyterian church as a teen and joined the (liberal) Congregational church, which he later left as well, dissatisfied with the teaching of Christianity altogether. At this meeting held by Barbour's associate, however, Russell felt his faith restored by what he heard.

Inspired by Wendell's prophetic chronology, Russell formed a Bible study group composed mostly of Second Adventists around 1870. He later met a Wendell associate named George Storrs, a former Millerite leader who had a profound theological influence upon Russell. He taught Russell many of the doctrines that Jehovah's Witnesses believe today, such as a restored paradise on earth, annual sacrament taking, conditionalism, annihilationism, soul sleep, and a second resurrection of the wicked dead who died in ignorance and will be given an opportunity to learn and to obey God's commands.

Sometime around December 1875, Russell came across a copy of a monthly issue of *Herald of the Morning* and invited Barbour to speak at a Bible study in Philadelphia in 1876. Russell was greatly impressed after meeting with Barbour, concluding that they had come to some of the same conclusions regarding Jesus's second coming and that he was also convinced that Jesus had invisibly returned in 1874. Unfortunately for Barbour, many of his original followers were unconvinced of this explanation after the Disappointment of 1874 and pulled back support of the magazine, forcing Barbour to suspend publishing. When Russell heard of it, he offered a largesse of several thousand dollars, agreed to back the periodical financially, and became the publication's assistant editor. During this time, Russell published his first pamphlet, *Object and Manner of Our Lord's Return*, and copublished Barbour's book *Three Worlds, and the Harvest of this World* in 1877, in which they detailed their mutual eschatological viewpoints.

Using elaborate scientific calculations, replete with charts, graphs, and Scriptures, Barbour outlines the following:

- The end times began in 1799.
- Christ's invisible presence occurred in 1874.
- Christ's visible return was to occur in 1878, during which time all Christians who already died would be resurrected and all believers would be raptured.
- 1914 would mark the end of a forty-year harvest of evangelism, consummating the Time of the Gentiles and the end of all human governments and ushering in Armageddon and God's kingdom on earth.

When Barbour's 1878 prediction of Jesus's return, the rapture, and the resurrection failed once more, he became disillusioned and had several disagreements with Russell over the failure of his calculations and the date of the rapture. Barbour felt as though his calculations were wrong, while Russell was convinced that Barbour had the dates right and that the dead were *invisibly* resurrected in 1878. The two also disagreed over Russell's view of the ransom atonement, which led to Russell resigning as assistant editor of the *Herald of the Morning* and officially parting ways with Barbour.

WATCHTOWER BIBLE AND TRACT SOCIETY

After the split, Russell took most of Barbour's subscriber base with him and published his own magazine called *Zion's Watchtower*, later changed to *Zion's Watch Tower and Herald of Christ's Presence*. Between the years 1879 and 1880, Russell managed to amass a global following by writing tirelessly, selling and distributing millions of his books and pamphlets worldwide, and printing his sermons in newspapers across the United States. These efforts expanded his preaching opportunities, leading him to form the organization *Zion's Watchtower Tract Society* in 1881 in Pittsburgh, Pennsylvania, and incorporated in 1884 for the purpose of tract distribution. Russell later changed the name in 1898 to *Watchtower Bible and Tract Society*. In 1909, after conferring with the Watchtower legal counselor J. F. Rutherford, Russell moved the society's headquarters from Pittsburgh, Pennsylvania, to Brooklyn, New York, incorporating the organization as a legal entity in the state of New York.

"Pastor" Russell was largely successful in propagating his message— which was still largely based on Barbour's eschatology and chronology—by writing voluminously, publishing and distributing massive quantities of pamphlets and booklets, and acquiring the financial capital to underwrite his own publishing. He employed business savvy to market and sell his books through colporteurs—traveling salespersons who made a living selling Russell's books for profit as independent contractors. He further incorporated the Watchtower Bible and Tract Society as a business corporation and received generous donations from investors and his follower base.

C. T. Russell's teaching continued the Millerite legacy of prophetic chronology, which he first became acquainted with through the teaching of Jonas Wendell, George Storr, and then later Nelson Barbour, whose eschatology and chronology (that 6,000 years from Adam had now come to an end) he continuously utilized to develop his own predictions for the coming of Jesus, the end of the harvest, the rapture, and Armageddon. Russell set dates of his own, first for 1881, then for 1914, 1915, and 1918. As each date came and went, he offered a diversionary explanation that what appeared to be failure was in fact the revelation of an invisible, spiritual event occurring. Russell had learned how to play the Adventist game very well—simply redirecting the disappointment and frustration of his followers by rolling it ahead another year and suggesting that something invisible and spiritual had indeed happened.

Between 1886 and 1904, Russell published his six-volume series *Millennial Dawn*, which was later renamed to *Studies in the Scriptures*, which sold over twenty million copies and was translated into several languages in his lifetime. These books were not merely designed to be an aid to studying the Bible but, by his own declaration, were deemed necessary to understand the Scriptures. Without them, an understanding of God's plan of salvation would be impossible. Russell boasted that it would be better *not* to read the Scriptures and read his books than to read the Scriptures without the aid of his books.

> Furthermore, not only do we find that people cannot see the divine plan in studying the Bible by itself, but we see, also, that if anyone lays the Scripture Studies [Russell's six-volume work] aside, even after he has used them, after he has become familiar with them, after he has read them for ten years—if he then lays them aside and ignores them and goes to the Bible alone, though he has understood his Bible for ten years, our experience shows that within two years he goes into darkness. On the other hand, if he had merely read the Scripture Studies with references, and had not read a page of the Bible, as such, he would be in the light at the end of two years, because he would have the light of Scriptures.[2]

Russell's entire ministry was built on one lie after the other, from false prophecy predictions to Scripture twisting, to selling "Miracle Wheat," to perjuring himself in a court of law about his ability to read the Greek alphabet. It should have been abundantly clear to his followers that failed prophecy built on failed prophecy was a faulty theological foundation. Not only did Russell write voluminously to peddle his doctrines, but he traveled far and frequently. According to Gerstner, "He spoke incessantly—often six and eight hours a day—and traveled as much as Bishop Asbury and the apostle Paul combined, averaging, according to Braden, 30,000 miles per year."[3] Russell died on October 31, 1916, while traveling by train on a cross-country preaching tour, in Pampa, Texas. Gerstner writes, "It was not inappropriate that this zealot, who compassed land and sea to make proselytes, should end his earthly life on an itinerary."[4] When he died, it left the Watchtower Bible and Tract Society (also referred to as the Bible Students) in a leadership crisis.

JOSEPH FRANKLIN RUTHERFORD

Shortly after Russell's death, on January 6, 1917, the society's legal counsel and longtime board member, Joseph Franklin Rutherford, was elected president of the Watchtower Society. Not everyone was welcoming of Rutherford's leadership, and over the next two decades, schisms developed over Russell's theological legacy and multiple groups split off from the organization. In 1931, at a convention in Columbus, Ohio, Rutherford adopted the name Jehovah's Witnesses in order to separate his movement from the other Russellite movements, to distance it from the past under Russell's leadership, and to distinguish it from Christianity.

Although not much is known biographically about Rutherford, his tenure as president of the Watchtower Society represented a transition between those who were Russell loyalists and those whose loyalties were to the organization and its proselytizing mission. The latter won out during Rutherford's presidency. Rutherford continued for a time to practice Russell's biblical chronology, but he made revisions to Russell's teaching: abandoning the year 1874 as the date of the invisible presence of Christ and 1878 as the date that Christ began to reign, identifying 1914 instead as the date for both events, and moving the date of the resurrection of the sleeping believers from 1878 to 1918. These revisions fueled even more schisms among the Russell loyalists.

Rutherford also made a number of doctrinal innovations which have characterized the Jehovah's Witnesses for almost one hundred years now. In a move to alienate the sect even further from worldliness, he condemned the celebration of birthdays in 1926, declared that Christmas was of pagan origin in 1927, and condemned Mother's Day in 1931. Rutherford rejected the symbol of the cross as pagan and taught that Jesus was crucified on a tree or stake made from wood rather than a Roman cross.[5] Rutherford, not to be outdone by his predecessor Russell, wrote as much as and perhaps even more than Russell, published, distributed, and sold millions more, and traveled just as far and as frequently. During his time leading the Jehovah's Witnesses, he added radio preaching to his list of accomplishments.

While Rutherford was greatly respected and even feared, he was rarely loved as Russell had been. Consequently, he was not much missed after his death on January 8, 1942, at the age of 72. When the announcement of Rutherford's death was made at "Bethel," the headquarters office in Brooklyn, NY, one Watchtower staff present reported, "The announcement was brief. There were no speeches. No one took the day off to mourn. Rather, we went back to the factory and worked harder than ever."[6]

A MILLENARIAN SECT

The Jehovah's Witnesses are classified as a millenarian sect because their fundamental beliefs and societal engagements are structured around the idea that the end of the world is near and that the return of Jesus is imminent and will be preceded by cataclysmic disaster and judgment. This will usher in a new age of earthly transformation. Religious millenarian salvation is experienced collectively as a result of the survival and vindication of the chosen remnant based on their obedience and adherence to the group's doctrines.

The Jehovah's Witnesses are also an ideological restorationist sect that is an outgrowth of the late eighteenth-century and early nineteenth-century Stone-Campbell restorationist movement, which sought to restore Christianity to its earlier or primitive beliefs and practices. It is built on the strongly held conviction of what is known as the Great Apostasy.[7] This is the belief that the church had become apostate, precipitating the need for God, through the teachings of a charismatic leader, to raise up a faithful remnant of believers who accept the restored truths that the church had abandoned. Restorationist groups viewed traditional Christianity as having become so corrupted, compromised, and fallen from the truth that the restoration of original Christianity could only be found by adhering to the teachings of the new remnant group whose beliefs, as taught by a visionary and charismatic founder, make them the elect and only true church. They see the church's acceptance of "pagan" holidays like Christmas and Easter and the existence of numerous Protestant denominations with their doctrinal differences as proof of the church's corrupt nature.

Typically, restorationist groups are exclusivistic; they reject the idea of denominations as well as the historical creeds and orthodoxy of Christianity in favor of "restored" beliefs and practices that, ironically, tend to be a radical departure from the historical doctrines of biblical Christianity. Restorationist cults tend to be very critical of traditional Christianity and mainstream churches; they often hold to revisionist ideas of church history, and they commonly view the Roman Catholic Church as the "mother of harlots" and Protestant churches as her daughters. Many of these groups, like the Jehovah's Witnesses, are known for their denial of the Trinity and the deity of Jesus, their perversion of the gospel of salvation by grace through faith in the person and work of Christ, and their rejection of other essential doctrines of the Christian faith.

How should Christians view a group like the Jehovah's Witnesses? Witnesses should not be regarded as Christians because they significantly deviate from biblical orthodoxy. Like many cults they deny the deity of Jesus and the Trinity, believing that Jesus was the first of God's creations and in his prehuman form was identical to Michael the Archangel. Jehovah's Witnesses deny the literal and physical resurrection of Jesus, believing instead that he rose in a spiritual body. They also deny the personhood and deity of the Holy Spirit, viewing him as an active force rather than as God. Jehovah's Witnesses also have a works-based salvation doctrine that bases salvation not on grace through faith in the person and work of Christ, but rather upon obedience and faithfulness to the Watchtower organization and its teachings.

BELIEFS, CORE VALUES, AND PRACTICES OF JEHOVAH'S WITNESSES

The hierarchical organizational structure of the Jehovah's Witnesses is very sophisticated. They consider themselves to be "theocratic"—God-ruled, or having their leaders appointed by God. Christian churches are considered apostate, so Jehovah's Witnesses' congregations meet in what they call *Kingdom Halls* to distinguish themselves from Christianity. Congregations are led by a body of male *elders* and a presiding elder. Twenty congregations make up a *circuit*, which is led by a circuit overseer. One circuit is made up of ten *districts*, which is supervised by a *district overseer*. There are twenty-two districts, which in cluster form *branches*, and clusters of branches are called *zones*, all of which are under the authority of the *Governing Body*.

Jehovah's Witnesses believe that their organization is the one and only true religion and that their Governing Body is the literal voice of God. As a result, they also prohibit studying the Bible independently and arriving at different views from the organization. To reject the teachings of the organization is tantamount to rejecting God, in their view. Witnesses are taught to shun any member who has been disfellowshipped, even if they are family members. The disfellowshipped person has been rejected by God and will be destroyed by God at Armageddon. There are several other offenses that can result in being shunned and disfellowshipped if the individual fails to demonstrate sufficient contrition, including the celebration of holidays such as birthdays,

Christmas, Valentine's Day, Mother's and Father's Day, and Easter. All of these are viewed as pagan in origin. Witnesses also prohibit receiving blood transfusions, which they view as equivalent to drinking blood (Gen. 9:4; Lev. 17:10; Deut. 12:23; Acts 15:28, 29). The organization has come under public scrutiny due to the deaths of some members who could have been saved through a blood transfusion if it had not been refused. Jehovah's Witnesses do not take up collections but operate the organization through publication sales, donations, and freewill giving.

Members are encouraged to attend the Lord's Supper or the Memorial of Christ's Death at Passover, which occurs once per year, but they are not allowed to partake in the elements, which are reserved only for the "anointed class"—also known as the "little flock," the living members of the 144,000. The Jehovah's Witnesses have a very low view of education and discourage attending college based on their belief that Armageddon is imminent and attending college is costly, materialistic, and influentially negative.

Socially, members maintain their closest relationships with other members and spend most of their time outside of work and home witnessing and attending the five meetings that are divided between the two weekly gatherings. They are apolitical, avoiding participation in all politics. They have an antimilitary/antiwar stance, and they discourage involvement in sports due to their competitive nature, which they liken to war.

In the following sections, we'll take a closer look at some of the core beliefs of the Jehovah's Witnesses and how they differ from accepted Christian teaching.

DEITY OF JESUS CHRIST[8]

Jehovah's Witnesses deny both the deity and the eternal preexistence of Jesus. According to their teaching, Jesus was the first of all God's created beings, the only direct creation of God, and he was created as a spirit being. In his prehuman existence, Jesus was called the only begotten Son of God, the Word, and even Michael the Archangel. Like the fourth-century heretic Arius, the Jehovah's Witnesses believe that Jesus is a god, divine-like but not the Almighty God. They believe that Jesus existed with God in prehuman form before all of God's other spirit sons and was made God's Chief Agent, through whom the coagency or instrumentality of creation occurred (not to be confused with Jesus being co-Creator).

While the Watchtower affirms the miracle of the virgin birth of Christ, they deny the incarnation. Instead, they teach that God transferred the Son's spirit life force into the womb of Mary, and he was born not as a spirit-human hybrid but as a perfect man. Thus, they deny what theologians call the "hypostatic union" or the dual nature that orthodox Christianity teaches exists within the person of Jesus.

The Christian View

Jehovah's Witnesses deny the deity of Jesus Christ and his eternal preexistence. While the Bible does describe Jesus as the firstborn (Greek *prōtotokos*) of all creation in Colossians 1:15, this description is meant to express his superiority in rank; it is not a reference to priority in time, as they allege. The description here is similar to the references in Genesis 22:2 and Genesis 25:5 to Isaac as the "only son" of Abraham who receives the blessing of the firstborn. He is described this way not because he was Abraham's only existing son, born first in time, but because he was chosen.

The Bible clearly teaches that Jesus is God in numerous passages. For instance, John 1:1–14 states that the *logos* was not only with God but is God (*theos*). Jehovah's Witnesses unwarrantedly change "God" in this verse to "a god" to deny it. Additional verses that identify Jesus as God are Romans 9:5, where Paul states that Christ is "God over all," and Titus 2:13, which states that Jesus is "God and Savior."

Witnesses also err in their belief that Jesus was formerly Michael the Archangel in his preexistence. Scripture tells us that Jesus not only created all things, including angels, but that all of the angels worship him as God; Jesus is even called "God" by God the Father (John 1:3; Col. 1:16; Heb. 1:2, 6, 8, 10).

In response to Jehovah's Witnesses' teaching on Jesus's birth and incarnation, the Bible clearly teaches that Jesus is called "God with us" (Matt. 1:23) in fulfillment of Isaiah's prophecy (7:14). Further, it teaches that he who eternally existed in the form of God and, in equality with God, dwelled physically on earth in the fullness of deity—a word that in Greek expresses the whole completeness or plenitude of everything that God is—existed in Jesus's physical body.

THE LIFE, DEATH, AND RESURRECTION OF CHRIST[9]

The Watchtower teaches that Jesus came to earth as a perfect man and became the Messiah upon being anointed at thirty years of age. Since Jesus, like Adam, was perfect, his life was given as a ransom to buy back what Adam had lost, which was the right to perfect human life on earth. In other words, Jesus's perfect sinless life qualified him to be the perfect sacrifice and ransom in order to offer up the equivalent of the loss that Adam forfeited for all humankind. The Watchtower does not teach the doctrine of original sin and therefore denies Jesus's atonement as paying the price for the sins of the world. Original sin, according to the Watchtower, refers not to bad deeds but rather to the inherited effects of Adam's sin—i.e., sickness, imperfections, and death—and does not alienate us from God, as he does not hold us culpable or guilty for Adam's sin.

Jehovah's Witnesses believe that Jesus was sentenced by Pontius Pilate, not to die on a Roman cross, but rather on a wooden pole or torture stake. After death, Jesus was asleep for three days until he was resurrected by Jehovah, not back to physical life but as a mighty, immortal spirit Son and glorious spirit creature. The Watchtower denies the physical resurrection of Christ on the grounds that Christ had given his life up to give the world a clean slate (not to pay for sin once for all), and taking it back physically would mean taking back the ransom price he had paid.

The Christian View

Jehovah's Witnesses wrongly teach that Jesus's death was a mere ransom payment to give humankind the right to live a perfect life on earth forever, which Adam forfeited in disobedience. In denying the inherited nature of sin, they claim that Jesus's death was a ransom for the effects of sin. Biblically, however, Jesus's death became the means by which our sins were taken away, remitted, and paid for; through his death we are cleansed and forgiven of actual sin guilt (John 1:29; Rom. 3:25; 5:9; 1 Cor. 15:3; Heb. 9:22; 1 Pet. 1:18–19; 2:24; 1 John 1:7).

Space does not permit me to explore the fallacy of the Watchtower in alleging that Jesus did not die on a Roman cross but rather on a pole or stake. Suffice it to say, the historical, linguistic, literary, and archaeological evidence overwhelmingly supports the fact that the word *stauros* means "cross" not "stake." The only purpose of such a baseless and irrelevant claim is to push the idea that the Watchtower alone has the correct interpretation of Scripture and Protestant Christianity does not.

Jehovah's Witnesses' teaching that Jesus only appeared visibly in a spiritual body can easily be refuted from New Testament passages like Luke 24:38–39. In this passage, Jesus explicitly tells his disciples, who were afraid and thought he was a ghost or a departed human spirit, to look at his hands and feet because spirits don't have flesh and bones "as you see *I have*" (emphasis mine). Elsewhere, in John 20:27, Jesus encourages Thomas's faith and tells him to place his fingers on his hands and into his side in order to prove that it was actually him in the same body that had the same marks from his crucifixion. It is this very physical proof that causes Thomas to exclaim with excitement, "My Lord and my God" (John 20:28)—yet another pronouncement of Jesus's deity. Just after the resurrection, as stated in Matthew 28:9, Jesus appears to the disciples and they "clasped his feet." Jehovah's Witnesses may counter that spirit bodies can be clung to and touched, just as Jacob wrestled with God at Peniel in Genesis 32. However, theophanies or appearances of God in human form like that in Genesis 32 were not just appearances in the sense of mere visibility but actually God in human form. Thus, Jacob grappled not with a spirit form but with God in human form (in the physical sense) because spirits in their immaterial form are considered noncorporeal or not tangible.

THE SECOND COMING OF CHRIST AND THE LAST THINGS[10]

Since the physical, bodily resurrection of Christ is denied in the teachings of Jehovah's Witnesses, it follows that they also deny his literal bodily return, teaching that he will come back as a glorious spirit person. Additionally, the Watchtower views Christ as having already arrived and been presently here since 1914, reigning as King through the Watchtower Society. The eschatology of the Jehovah's Witnesses is one big spaghetti bowl of millennial madness, filled with biblical chronology calculations, date-settings, and false claims about Christ's return, Christ's reign, the start of Armageddon, and the rapture. There are numerous changed dates, revised interpretations of date meanings, adjustments in doctrine, failed prophecies, and denials. When Watchtower prophecies fail, they blame readers for misunderstanding. The clearest position that Jehovah's Witnesses have regarding end-time events is their teaching that unbelievers will be destroyed by God in Armageddon and then annihilated or wiped out of existence rather than experience eternal conscious punishment.

Witnesses also teach that there are two classes of believers, both of which are composed of Jehovah's Witnesses. The first group, called the "anointed class," are considered the 144,000 from Revelation 7:4 and are made up of believers who will actually live in heaven with God and rule with Christ. The anointed class closed in 1935. This group is also referred to by Witnesses as "the little flock" from their interpretation of Luke 12:32. The second group, "the great crowd," is composed of all Witnesses who survive Armageddon but are not part of the anointed class. They will be resurrected and will live forever in paradise on earth.

The Christian View

The second coming of Christ is an essential doctrine of the Christian faith and, as such, what we believe about it must align with what Scripture says about it. The Bible states clearly in Revelation 1:7 that when Christ returns, "Every eye will see him." In Acts 1:9–11, the angels assure the disciples that Jesus, who was ascending into heaven, will return from heaven in the same way. This can mean nothing other than exactly what is stated: that since Jesus's physical resurrection was attested to by "many convincing proofs" (Acts 1:3) and we have proven from Scripture that he was raised physically, then he ascended physically. Therefore, it is an eschatological fact that he will return in that same manner—physically. We are also promised that upon his return the bodies of all believers will be changed into glorified physical bodies (Rom. 8:23–25, 30; 1 Cor. 15:12–14, 50–55). If Christ returned in 1914, why aren't believers glorified? The idea of Christ's invisible return is heresy.

Nowhere in Scripture is it taught that there are two classes of redeemed people, those who get into heaven and those who live forever on earth. In fact, the Bible clearly states in Revelation 7 and 14 that both the 144,000 and the "multitude" are made up of all nations of believers who will be gathered around the throne of God worshiping. In Revelation 21 and 22, the throne of God and God's tabernacle will dwell with humanity in the new Jerusalem in the new earth, where all believers, including the 144,000, will live. John uses the same word (Greek *skene*) in Revelation 21:3 to refer to God's dwelling or tabernacling with humanity that he used in John 1:14 when he stated that the *logos* or the word became flesh and dwelled (Greek *skene*, "tabernacled") among us, an echo of God telling Moses in Exodus 25:8, "They are to make a sanctuary for me so that I may dwell among them" (CSB).

SALVATION[11]

According to the Watchtower, salvation is not "gained" by faith in Jesus but by obedience and good works, which are based on four requirements: (1) learning about Jehovah, (2) obeying his laws, (3) being a member of the Jehovah's Witnesses, and (4) demonstrating loyalty by telling others about the kingdom message.[12] Part of obedience is baptism, which Witnesses view as essential to salvation.[13]

The Christian View

Jehovah's Witnesses are blatant in teaching salvation by good works. However, the Scriptures are quite clear that we are saved by grace through faith and not by works, a point Paul makes repeatedly for greater emphasis (Eph. 2:8–9). Scripture also repeatedly teaches that we are justified by faith apart from works (Rom. 3:28; Gal. 2:16; Phil. 3:8–11).

GOD[14]

The one true God, according to the teachings of Jehovah's Witnesses, is properly named Jehovah. They have a unipersonal view of God, teaching that there is one God, who is an individual spirit person that is omniscient and omnipotent, but *not* omnipresent. According to their teachings, God has a spiritual body that resides in a specific dwelling place in a very specific location. Witnesses condemn the doctrine of the Trinity as pagan and idolatrous and credit the idea to Satan. Jehovah's Witnesses reject the Trinity admittedly because it is confusing to them, not easily understandable, and because 1 + 1 + 1 = 1 is not scientifically calculable.

The Christian View

Jehovah's Witnesses, in their rejection of the Trinity, like to point out that the word "Trinity" is found nowhere in Scripture. However, they are comfortable using words like "omniscient" and "omnipotent" to refer to God, which are also not found anywhere in Scripture. The question is whether the *concept* is actually taught in Scripture—and the Bible clearly affirms that there is one God who eternally exists in three persons: the Father, the Son, and the Holy Spirit. In Scripture, the Father is called God (1 Pet. 1:2), Jesus is called God (John 20:28; Heb. 1:8), and the Holy Spirit is called God (Acts 5:3–4). Further, as to the attributes of deity, the three persons are said to be omnipresent

(Ps. 139:7; Jer. 23:23–24; Matt. 28:20), omnipotent (Jer. 32:17; John 2:1–11; Rom. 15:19), omniscient (Ps. 147:5; John 16:30; 1 Cor. 2:10–11), and eternal (Ps. 90:2; Heb. 9:14; Rev. 22:13). There is no single activity that identifies one as being God quite like the work of creation, and all three persons in the Godhead are ascribed a role in the creation. The Father is Creator in Genesis 1:1 and Psalm 102:25; the Son is Creator in John 1:3, Colossians 1:16, and Hebrews 1:2; and the Holy Spirit is Creator in Genesis 1:2, Job 33:4, and Psalm 104:30.

THE HOLY SPIRIT

According to the Jehovah's Witnesses, the Holy Spirit is not a person, it is God's active force which God uses to accomplish his will. The Holy Spirit is therefore subordinate to God.

The Christian View

Scripture refutes the idea that the Holy Spirit is just the active force of God. The Holy Spirit has all of the divine attributes. Notice that Peter tells Ananias that he has lied to the Holy Spirit and then states, "You have not lied to people but to God" (Acts 5:3–4 CSB). The Holy Spirit, unlike a force, has intelligence (Rom. 8:27), actually knowing the mind of God. He also has will (1 Cor. 12:11) and emotions so that he can be grieved (Eph. 4:30). These attributes, along with his ability to teach (John 14:26), send (Acts 13:4), command (Acts 8:29), intercede (Rom. 8:26), testify (John 15:26), and search (1 Cor. 2:11), demonstrate personhood.

HUMANITY, THE SOUL, AND THE DESTINY OF THE WICKED[15]

Jehovah's Witnesses teach the mortality of the human soul and the annihilation of the wicked, both of which originate from Russell's early Adventist teachings. The Watchtower, like Adventism which predates it and even the Sadducees of Jesus's day, has a materialist view of humanity, believing the soul dies with the body. Humanity is merely a combination of material components and the breath of life, according to Witness doctrine. The Watchtower's position is that hell is the grave of the body and that the spirit or life-force of man is extinguished. It is from this view that they justify the belief that God will destroy the wicked by annihilating or wiping their existence out, rather than through eternal conscious judgement, which Russell, from a young age, found to be irreconcilable to his personal view of God.

The Christian View

Biblical evidence that the soul survives the death of the body is clearly demonstrated in the transfiguration scene where Moses and Elijah are both present and talking to Jesus, something that cannot be done if the soul is not conscious after death (Matt. 17:3). Further, eternal separation from God is not just an eternal judgment but an eternal state of existing in sin according to John 3:36, which contrasts the eternal life had by the elect who have believed in Christ with the one who doesn't believe (who rejects the Son and therefore doesn't see life because the wrath or the judgment of God remains upon him). The Greek verb translated "remains" is in the present active indicative, meaning the one who rejects the Son always has the wrath of God abiding on him just as the one believing in the Son always has eternal life. Conclusively, the wrath of God is as much a continuous state for the unbeliever as eternal life is a continuous state for the believer! This same contrast between the eternal state of the believer and unbeliever is used by John in Revelation 14:11–13 to communicate the same idea. John states that the smoke of the torment of the wicked is said to rise forever, which is in contrast to the smoke of the incense of the prayers of the believers being offered to God in Revelation 8:3–4. Like the smoke of incense continuously rising, the torment of wicked will never rest (Greek *anapausis*)—that is, cease from God's wrath. This is in contrast to the never-ending rest (*anapausis*) experienced by those in Christ who have been killed for their faith (14:13) and their never-ending worship of the Lord in Revelation 4:8, which is stated to also never cease (*anapausis*). The same word is used to describe the continuous nature of God's judgment on the wicked, disproving once and for all the doctrine of the annihilation of the wicked.

JEHOVAH'S WITNESSES AND THE NEW WORLD TRANSLATION

In 1950 the Watchtower published its own translation of the New Testament called the New World Translation of the Christian Greek Scriptures. In 1961 they completed the Old Testament, called the New World Translation of the Holy Scriptures. It has been revised four times, most recently in 2013. Overall, the New World Translation (NWT) has been criticized by biblical scholars and theologians for being intellectually dishonest, ignoring widely accepted scholarship, containing erroneous renderings of the biblical languages, utilizing theological interpretations that support its doctrines, and proposing biased translations.[16]

While the Watchtower claims the NWT was the work of competent scholars, not one person on the committee—including the committee's head and the principal translator himself—had an earned and recognized degree in Hebrew or Greek grammar or exegesis. Fredrick W. Franz, the publisher and head of the New World Bible translation committee, who was responsible for the oversight of the translation work and revisions, was at the time also serving as the vice president of the Watchtower Society. At the time, Franz was considered the Watchtower's only Bible scholar and the only person on the translation committee "with sufficient knowledge of the Bible languages to attempt translation of this kind. He had studied Greek for two years in the University of Cincinnati but was only self-taught in Hebrew."[17] The Watchtower has never released the names of the translators, claiming that they desired to remain anonymous so as to not "advertise themselves but let all the glory go to the Author of the Scriptures, God."[18] Former members of the Watchtower's governing board mention Knorr, Fredrick Franz, and three others, while Penton states that the NWT was the work of one man, Fredrick W. Franz.[19] Franz claimed under oath to be able to read the Bible in Hebrew, Greek, Latin, Spanish, Portuguese, German, and French, but during cross-examination admitted he was unable to translate Genesis 2:4 from the Hebrew. This is oddly reminiscent of Charles Taze Russell's perjury under oath when he made a similar claim.

Deliberate scriptural distortions and forced translations can be found in passages in the NWT that clearly express the deity of Christ. Several examples are shown below:[20]

	NWT	CSB	Notes
Titus 2:13	We wait for the happy hope and glorious manifestation of the great God and of our Savior, Christ Jesus.	While we wait for the blessed hope, the appearing of the glory of our great God and Savior, Jesus Christ.	The NWT changes the reading from "the glory of our great God and Savior" (CSB) to avoid identifying Jesus as God.

continued

	NWT	CSB	Notes
Col. 1:15–17	He is the image of the invisible God, the firstborn of all creation; because by means of him all other things were created in the heavens and on the earth, the things visible and the things invisible, whether they are thrones or lordships or governments or authorities. All other things have been created through him and for him. Also, he is before all other things, and by means of him all other things were made to exist.	He is the image of the invisible God, the firstborn over all creation. For everything was created by him, in heaven and on earth, the visible and the invisible, whether thrones or dominions or rulers or authorities—all things have been created through him and for him. He is before all things, and by him all things hold together.	The NWT adds the word "other," a word not present in the original Greek, in order to make Jesus appear to be part of God's creation, simply being the first of all creation.
Heb. 1:8	But about the Son, he says: "God is your throne forever and ever, and the scepter of your Kingdom is the scepter of uprightness."	But to the Son: Your throne, God, is forever and ever, and the scepter of your kingdom is a scepter of justice.	The NWT reverses the order of the text from "your throne, O God, is forever," because God the Father here calls the Son "God."
John 1:1	In the beginning was the Word, and the Word was with God, and the Word was a god.	In the beginning was the Word, and the Word was with God, and the Word was God.	The NWT adds the indefinite article "a" before "god," which mistranslates the text in order to emphasize the idea that Jesus was inferior to God the Father.

THE JEHOVAH'S WITNESSES AND BLACK COMMUNITIES

How have the Jehovah's Witnesses affected Black communities? The Watchtower has elements of racism in its past. It was racially segregated and evidence of racist teaching—Blacks being inferior to whites and having cursed skin—are part of that shameful history. Most embarrassing of all is Russell's teaching that Black people's racial plight in America can be solved through their transmogrification into whiteness. Literally, he taught that with the help of God, Black people's skin color could be changed to white. He attempted to justify this teaching with the famous biblical question in Jeremiah 13:23, "Can an Ethiopian change his skin or a leopard its spots?"

Studies show that Blacks in the US are most likely to identify as Christian or Protestant (72 percent) whereas less than 1 percent identify as a Jehovah's Witness. Nevertheless, while the Watchtower organization does not track or keep racial demographic data of its own, Pew Research's ten-year Religious Landscape Study, last conducted in 2014, revealed that the Jehovah's Witnesses are among the most racially and ethnically diverse religious groups in America: 36 percent are white, 32 percent are Hispanic, 27 percent are Black, and 6 percent are another race or mixed race.

Since the culture and values of Jehovah's Witnesses are apolitical and antieducation, participation in the Watchtower Society only serves to further marginalize Blacks in America. Economically, it limits postsecondary education and discourages their participation in elections that impact the quality of life Blacks can enjoy in America. Historically, the lack of voting rights and education equality are among the two highest contributing factors to the disproportionate wealth gap between whites and Blacks in the US, a gap that only grows wider when Blacks participate in socially isolating cults. Heyward reasoned that Blacks in America might have found the Jehovah's Witnesses appealing because the Watchtower's obsession with eschatology made it possible for them to see the problems of racism as issues that have imminent expiration dates.[21]

The Jehovah's Witnesses prioritize their "kingdom mission" over issues of fighting racial segregation—a practice that works against Black Witnesses today just as much as it did in the past. The Jehovah's Witnesses spend millions of dollars annually in the US and other countries litigating for the right to preach, their right to proselytize, and their right of refusal to pledge allegiance to the flag. These reforms suit the agenda of the organization, but on matters of social justice—which includes challenging the structural and systemic injustices surrounding housing discrimination, education, economic, and health care disparities caused by laws, practices, and policies that perpetuate oppression and unfair treatment of Black people—the position of the Jehovah's Witnesses is to remain neutral. Efforts to promote societal change are considered "worldly."

ENGAGING WITH WITNESSES

What, then, is the best way to effectively engage with a Jehovah's Witness? While it can be difficult, there are several strategies that can lead to positive engagement.

1. Demonstrate that the Watchtower is a false prophet by recounting the numerous times they have been wrong about prophecies that have not come to pass as and when predicted. Use Deuteronomy 18:20–22 to show that Russell, Rutherford, and the entire Watchtower organization fits the character of a false prophet. To be clear, the Watchtower predicted Christ's return in 1878, 1914, 1925, and as recently as 1975![22]

2. Show them the NWT's mistranslations using an English-Greek Interlinear so that they can see where certain words were added, changed, or removed.

3. Research the New Testament for those passages that clearly affirm the deity of Christ. No other tenet of the Jehovah's Witnesses' faith is more central than the idea that Christ is not God and that he was a created being.

4. Show from Scripture that the gospel assures believers today of eternal life—not on the basis of "witnessing" or the hope of being spared from Armageddon but on the basis of the work of Christ at the cross, which is received by trusting in him, not by our efforts. They need to know that the true good news is not the possibility of living forever in paradise on earth but having eternal life and actual fellowship with God right now, knowing that our sins were judged in Christ at the

cross so that we don't have any future judgment looming over us that would jeopardize our eternal state. Future judgments for the believer are rewards for our work, and no one will be lost (2 Cor. 5:10).

Clearly, the teachings of the Jehovah's Witnesses are incompatible with the biblical Christian faith and should be considered heretical. The Jehovah's Witnesses are considered a cult because they deny essential biblical doctrines such as the Trinity, the deity of Jesus, the physical bodily resurrection of Christ, and the personhood and deity of the Holy Spirit. In addition, they plainly teach that salvation is a matter of works done to spread their teachings rather than a gift of grace to those who place their faith in the Lord Jesus Christ.

Charles Taze Russell, Joseph Rutherford, and the Watchtower organization collectively, as the official voices of Jehovah's Witnesses' doctrine and teaching, have a documented history of making numerous failed prophecies concerning the date and manner of Jesus's second coming, as well as blatantly changing the wording of Scripture to support their doctrines. Scripture warns against this and promises God's judgment for those guilty of adding and taking away from the words of Scripture (Mark 13:32–33; Rev. 22:18–19). According to Scripture, the Watchtower should be regarded as a false prophet; the Bible warns us to avoid their teachings. These teachings not only create divisions among professing Christians who affirm the true apostolic faith, but those same teachers also create obstacles to hearing the gospel that are deceptive and ultimately damnable to those who follow them (Rom. 16:17).

Peter warns believers to be on guard against unstable and unlearned false teachers who distort Scripture to their own destruction and lead away from the truth those who are spiritually unstable (2 Pet. 2:14; 3:16). While the tireless dedication of the Jehovah's Witnesses who spend hours weekly propagating their faith may appear admirable and honorable, there is nothing noble or glorious about the cruel slavery of attempting to earn eternal life and good standing before God with one's own works. Sadly, those who do will only be compensated in the end with eternal separation from God, the penalty for sin. They have rejected the gift of God, which is eternal life through Jesus Christ (Rom. 6:23).

THE GLOBAL CHURCH

CRISTEN CAMPBELL

A conviction is defined as "a strong persuasion or belief."[1] As believers, our convictions should always be informed by a sound biblical and theological foundation. In other words, what we believe is not only shaped by what the Bible says, but more importantly, by what God has revealed about who he is. Our convictions are solidified based on our knowledge of God, his work in creation, his work in the community of faith (the church), and his work in our lives.

The living organism that is the church is foretold by the Lord upon the confession of faith of the apostle Simon Peter. In Matthew 16:18, Jesus says to Simon, "You are Peter, and on this rock I will build my church, and the gates of Hades will not overpower it" (CSB). This prophetic declaration follows Simon Peter's pronouncement that Jesus is the Messiah, the one foretold by the prophets to deliver Israel. Jesus's substitutionary death and atonement for all who would believe in him inaugurated the establishment of the church. Its growth was spawned by the coming of the Holy Spirit in Acts 2, the persecution of its early followers, and the subsequent expansion of the community of faith beyond the borders of Israel through evangelization.

Since its birth, the church has withstood attacks from within and without, and it is still standing. This is a testament to its prophetic roots, its purpose, and its global presence. In his book entitled *The Lost History of Christianity*, Phillip Jenkins states,

> The particular shape of Christianity with which we are familiar is a radical departure from what was for well over a millennium the historical norm: another, earlier global Christianity once existed. For most of its history, Christianity was a tricontinental religion, with powerful representation in Europe, Africa and Asia. . . . Christianity became prominently European not because this continent had any obvious affinity for the faith, but by default: Europe was the continent where it was *not* destroyed.[2]

According to Jenkins, the Middle Ages ripped Christianity from its cultural, geographic, and linguistic roots. Over time, the church's center of gravity shifted from prominence in the Near East, where it thrived for centuries, to Europe and the Atlantic world, and now to what is being called the global South.[3]

GLOBAL CHURCH CULTURE

When we think about global church culture, we want to consider what believers everywhere around the globe share in common—namely, a conviction that Jesus is Lord, and that through his death, burial, and resurrection:

1. We have been reconciled to the Father.
2. We have been delivered from the power of sin and death.
3. We are eternally connected as brothers and sisters, with Jesus as our head.

Our faith in Christ and his power to save and deliver us is what unites us eternally to the Father and to one another.

The global church transcends the church where it exists locally, because the universal church is larger than any one church or churches in a certain region. The global church values the unity of all believers everywhere for all times. It also values the fact that the church is vast and diverse. Historically, Christianity did not appeal to the elite, but to the lowly. It elevated the status and worth of the poor, the slave, the illiterate, the disenfranchised, and women. From its inception, it was countercultural, welcoming those who lived in the margins of society and placing them squarely in the center of God's divine purposes. William Bennett writes in his book *Tried by Fire: The Story of Christianity's First Thousand Years*, "The Christian faith also put no intellectual, ethnic, racial, gender, or class restriction on who could be a member. . . . This concern for the lowest stratum of society revealed a valuation of human life that was vastly more empathetic than Greco-Roman notions."[4]

The conviction that life is valuable has implications for the church today because, in Christ, all life is valued. This is why the voice of the church in heralding the dignity and value of all human life in all phases (from the womb to the grave) against a culture that diminishes and devalues life is so important. This very notion is what makes the Western church (in particular) complicit if it fails to speak up for what God has called "good," since he pronounced everything he created as such (Gen. 1:4, 10, 12, 18, 21, 25, 31).

VOICES FROM THE GLOBAL CHURCH ON ECCLESIOLOGY

The Majority World Theological Series promotes the voices of prominent non-Western theologians and biblical scholars, who add their perspectives on the major doctrines of the faith, including the doctrine of ecclesiology (the teaching about the church). The fifth book in this series, entitled *The Church from Every Tribe and Tongue: Ecclesiology in the Majority World*, deals with the theology of the church from a non-Western perspective.[5] These theologians and Bible scholars help us to appreciate the elements that make the church unique in its expression in the culture where it exists. They also help us to understand that a comprehensive ecclesiology of the global church is not complete without global voices contributing to the discussion. In the eight essays that comprise this volume, each author reflects on the doctrine of ecclesiology from the perspective of the Niceno-Constantinopolitan Creed. As they do, several key themes emerge.

In the opening essay, the only Western theologian in this volume, Kärkkäinen, discusses the classical marks of the one holy, catholic (universal), and apostolic church found in the Niceno-Constantinopolitan Creed of 381 AD.[6] For Kärkkäinen, the global church must include the following elements: worship, liturgy, sacramental celebration, the proclamation of the gospel, mutual fellowship (*koinonia*), and *diakonia* ("service," e.g., meeting the needs of those in the community). He also adds that in the larger purposes of God, the global church should also concern itself with promoting and affirming equality and justice, peace and reconciliation at all levels within and outside the church, as well as care for nature and the environment.[7] In other words, the church must be engaged in holistic ministry to all humankind and creation. This universal concern for the totality of God's creation is rooted in Genesis 1, where the Lord delegates dominion over creation to Adam and Eve (Gen. 1:26, 28).

In another essay, Stephanie Lowery, a missionary kid who grew up in Kenya, writes to promote an African ecclesiology modeled on the idea of the "church as family" that is popular among Roman Catholics in Africa. She demonstrates that this theme is supported in Scripture with many references to the familial language used to describe the church, showing that it also has cultural appeal to African ears. In Africa, "family" connotes not just bloodlines, but ethnicity, tribal connections, and connections to ancestors.[8] The idea of the church as family has cultural significance in the African context. Lowery also highlights the contributions of African ecclesiologies across the continent, including how they value solidarity (how the church visibly models unity), their reliance on biblical models (with an emphasis on the application of the Scriptures in the life of a believer), and promotion of the radical nature of what it means to follow Christ.[9]

Additionally, she details what African Independent Churches (AICs) have contributed to the study of the church and why they have such an appeal in Africa and in the global church context. She lists five reasons AICs appeal to people. First, they provide or are based on divine revelation to the founder— that is, direct communication from God to his people through the leader. Second, many of them offer a holistic salvation (e.g., divine healing, casting out of spirits). Third, they provide freedom and dignity (e.g., freedom from Western control and dignity to express their faith as African believers). Fourth, they provide more equality among men and women, including opportunities to lead (egalitarianism). And fifth, they rely heavily on the Holy Spirit's power.[10]

Majority World theologians like Kärkkäinen and Lowery help us to appreciate the elements that make the church unique in the cultural context in which it exists, but they also help us to see that they view themselves as a part of the greater, universal body of Christ. They remind us that marginal voices have a contribution to make to an understanding of what it means to be the global community of faith, and without their voices, no proper ecclesiology is complete.

CONVICTIONS FROM THE GLOBAL CHURCH

What, then, are the core convictions of the global church? These seven qualities, informed by my years of ministry outside the North American context, reflect many of the values and convictions of the global church context.

1. **The church views itself as a part of the whole, not separate from believers in other parts of the world.** Often, the Western church focuses on the needs at home and fails to live out its responsibility to the church abroad.

2. **Ministry must meet the needs of the entire person (holistic).** In other words, ministry is not compartmentalized. Ministry in the Western church can often appear to be programmatic in nature and sometimes fails to address the needs of the whole person.

3. **Relationships must be preserved at all costs.** This is a high cultural value in most Eastern cultures. In Western culture, individualism tends to be regarded more highly; therefore, commitment to community and relationships often suffers. From the global church perspective, this can be summed up in an African proverb that says, "I am, because we are."

4. **Ministry must include elements of the surrounding culture (e.g. handmade musical instruments, dancing, clothing, food, etc.) that does not contradict the Word of God.** In other words, the church must be committed to being culturally authentic without being syncretistic. For example, in some Western church contexts, the use of some or all musical instruments is discouraged or viewed as less "spiritual" than others. This also extends to what kind of music is used during worship and how it is categorized, which has led to what some call "worship wars."

5. **Table fellowship (i.e., the breaking of bread or sharing a meal) and hospitality are an essential part of building and maintaining community and discipleship relationships.** Though Christian fellowship over meals is common in the Western church, we often do not place as much significance on the act of sharing a meal with others as early believers did or cultures of the East still do to this day.

6. **Suffering is a necessary part of the Christian experience, especially as it relates to the building of one's faith and the work of sanctification.** Unlike most of the global church, the Western church seems uncomfortable and adverse to embracing the reality of suffering as a part of the Christian life. A theology that fails to embrace suffering as a component of our spiritual life is unbiblical and robs the believer of the opportunity to grow by quenching the Holy Spirit (1 Thess. 5:19).

7. **Cultural norms do not take precedence over biblical teachings.** In other words, the church should never conform to the culture; rather, the church should influence the culture. Where the church conforms, it proves to be ineffective and irrelevant. Where the church conforms, it proves to be syncretistic rather than salvific.

We must never forget that the church itself is an apologetic. It has survived, often despite persecution, suffering, and difficulty, for more than two millennia, and it continues to fulfill the prophetic words spoken by Jesus that "the gates of Hades will not overpower it" (Matt. 16:18 CSB). As we consider the Black church experience within the context of the larger, global church culture, we see many similarities. Like the early church, the Black church has endured much in order to survive, including facing abuses from fellow believers within the church while battling forces outside the church. Today, those forces remain, and the church must be poised with an apologetic that combats these ideologies. According to Kärkkäinen, the global church today is facing the challenges of secularism and religious pluralism: "The rise of both secularism and religious pluralism means that the ecclesiologies of the third millennium have to pay attention not only to what is inside the church and within Christian tradition, but also to the teaching of other religious traditions and the mindset of the secular public."[11] This is key in helping the church to develop an apologetic that will combat heresies and ideologies that are contrary to the gospel, just like the early church did. We must always be ready to give a defense for the hope that is within us (1 Pet. 3:15). As believers, we are called to endure hardships and persecutions, but at the end of the day to "consider it pure joy" (James 1:2). As the church, we long for the day when our purpose will be culminated at the marriage supper of the Lamb (Rev. 19:6–9).

ELEVEN

THE PROSPERITY GOSPEL

DAMON RICHARDSON

You've likely seen them on billboards and TV: ministers with bright, toothy smiles and perfectly pressed suits pacing the stage of their expansive church and declaring to their well-dressed and manicured congregations the health and wealth they're sure to attain when they put their faith in Christ. Those who preach and teach this message of health, wealth, and prosperity are largely associated with the Word of Faith movement, a nondenominational multinetwork of churches, ministries, and teachers that are loosely connected, not by formal creed or confession, but by a distorted view of biblical faith. Proponents of this movement contend that this "faith" is the means by which believers appropriate the will of God, resulting in prosperity and success in life—better health and the blessing of wealth. The movement was founded by the teachings of Essek William Kenyon (1867–1948), whose teachings range from concerningly heterodox to egregiously heretical, and much of Kenyon's teaching was later popularized by Kenneth Hagin Sr.

Why address this in the current volume? Because the influence of the prosperity gospel, as it is commonly called, is a far cry from the original emphasis of the Black church. The Black church had its roots in a lived and shared experience of suffering and lament, having grown out of the evils of slavery and racial injustice. This biblically informed experience led to the civil rights movements, created universities and schools, and produced many fine teachers, lawyers, and sound preachers. Yet this new gospel of prosperity rejects all of that and no longer requires believers to turn the other cheek or care about the social and political problems plaguing the Black and Brown community. The new gospel of prosperity promises health and wealth by sowing a seed—but it never offers true salvation. The prosperity gospel sounds like a promise of salvation when you have experienced systematic and systemic racism, but it fails to deliver what it promises. It is unbiblical, and in this chapter we will learn why it is unbiblical and is a danger to the Black church and the Black community around the world.

HISTORICAL DEVELOPMENT

To understand the development of the Word of Faith movement, one needs to understand a little of the zeitgeist of the mid- to late nineteenth century in America. This period in history was a time of immense change across the nation. A crisis of faith began reshaping the religious landscape, which led to several historical reactions.

The Civil War had claimed greater than half a million lives, lost not only to battle but also to civilian conflicts, the spread of disease from soldier encampments, and high mortality rates among children. The reality of death weighed heavily upon many Americans. As a result, many began to seek theological alternatives to the pessimistic outlook of Calvinism, which had dominated the theology of churches during the eighteenth century. The doctrine of predestination had become particularly troubling as many wrestled with the notion of their deceased loved ones, especially their children, being eternally lost because they were not among the elect.

This concern led to a theological shift among many denominations away from Calvinism as people sought to take responsibility for their own spiritual outcomes by embracing theologies that focused more upon human action in effecting salvation. Revivalist preachers like Charles Finney began to emphasize decision-making, individual responsibility for repentance, and participation in the call of the gospel of grace. Baptist and Methodist preachers preached free will—every person could choose salvation because salvation was open to all willing human beings rather than to only those whom God had predestined. Because Calvinists like Edwards and Whitefield had placed so much emphasis on human depravity, many felt hopeless at being able to do anything about their own sinful condition and even less, their social situation.

The new evangelical revival expression, essentially a practical Arminianism, was no less adamant about preaching the sinfulness of humanity as Calvinist preachers had done. Yet it also stressed the ability of humans to turn away from sinful behavior and embrace moral action and social change. The revivalism of the latter phase of the Second Great Awakening stirred a conviction within many Christians that society could be spiritually and morally transformed, and as a result they partnered with abolitionists, suffragists, and other networks of social reform that sought to eradicate social and moral ills such as slavery, women's inequality, and alcoholism. All of this ultimately led to greater public roles for women and increased African American participation in Christianity.

THE ENLIGHTENMENT

By 1860, Lyell's *Principles of Geology* and Darwin's *Origin of Species* had created a firestorm of controversy in the scientific and Christian communities. Both works challenged traditionally held notions of a young earth and proposed that humans evolved, as did other animals, from earlier species. This kindled a growing attraction to and interest in science, fueled by the growing disinterest of many with the answers they were seeking from Protestant Christianity. Not everyone got caught up in the revival fervor, however. Others sought comfort in their crisis of faith by embracing new ways to think about and understand topics such as life, death, and humanity's place in the universe.

By the late nineteenth century, Enlightenment-era rationalism and Romanticism, evolutionary science, and higher biblical criticism had gained a foothold in educational institutions like Harvard and Yale, which in turn led some Protestant denominations to question traditionally held orthodox views such as the divine inspiration and authority of Scripture, the virgin birth, the deity of Christ, the resurrection, and the Trinity. These were often replaced with theologically liberal views and a social gospel. Longing for a modern and scientifically intellectual Christianity, some turned to more theologically liberal churches and movements like Unitarianism for answers, while others turned to science. There was also a burgeoning interest in spiritualism, which provided the perfect balance between the growing American interest in scientific empiricism and their hunger for spiritual fulfillment. Spiritualism and the metaphysical sciences invited those seeking to explore spirituality apart from traditional Christian spirituality while also feeding their curiosities regarding scientific naturalism.[1]

ESSEK KENYON: FATHER OF THE PROSPERITY GOSPEL

It was during this shifting religious landscape in postbellum America that we meet the father of the Word of Faith / prosperity gospel movement, Essek William Kenyon. Kenyon was a New England Baptist pastor who attended Emerson College in Boston in 1892, where he was first exposed to and influenced by metaphysical mind science cults such as New Thought, Christian Science, Unity School of Christianity, and Science of the Mind. Born April 25, 1897, in Saratoga County, New York, Kenyon experienced a conversion to Christianity around age eighteen and a year later preached his first sermon at a Methodist Church in Amsterdam, New York, while working in a factory. By twenty-one years of age, Kenyon, who was working as an uneducated door-to-door salesman, was called to pastor his first church and then pastored several churches throughout New England. He also sought to supplement his education by attending various institutions until he moved to Boston in 1892 and enrolled in Emerson College of Oratory.

Scholars believe that it was likely during Kenyon's year-long study at Emerson that he first was influenced by the metaphysical science and New Thought ideas popularly espoused by Phineas Quimby, Mary Baker Eddy, and Ralph Waldo Trine among others. Emerson College's curriculum was replete with transcendental, New Thought, and Unitarian courses taught by professors like Trine who espoused the mind sciences. Strands of these mind-science ideas are undisputedly reflected in Kenyon's teaching.

The general consensus of Kenyon scholarship is that Kenyon saw the metaphysical sciences as false religions, yet he agreed with certain ideas they had about deification, the power of the mind, and the power of faith to produce healing and overcome sickness and poverty. Kenyon sought to combine certain elements from the metaphysical sciences that he liked with Christianity in order to develop a new Christianity that underscored the

power of faith to receive healing, wealth, and greater supernatural authority. Kenyon syncretized Christianity with aspects of New Thought that he
believed were true and redeemable to Scripture. He viewed both Christianity
and the metaphysical sciences as valid truth in some areas yet falling short
of the truth in other areas.[2]

KENNETH ERWIN HAGIN: POPULARIZING PROSPERITY TEACHING

Many of the core teachings of the Word of Faith movement were later
popularized by Kenneth Hagin. Several of his teachings directly originate
with Kenyon, except in areas where Hagin or later Word of Faith teachers
have theologically innovated. Hagin claimed that in 1934, a year after his
conversion to Christianity, he fell deathly ill due to a deformed heart condition that he had since birth, and while on his deathbed God revealed to
him the message of faith in God's Word after reading Mark 11:23–24. He
was subsequently miraculously healed. In 1950, Hagin, then an itinerant
Assemblies of God minister, was introduced to several of Kenyon's books and
began teaching Prosperity—the application of faith to finances and healing.
Hagin relocated his Texas-based evangelistic ministry to Tulsa, Oklahoma,
in 1966 and began numerous ministries and outreaches via a nationwide
radio broadcast and a publishing house which printed tens of millions of
books, magazines, and booklets, all of which heavily promoted the Word of
Faith message.

Perhaps no other entity was as influential in spreading Prosperity theology as the Rhema Bible Training Center, an unaccredited Bible college that
he founded in 1974. Forty-eight years later this center has more than 30,000
US graduates and over 93,000 graduates worldwide, with over 250 campuses
in more than 50 countries. Although much of Hagin's writings were unques-
tionably plagiarized from Kenyon (who directly influenced his own teaching),
Hagin's influence was the driving force behind many of the movement's most
popular teachers, such as Frederick K. C. Price, Kenneth Copeland, Charles
Capps, and television networks like Trinity Broadcasting Network. Many of
the major "faith" ministries have spread Prosperity theology globally, which
has significantly redefined the way hundreds of millions of Christians understand Scripture as it relates to faith, sin, sickness, healing, wealth, and, more
importantly, the gospel.

WHAT IS THE PROSPERITY GOSPEL?

The prosperity gospel is sometimes referred to as "name it and claim it theology," the "health and wealth gospel," the "positive confession movement," or more popularly as the "Word of Faith movement." We include it in our section on cults because it is a glaring aberration of the true gospel of Jesus Christ. It is built upon several erroneous presuppositions that misrepresent God and his Word, including the following:

1. God has faith and exercised his faith in creation by speaking words.
2. God created man in the "god class" and, by positive and/or negative confession, people exercise their faith, which creates certain realities in their lives.
3. God wills that every believer walk in health, healing, and wealth for his glory.
4. God is contractually obligated to heal and materially prosper all believers who claim their new covenant rights and exercise faith by speaking God's Word and claiming his promises.
5. Should a believer not receive healing or prosperity, it is not because the Word of God failed but rather due to a lack of faith appropriation or hidden and unconfessed sin in the believer's life.

While specific views may vary from Prosperity teacher to Prosperity teacher and not all doctrines are uniformly held, there are core tenets that are propagated by the majority of Prosperity or "faith" teachers that can be traced back to Kenyon. Those core tenets are as follows:

1. Humanity is divine.
2. Born-again believers have the abilities of God.
3. Jesus died spiritually.
4. People are trichotomous; a person is a spirit, that has a soul, that lives in a body.
5. Jesus was born again in hell.
6. Jesus took on a satanic nature on the cross and suffered in hell to secure our redemption.
7. God created the world by using faith expressed through words.

8. We can use the God kind of faith to make positive confessions to receive the healing and health that rightfully belong to us and to overcome poverty and sickness.

9. When Adam sinned, he forfeited his dominion to Satan, and Jesus's death and suffering in hell legally restored dominion back to those who are born again like Jesus.

In this next section we will explore several of these claims and unpack the errors of the prosperity gospel as taught by its proponents, along with the correct biblical response to each of those views.

PROSPERITY TEACHERS AND THE DOCTRINE OF GOD

The God of the prosperity gospel is not the God of Scripture. God, according to Prosperity teachers, has no "legal entrée into the earth."[3] As Frederick K. C. Price explains,

God has to be given permission to work in this earth realm on behalf of man. . . . Yes! You are in control! So if man has control, who no longer has it? God. . . . When God gave Adam dominion, that meant God no longer had dominion. So, God cannot do anything in this earth unless we let Him. And the way we let Him or give Him permission is through prayer.[4]

Word of Faith teachers view God similarly to Mormons and Jehovah's Witnesses in that they teach that God has a spiritual body, "a face and hands, a form of some kind,"[5] and lives in a specific geographical location or "mother planet"[6] called heaven. Kenneth Copeland has taught that God "stands somewhere around 6'2", 6'3"" and "weighs somewhere in the neighborhood of a couple of hundred pounds."[7] While this particular view is a departure from Kenyon, the view that God is a faith being, who by faith created the universe, comes directly from Kenyon's teaching.[8]

Prosperity teachers misinterpret Scriptures such as Hebrews 11:3 to teach that God created the world by faith expressed in his words "Let there be."[9] To further support this idea, Word of Faith (WF) teachers interpret Mark 11:22, "Jesus replied to them, 'Have faith in God,'" to mean that believers should have the kind of faith that God had, the "God-kind of faith." As Hagin has said: "God believed in His heart that what He said with His mouth would come to pass, and He dared to say it. . . . If our Father is a faith God, then we must be faith children of a faith God."[10] This means believers should speak to situations by faith and expect their faith-filled words to create and physically manifest the very thing you spoke in faith.

PROSPERITY TEACHERS AND THE DOCTRINE OF MAN

Prosperity teachers have a heretical view of humanity because they teach that people are little gods, created in the "god class." When WF teachers speak of Adam as having had dominion, they do not mean ruling in the sense of stewardship but in the sense of an autonomous and temporary ownership. In other words, they believe that God literally turned the earth completely over to Adam to rule as he pleases as the god of the earth. This substitutes the biblical concept of dominion for an unbiblical view of man's deification. Having dominion, according to WF teachers, means that God gave to Adam the ability to rule creation with his spoken word, just as God had used his voice to create. Consider these examples from Kenyon and Hagin:

> Hebrews 1:3 gives to us a suggestion as to the way Adam ruled God's creation. . . . Adam ruled creation by his word. His voice was like the voice of his Creator in its dominion over creation.[11]
>
> —E. W. KENYON

> Originally, God made the earth and the fullness thereof, giving Adam dominion over all the works of His hands. In other words, Adam was the god of this world.[12]
>
> —KENNETH E. HAGIN

According to Bowman, the argument in WF theology for the "little gods" doctrine goes something like this:

1. God is a spirit; that is, God is in the spirit class of being.
2. Man is also a spirit; that is, man is in the spirit class of being.
3. Therefore, man is in the same class of being as God.
4. Any being in the same class as God is a god.
5. Therefore, man is a god.[13]

The logic here follows from the idea that God created man in his likeness, which WF teachers interpret to mean a copy—a reproduction of himself—just as other living things did in the Genesis 1 account.

Here are some examples of quotes from WF writings that demonstrate their "little gods" doctrine:

You understand that man is in God's class of being. When he was created in the Garden he was made in the image and likeness of God. He had to be a spirit being because God is a Spirit. . . . He had to be a spirit being, an eternal being who would live as long as God lives. Man had to be in God's class.[14]

—E. W. KENYON

Man . . . was created on terms of equality with God, and he could stand in God's presence without any consciousness of inferiority. . . . God has made us as much like Himself as possible. . . . He made us the same class of being that He is Himself. . . . Man lived in the realm of God. He lived on terms equal with God.[15]

—KENNETH E. HAGIN

You don't have a god in you, you are one.[16]

According to the law of genesis, every living thing was created by God to reproduce after its own kind. Man was no exception to this rule. God is a Spirit, and Adam was created in God's own image and likeness, a spirit-being.[17]

Man was created in the god class. . . . He is in the god class . . . and that is the God-given right to choose his own words, and speak them, thereby setting his own divine destiny, his own destination. . . . All right—are we gods? We are a class of gods![18]

[Adam] was the copy, looked just like [God]. If you stood Adam upside God, they look just exactly alike. If you stood Jesus and Adam side-by-side, they would look and sound exactly alike.[19]

—KENNETH COPELAND

In the Word of Faith view, mankind is a spirit being like God that has a soul and lives in a body. Prosperity teachers utilize a trichotomous view of man in order to teach that man is a spirit being like God and can, as a result, act like God by using the same faith God used. They also utilize a rigid form of trichotomy in order to teach that one's spirit should rule over one's soul and body. In WF trichotomy, man's spirit existed first and was placed in the body, therefore the spirit is the *real* you. Similar to Mormon teaching, this suggests spirit preexistence.

Again, here are several quotes showing the false trichotomous view of man espoused by many of the WF teachers:

> The spirit is the real man, created in the image of God. . . . Your body is not you. Your mind is not you. You have a mind which you use. You possess a body which you use. Your mind and body are merely the instruments of your spirit, the real YOU.[20]
>
> —E. W. KENYON

> The real man is the spirit. The spirit operates through the soul: the intellect, sensibilities, and will. And the soul operates through the body.[21]
>
> —KENNETH E. HAGIN

PROSPERITY TEACHERS AND THE FALL, SIN, SATAN, AND DOMINION

The prosperity gospel's version of the fall of mankind into sinful rebellion differs significantly from Scripture. In this version, man's dominion was a short-term lease, and when Adam sinned by disobedience, he forfeited his dominion. In other words, Adam legally transferred the lease over to Satan, who then assumed dominion over all creation and the remaining balance of the lease.

In this version of the fall, mankind became a sinner, was separated from God, and, as a result, lost their divine nature and consequently took on the nature of Satan. Once Satan obtained the lease, he became the legal god of the earth, unable to be evicted until his lease runs out. This means that, as noted earlier, God doesn't have control over the earth—Satan does. God is thus locked out and essentially an illegal alien to the earth realm. This schema demotes God from omnipotent to impotent and promotes Satan from seducer to sovereign god of the whole earth—a ruler whom even God himself could not legally evict. The following quotes articulate this belief:

> The Fall of Man was a lawful act; that is, Adam had legal right to transfer the authority and dominion that God had placed in his hands into the hands of another. This gives Satan a legal right to rule over man and over creation.[22]

> God gave to man a Time-Limit Dominion; by accommodation we might call it a Lease of Dominion. This Lease of Dominion is called in Daniel and in Mark, "the age of the Gentiles," that is; the age of the nations, or the age of the Dominion of Man.[23]

> He is more than a sinner; he is sin. A new Nature enters into him. It is not the nature of God but of this enemy, the Devil. A similar nature is breathed into the Animal Kingdom, devilish, cruel, and malignant. Man's spirit undergoes a change; he has become a partaker of the Satanic nature, spiritual death, and he dies spiritually.[24]

> It is very noticeable that the moment Man sinned His Nature underwent a complete change. This change has no parallel in Nature except in that which is known as the New Birth, for when one is born of God he undergoes as instantaneous a change. This proves to us that Man was actually Born Again when he sinned. That is, he was born of the Devil. He became a partaker of Satanic Nature just as man today becomes a partaker of Divine nature when he is born of God by accepting Jesus Christ.[25]

—E. W. KENYON

> Adam was the god of this world. But Adam committed high treason and sold out to Satan. Thus Satan became the god of this world.[26]

—KENNETH E. HAGIN

> But when Adam bowed his knee to Satan, he shut God out. God found Himself on the outside looking in. His man, Adam, had lost his authority. Satan . . . had become the god of the world system. . . . Satan had gained ascendancy in the earth by gaining Adam's authority, and God was left

on the outside. God couldn't come here in His divine power and wipe them out.[27]

—CHARLES CAPPS

The Bible says that God gave this earth to the sons of men . . . and when [Adam] turned and gave that dominion to Satan, look where it left God. It left Him on the outside looking in. . . . He had no legal right to do anything about it, did He? . . . What Satan had intended for Him to do was to fall for it—pull off an illegal act and turn the light off in God, and subordinate God to himself.[28]

—KENNETH COPELAND

PROSPERITY TEACHING ON THE PERSON AND WORK OF JESUS CHRIST

The Word of Faith view of the person and work of Christ and the meaning of the gospel is heretical, reflecting the ancient Monarchian heresy. At least several prominent Prosperity teachers hold a view of Christ that denies his preexistence by claiming that the word or the *logos* was spoken into existence by God the Father, who planted the seed of the word into Abraham and others all the way down to Mary, who, by a positive confession that the Messiah would come, manifested Jesus. This notion that the spoken word of God *became* Jesus is quite common in WF teaching:

The faith it took to make fingers was loosed, the faith it took to make arms was loosed in the earth, and now God had a way to hover over a little woman by the name of Mary.[29]

The Word became flesh and dwelt among us. What Word? The Word of the Covenant that God cut with Abraham way back there years before. . . . That covenant was the door that opened up to heaven that caused God to be able to come to Mary and speak words of life to her and that those words that that angel brought to her became seed inside her womb that produced the blood that flowed in the veins of Jesus. Literally produced it. That's the reason He had to be born of a virgin. It was a creative miracle of God. He created with His words the blood that flowed in His veins.[30]

Now you see, God is injecting His Word into the earth to produce this Jesus—these faith filled words that framed the image that's in Him.[31]

—KENNETH COPELAND

God's Word spoken by the angel became the Seed, the physical manifestation of a promise of God. He declared it would come to pass and centuries did not hinder the ultimate fulfillment of His spoken Word. . . . Joseph himself had to exercise faith and accept the Word that Jesus' conception was the Word spoken by the Holy Spirit. The Word was made flesh. Jesus, the Messiah to the world, co-existed with God from the beginning as the Word. Through Him were all things created that exist. Mary conceived God's Word in her spirit. Once it was conceived in her spirit, it manifested itself in her physical body. The Bible said, "The Word was made flesh . . ." The embryo in Mary's womb was the Word of God—and it took flesh upon itself. The Word of God was conceived by an act of the God-kind of faith and was born on the earth. Jesus was the Living Word of God—the Word in flesh form! He was the seed of righteousness that God planted in the earth. Mary dared to believe and receive the seed sent from God.[32]

—CHARLES CAPPS

Additionally, according to Kenyon and all major Word of Faith teachers, Jesus did not just die physically on the cross, he also died spiritually. He essentially died "twice on the Cross."[33] To WF teachers, spiritual death means that Jesus was not just separated from the Father on the cross, but that he also had his nature changed to the nature of Satan—just as Adam's nature had been changed to the nature of Satan when he disobeyed God in the garden. Once Jesus's nature had been changed to the nature of Satan, he literally became the very essence of sin and, as a result, temporarily lost his divinity. This is taught by WF leaders, as we see below:

Here is a picture of the Substitutionary Sacrifice of Christ. In the ninth verse, Isaiah says, "He made his grave with the wicked and with the rich man in his death." The word, "death," is plural in the Hebrew, indicating that Jesus died twice on the cross. He died Spiritually the moment that God laid our Sin upon Him. The moment that "Him who knew no sin became sin."[34]

He is spiritually dead. The worm. He has become what John's Gospel, 3:14, said. "And as Moses lifted up the serpent in the wilderness, even so must the Son of Man be lifted up." He had been lifted up as a serpent. Serpent is Satan.[35]

He is to satisfy the claims of Justice against the human race. He could not do that in His physical life. Sin basically is a spiritual thing, so it must be dealt with in the spirit realm. If Jesus paid the penalty of Sin on the cross, then Sin is but a physical act. If His death paid it, then every man could die for himself. Sin is in the spirit realm. His physical death was but a means to an end.[36]

—E. W. KENYON

Spiritual death means something more than separation from God. Spiritual death also means having Satan's nature. . . . Jesus tasted death—spiritual death—for every man. Sin is more than a physical act; it is a spiritual act. He became what we were, that we might become what He is. . . . Jesus became sin. His spirit was separated from God.[37]

—KENNETH E. HAGIN

The righteousness of God was made to be sin. He accepted the sin nature of Satan in His own spirit. And at the moment that He did so, He cried, "My God, My God, why hast thou forsaken Me? . . ." I said, "Why in the world would you want to put a snake up there—the sign of Satan? Why didn't you put a lamb on that pole?" And the Lord said, "Because it was a sign of Satan that was hanging on the cross."[38]

—KENNETH COPELAND

Somewhere between the time He [Jesus] was nailed to the cross and when He was in the Garden of Gethsemane—somewhere in there—He died spiritually. Personally, I believe it was while He was in the garden.[39]

—FREDERICK K. C. PRICE

The rabbit hole goes even deeper here as WF theology further teaches that Jesus did not offer himself as a complete atoning sacrifice at the cross and did not purchase our redemption there. Rather, he purchased it in hell, where he had to suffer in torment at the hands of Satan and demons for our sins. It was necessary, the WF teachers argue, that Jesus taste spiritual death for every man.

> When Jesus cried, "It is finished!" He was not speaking of the plan of redemption. There were still three days and nights to go through before He went to the throne. . . . Jesus' death on the cross was only the beginning of the complete work of redemption.[40]
>
> —KENNETH COPELAND

> Do you think that the punishment for our sin was to die on a cross? If that were the case, the two thieves could have paid your price. No, the punishment was to go into hell itself and to serve time in hell separated from God. . . . Satan and all the demons of hell thought that they had Him bound. . . . They dragged Him down to the very pit of hell itself to serve our sentence.[41]

> The thing that redeemed us was not Jesus being nailed to the cross. His spirit and soul went into Hades.[42]
>
> —FREDERICK K. C. PRICE

As a result of dying spiritually for the sins of mankind and not for any sins that he himself had committed, Jesus was being held on a technicality until he was reborn in hell. Satan had not realized that Jesus's lease in hell was short term. WF teachers teach that Jesus became the first born-again man, which was necessary in order for his fellowship with the Father to be reconciled after he took on the Satanic sin nature which had alienated him from his Father. Upon being born again, Jesus immediately had his divinity restored and rose again from the dead, having defeated Satan in hell.

> When Jesus died, His spirit was taken by the Adversary, and carried to the place where the sinner's spirit goes when he dies. . . . He is the first born out of spiritual death, the first person who was ever born again. This is a remarkable fact, that Jesus was born again before He was raised from the dead.[43]
>
> —E. W. KENYON

> Why did He need to be begotten, or born? Because He became like we were, separated from God. Because He tasted spiritual death for every man. His

spirit, His inner man, went to hell in our place. Physical death would not remove our sins. He tasted death for every man—spiritual death. Jesus is the first person ever to be born again. Why did His spirit need to be born again? Because it was estranged from God.[44]

—KENNETH E. HAGIN

You have to realize that He went into the pit of hell as a mortal man made sin. But He didn't stay there, thank God. He was reborn in the pit of hell.[45]

The Spirit of God spoke to me and He said, "Son, realize this . . ." He said, "Think this way—a twice-born man whipped Satan in his own domain . . ." He said, "A born-again man defeated Satan, the firstborn of many brethren defeated him." He said, "You are the very image, the very copy of that one. . . . If you had the knowledge of the Word of God that He did, you could've done the same thing, cause you're a reborn man too."[46]

—KENNETH COPELAND

PROSPERITY TEACHING ON REGENERATION, REDEMPTION, INCARNATION, AND DEIFICATION

If Christ, according to WF teachers, had to take on Satan's nature at the cross and die spiritually and physically in order to provide redemption and then be born again, after having suffered as our substitute in hell rather than on the cross, the question becomes: What are the spiritual implications of this redemptive work of Jesus in hell for the believer? According to the most notable WF proponents, including Kenyon, born-again believers have the forfeited dominion of Adam restored, and the substance and nature of God is imparted into their nature, thus restoring deification along with the creative ability of God to speak faith-filled words and speak things into existence. The regenerated believer becomes an individual incarnation of God; they begin to operate in faith rather than from sense, as the believer continues to grow in the understanding of their true identity.

The Son, by taking a human body, forever linked humanity with Deity, proving that Deity can partake of humanity just as much as humanity can partake of Deity. If God has taken over a human body, then men can take over God's Nature and God's Spirit. If Jesus is the union of Deity and humanity, the two forms of life mingling and becoming one then man can partake of God's Nature, God's very Substance and Being and become one in relationship with God.[47]

Every man who has been born again is an Incarnation. The believer is as much an Incarnation as was Jesus of Nazareth.[48]

—E. W. KENYON

Growing into sonship means that you grow in your ability to operate as a "little God" in the earth.[49]

—CREFLO DOLLAR

God is God, He is a Spirit. . . . And He imparted in you when you were born again—Peter said it just as plain, he said, "We are partakers of the divine nature." That nature is life eternal in absolute perfection. And that was imparted, injected into your spirit man, and you have that imparted into you by God just the same as you imparted into your child the nature of humanity. That child wasn't born a whale! [It was] born a human. Isn't that true? Well, now, you don't have a human, do you? No, you are one. You don't have a god in you. You are one.[50]

—KENNETH COPELAND

God created everything; then He made man, Adam, and gave him dominion over all of it. God made it all for His man Adam. He gave Adam dominion over the cattle on a thousand hills, over the silver and gold, over the world and the fullness thereof. In other words, Adam was the god of this world. But Adam committed high treason and sold out to Satan. Thus, Satan became the god of this world. . . . Jesus, however, came to redeem us from Satan's power and dominion over us. Romans 5:17 says, "For if by one man's offence death reigned by one; much more they which receive abundance of grace and of the gift of righteousness shall reign in life by one, Jesus Christ . . ." We are to reign as kings in life. . . . That means that we have dominion over our lives. We are to dominate, not be dominated. Circumstances are not to dominate us. We are to dominate circumstances. Poverty is not to rule and reign over us. We are to rule and reign over poverty. Disease and sickness are not to rule and reign over us. We are to rule and reign over sickness. We are to reign as kings in life by Christ Jesus, in whom we have redemption.[51]

—KENNETH E. HAGIN

FAITH FALLACIES IN PROSPERITY TEACHING

Because WF proponents teach that God is a faith being and exercised his faith through words, they also teach that man, who was made in the god class, has the same ability and can therefore create or speak things into existence through positive confession. This is an idea that Kenyon borrowed from New Thought and attempted to syncretize with the biblical concept of faith. The prosperity gospel views faith as a force which causes spiritual laws to function.

Word of Faith theology (which is rooted in the earlier metaphysical sciences of mind-cure) sees faith as a force that is released through words, similar to the way that the force of electricity flows through conductors like copper or aluminum. WF teachers further interpret Hebrews 11:1 from the KJV, reading "Now faith is the substance of things hoped for, the evidence of things not seen," to mean that faith is the "stuff" that the universe is actually made of, literally the substance God used to create. Interestingly, WF teachers also read the conjunctive "now" as a present-tense adjective which should be read "now faith." This present-tense view is used to teach that we claim or receive right now by faith what is ours rather than having hope (future tense) for what we want to happen. Faith then creates and produces in the seen and visible realm that which is a reality in the unseen and invisible realm.

This view that the words of Christians need to be "faith filled" is one of the reasons that the prosperity gospel is often referred to as Word of Faith theology. The believer, according to their teaching, needs faith to release God's will in a given area such as healing and prosperity. Word of Faith theology believes that the force of faith works by spiritual laws or principles that govern all things, including God! These spiritual laws govern things like prosperity or material wealth and healing, and it is faith that sets these laws in motion. In this view, God works within these laws and is himself limited or restricted to acting according to these laws. Confession, according to WF teachers, is the formula by which the believer releases faith, which in turn produces the results.

Prosperity teachers offer numerous scriptural prooftexts to support the idea that our words are powerful and that we can have whatever we confess. Romans 4:17 is often referenced to support the idea of speaking things into existence, while Mark 11:22–24 is interpreted to mean that we need to have the "God-kind of faith"—faith just like God. By saying what we believe—and if you truly believe it—you will have exactly what you say. Prosperity gospel teachers see faith as working by positive and negative laws, so if you speak negative things, you will have those things also. This is also one of the reasons why WF teachers warn against verbally claiming certain realities like poverty and sickness, which they teach are merely symptoms that we must either accept or reject in order for them to become true. Proverbs 6:2, 18:21, and Matthew 12:37 are used as proof texts to reinforce the teaching that our words produce whatever we speak: from snares, to condemnation, to death. In WF theology, it is equally important for the believer to also have right thinking, which comes through reading and confessing Scripture repeatedly.

The perverted view of faith within WF teachings leads to replacing faith in God with faith in faith. It argues that God is not only a faith being but that he, too, had to trust his own faith and believe that what he said would come to pass. Thus, the believer must also release faith through words and trust his or her faith to work. Confession becomes the magical mantra to get whatever you want according to whatever God has said in his Word that we can have. This is also one of the reasons that WF teachers often use the word *rhema*, distinguishing "*logos* Word," which refers to the written Scripture, from "*rhema* word," which refers to faith expressions such as glossolalia, prophecy, and the spoken word of God to believers.[52] Word of Faith teachers emphasize each person developing their own faith for healing, miracles, and finances rather than depending upon the prayers of the faith evangelist.

Faith is the creative force in man. Faith is the creative force in the Creator. God simply said, 'Let there be . . .'[53]

I began to examine myself and ask the question, "Why is it that people haven't faith in their own faith?" They have faith in my faith. I receive letters from many far away countries asking for prayer. Why? Because the people who ask for prayer haven't confidence in their own faith. For some reason they do not believe in themselves. They do not believe in what Christ has wrought for them, or what they are in Christ.[54]

Remember that your lips give expression to your faith. Your words are your faith. You say, "I believe; I have." Then you thank Him for it. You do not need to see or hear or feel. The Word is your evidence. He says you are, and because He says you are, you are. WHAT I CONFESS, I POSSESS. It took me a long time to see this truth. After I saw it and thought I understood it, I still could not act upon it. Christianity is called "the great confession." The law of that confession is that I confess I have a thing before I consciously possess it.[55]

—E. W. KENYON

Confession is faith's way of expressing itself. Faith's confession creates reality. It is always possible to tell if a person is believing right by what he says. If his confession is wrong, his believing is wrong. If his believing is wrong, his thinking is wrong. If his thinking is wrong, it is because his mind has not been renewed with the Word of God.[56]

Jesus used the fig tree to demonstrate that He had that God-kind of faith, then He said to the disciples—and to us—"You have that kind of faith." . . . Jesus said He had the God-kind of faith; He encouraged His disciples to exercise that kind of faith; and He said that "whosoever" could do it. . . . That is why Jesus said, "whosoever shall say . . . and shall not doubt IN HIS HEART."[57]

—KENNETH HAGIN

If you can remember this law, and make it part of your daily life, it will guarantee your success. The law I am referring to is this: Your faith will never rise above the level of your confession. In other words, your faith is governed by your confession. If you confess doubt, that is where your faith will operate—at the level or in the area of doubt. Your words will determine where your faith operates.[58]

—FREDERICK K. C. PRICE

Spiritual law gave birth to physical law. The world and the physical forces governing it were created by the power of faith—a spiritual force. God, a Spirit, created all matter and he created it with the force of faith. . . . Faith is a spiritual force, a spiritual energy, a spiritual power. It is this force of faith which makes the laws of the spirit world function.[59]

As a born-again believer, you are equipped with the Word. You have the power of God at your disposal. By getting the Word deep into your spirit and speaking it boldly out your mouth, you release spiritual power to change things in the natural circumstance.[60]

—KENNETH COPELAND

Some think that God made the earth out of nothing, but He didn't. He made it out of something. The substance God used was faith. . . . He used His words as a carrier of that faith.[61]

—CHARLES CAPPS

PROSPERITY TEACHING ON SICKNESS, HEALTH, FINANCES, AND MATERIAL WEALTH

"Prosperity," according to most proponents of the Word of Faith movement, refers to the spiritual blessings of Ephesians 1:3 to which every believer has a right. If positively confessing faith just as God did in creation is the emphasis of Word of Faith doctrine, then prosperity, health, wealth, and success are the end goals. The formula of faith and financial "seed sowing" are the two primary ways that believers are taught to appropriate and claim the blessings that belong to them already. Much of the teaching surrounding the prosperity gospel is focused upon believers "learning" to walk in their identity, understanding their position and authority in Christ, and learning their "rights."

Word of Faith teachers claim that the covenant that God made with Abraham (Gen. 12, 15, 17, and 22) is primarily about material blessing and that Christians, who by means of faith in Christ become joint heirs with Christ, receive or inherit the blessing of Abraham (Gal. 3:14). The prosperity gospel teaches that the new covenant, which Jesus provided in the atonement, removes the curses of sin, sickness, and poverty. As we have explored above, the basis upon which the Word of Faith teachers uphold their views of prosperity is the teaching that people are created in God's class, that God uses faith-spoken words to create, and that every born-again believer has the same ability of God to release their creative faith through positive confessions.

Prosperity gospel preachers also falsely proclaim that because healing and wealth are provided for in the atonement, health and material prosperity is God's will for every believer. Those who do not appropriate their blessings by faith are forfeiting the rights to what already belongs to them and living beneath their rights and privileges. Prayer is not asking God if anything in particular be his will, but rather reminding God of his promises. Since God is legally bound to his Word and to the spiritual laws that govern faith, he must make provision for what you have asked in faith, believing that you will receive it. Believers are taught to only make positive confessions until the blessing manifests from the spiritual into the physical; they are taught to resist the urge to "claim" by negative confession symptoms of sickness or conditions of poverty, which don't legally belong to believers but rather to Satan. According to WF teachers, Jesus, who was rich in heaven, became poor in the incarnation so that we might become materially rich. Likewise, Jesus also "became sin and sickness" for us so that we might be healed and enjoy physically healthy lives.

> Jesus was made sick with our sicknesses. He was made sin with our sin. This was God's method of dealing with the sin problem. He settled the sin problem. There is no sin problem. Christ put sin away, and satisfied the claims of justice for man. The real problem is the "sinner problem." There is no sickness problem. There is simply a problem of the believer's coming to know his inheritance in Christ.[62]

> He wants us to know in the second place, that sickness and disease do not belong in the Family of God. If there should be any sickness among us, it is because of a low state of knowledge of our rights and privileges in our Redemption. It is due to a lack of knowledge of the fact that God, by laying our diseases on Christ, has settled the disease problem in Redemption. We should be as free from the fear of sickness as we are free from the condemnation of sin. Both are of the adversary. At the New Birth, sins are all remitted. The sin nature is displaced by the nature of God. Disease leaves with the sins.[63]
>
> —E. W. KENYON

I am fully convinced—I would die saying it is so—that it is the plan of Our Father God, in His great love and in His great mercy, that no believer should ever be sick; that every believer should live his full life span down here on this earth; and that every believer should finally just fall asleep in Jesus.[64]

—KENNETH HAGIN

It's a matter of your faith. You got one-dollar faith, and you ask for a ten thousand-dollar item, it ain't gonna work. It won't work. Jesus said, "According to your faith," not "according to His will, if He can work it into His busy schedule." He said, "according to your faith be it unto you." Now I may want a Rolls Royce and don't have but bicycle faith. Guess what I'm going to get? A bicycle.[65]

—FREDERICK K. C. PRICE

You must realize that it is God's will for you to prosper. This is available to you, and frankly, it would be stupid of you not to partake of it.[66]

Sadly, many Christians have been falsely accusing God of being the cause of their troubles. They wrongly believe that trials and tribulations are God's tools for developing and strengthening our character. . . . This is absolutely against the Word of God. Why? Because the very basic principle of the Christian life is to know that God put our sin, sickness, disease, sorrow, grief and poverty on Jesus at Calvary. For God to put any of this on us now to teach us or to strengthen our faith would be a miscarriage of justice. To believe that God has a purpose for sickness would mean that Jesus bore our sickness in vain. What an insult to His love, care and compassion for us![67]

—KENNETH COPELAND

The Lord redeemed us from sickness just as much as He redeemed us from sin. He would no more want us to be sick than He would want us to sin. Those are radical statements to many Christians because we've been taught that forgiveness of sins is what salvation is all about. Well that's certainly a vital part of salvation, but that's not all that Jesus accomplished. We were also healed by His stripes. Sickness is not of God just as sin is not of God. Thank You, Jesus![68]

Here's another indispensable basic truth you must know and understand about healing: It's never God's will for us to be sick; He wants every person healed every time. That's nearly-too-good-to-be-true news, but that's the Gospel. Most Christians don't know or believe that. They think the Lord makes them sick, or at the very least, He allows Satan to make them sick to either punish or correct them. That kind of thinking will get you killed; it's not what the Bible teaches.[69]

—ANDREW WOMMACK

When we pray, believing that we have already received what we are praying, God has no choice but to make our prayers come to pass.[70]

—CREFLO DOLLAR

Give $10 and receive $1,000; give $1,000 and receive $100,000; . . . in short, Mark 10:30 is a very good deal.[71]

—GLORIA COPELAND

God has already done everything He's going to do. The ball is now in your court. If you want success, if you want wisdom, if you want to be prosperous and healthy, you're going to have to do more than meditate and believe; you must boldly declare words of faith and victory over yourself and your family.[72]

—JOEL OSTEEN

CAPITALISTIC CHRISTIAN SYNCRETISM

While the Word of Faith movement represents the largest expression of what is termed the prosperity gospel, it is not the only form. American capitalism has imbued Christianity with a more subtle—yet perhaps even more pervasive—type of prosperity gospel. It is the notion that following Jesus necessarily results in positive outcomes for the believer, as evident in the popularity of texts like Philippians 4:13 and Jeremiah 29:11. It presents to the world a Jesus who in effect only cares for marginally wealthy and middle-class Christians. The "blessings" that this type of prosperity gospel offers are not available in many parts of the world where Christians walk out their faith in Christ in hostile, deplorable conditions of poverty and persecution.

Without subscribing to the errant doctrines of Kenyon and Hagin, this more subtle form of prosperity theology thrives in even the most theologically conservative churches. It accepts the idea that one aspect of the abundant life Christ offers is a general happiness or well-being, a state of entitlement as children of God to material blessings. The "rugged individualism" of Hoover somehow became the hermeneutical lens of the average American believer who heard Scripture preached and learned to read Scripture more from the perspective of individual application rather than the collective and communal sense. Hence, the New Testament letters are read with greater concern for the individual believer's particular circumstances than the good of the community.

PROSPERITY IN THE AFRICAN AMERICAN CONTEXT

Health and wealth peddlers have often targeted Black communities because their message is particularly attractive to the poor, oppressed, and underserved populations. In African American communities, the result is often the opposite of what WF teachers promise: those who teach this false gospel become wealthy by convincing the desperate and needy that if only they give a certain amount, sacrifice their last, and make sure that the prophets' needs are met first, then—and only then—will God perhaps relieve their economic plight and bring justice to the unfairness and economic disparities that racism created.

The Reverend Frederick J. Eikerenkoetter (1935–2009), better known as Reverend Ike, was the prototypical Black prosperity gospel preacher. Like Kenyon before him, he employed a syncretism of spiritualism, metaphysical science, self-help, and Christianity in his preaching. He tended to blatantly disregard Scripture, often openly disagreeing with Scripture in favor of his own maxims: "The lack of money is the root of all evil," "Never say money is hard to get; money will hear you, and that's just what she'll be," "The best thing you can do for the poor is not be one of them," and "You can't lose with the stuff I use!"

Reverend Ike amassed a following of millions nationwide with his radio broadcasts and became a multimillionaire by selling a pseudo-Christianity to Black people he called "the Science of Living." Cloaked in a false prosperity gospel, he taught his poor followers to utilize the power of positive thinking based on Norman Vincent Peale's teaching and New Thought. He urged his followers to visualize and actualize the life they want to live. Rev. Ike provided the false hope that if only his followers change the way they think and tap into the power of the mind, they too could attract success and wealth and change their circumstances for the better.

Milmon Harrison, associate professor of African American and African Studies at the University of California, Davis, in his book *Righteous Riches: The Word of Faith Movement in Contemporary African American Religion*, offered an insider's perspective of life within the Word of Faith movement. Harrison found that many of the interviewees that came from more traditional churches were drawn to WF/Prosperity churches because they were looking for something "more." Harrison found that the following characteristics of Prosperity teaching appealed to African Americans:

1. A focus on the here and now as opposed to the by-and-by
2. An emphasis on prosperity
3. An emphasis on self-development
4. An emphasis on self-actualization
5. An emphasis on self-empowerment
6. An emphasis on control over one's own life and circumstances[73]

In addition, the economic and social effects of racism make the prosperity gospel attractive to Black people, many of whom are Christians seeking churches that understand the need to contextualize the Word of God and the gospel to their specific issues and situations. This is one of the reasons that African American Prosperity teachers like Frederick K. C. Price, Creflo Dollar, I. V. Hilliard, and Bill Winston have had incredible success as profiteers by preaching the prosperity gospel in the Black community. They have made millions by selling others on the idea that if only their followers would "work their faith," sow financial seeds, and tithe faithfully, God will perform supernatural debt cancellations, job promotions, and grant financial prosperity and increase. Black American Word of Faith members come to believe this will help them close the wealth gap and overcome economic poverty, which is a curse. It is not difficult for them to conclude that if the poorest people are Black, then Black people are also the most cursed people.

ANSWERING THE PROSPERITY GOSPEL

Many members of prosperity gospel churches, including many in the Black community, have had their faith shipwrecked. They struggle to understand why the faith message didn't work for them, and they are left disillusioned and disgraced after they have given significant earnings and life savings in hopes of being able to reap the increase that Prosperity teachers offer. What happens to the subscriber of Word of Faith theology when the sick die or they experience financial distress, despite their positive confessions and giving? Their fellow church members might tell them, "Well, I can only speak for myself, but it worked for me." Others will say, "You obviously lacked faith or doubted somewhere." Yet still others will say, "Whatever happened, I don't know, but the Word of Faith is true no matter what, and I choose to stand on it!"

This can be incredibly harmful, and it is not rooted in biblical truth. Sadly, among adherents of the prosperity gospel we see the promises of wealth and prosperity overshadowing the greater truth of our sanctification, justification, and God's love. It is a self-centered theology that negates justice and fails to take seriously the effects of socioeconomic injustices on poor communities. The Bible provides wonderful perspective on these matters of justice that the body of Christ needs to hear. We must be involved with meeting one another's needs, especially in times of hardship and suffering. Yet the teachers of the prosperity gospel rarely speak about the reality of suffering, the problem of evil, or the persecution of Christians. They replace the gospel of God with a gospel of self.

It can be difficult to engage with those who stubbornly hold to a false gospel, but it's worth the effort to bring people to the truth about God. In the following paragraphs, we'll provide some pointers for engaging with those influenced by prosperity gospel teachings.

DOES GOD HAVE FAITH?

Prosperity gospel preachers espousing Word of Faith theology teach that God has faith based on misinterpretations of Mark 11:22 and Hebrews 11:3. These false interpretations are easily corrected by looking at the grammatical construction of the Greek words that make up these verses.

Mark 11:22

Prosperity gospel teachers argue that in Mark 11:22 the words *echete pistin theou* should be translated as "Have the God-kind of faith." The noun *theou* ("God") in this verse is in the genitive or the possessive case. A genitive can be either subjective or objective. In this case, if the genitive is subjective, then God would be the subject of faith, resulting in the translation "Have the faith [or even "faithfulness"] of God" or "Have God's faith." If the genitive is objective, then God is the object of the action implied in the noun *pistis* ("faith"), resulting in the translation "Have faith in God." Every Greek New Testament grammarian translates *theou* in this verse as an objective genitive.

Hebrews 11:3

Hebrews 11:3a reads, "By faith we understand that the universe was created by the word of God" (CSB). The WF interpretive reading connects "by faith" and "by the word of God" together with "created" in order to support their doctrine that God not only has faith but that he spoke the Word to communicate *his* faith. Grammatically and theologically, this is impossible as the text is telling us that it is by faith that *we* understand that God created the universe by his Word. God is not the one with faith in this passage; we have faith in the God who spoke creation into being!

Ironically for Prosperity teachers, Romans 4:17c identifies Abraham's God as "*the one who gives life to the dead and calls things into existence that do not exist.*" This verse completely undermines the Prosperity doctrine of speaking things into existence because it stresses that it was not Abraham or any born-again person that has this ability to create *ex nihilo* (out of nothing) but God alone. We are to believe in God's ability, not our own. It is wrong to have "*faith in our own faith*" rather than faith in God.

The view that God has faith challenges both God's sovereignty and his omnipotence, since faith means to trust. God need not put his trust in himself, and certainly there is none greater than he. God simply acts out of his divine sovereign prerogative (Isa. 45:1–25).

WHAT IS BIBLICAL FAITH?

Since we have addressed the false teaching that God doesn't have faith, we can be assured that there is nothing like what the WF teachers describe as the "God-kind of faith." However, the question remains: What *is* faith? Hebrews

11, a chapter that prosperity gospel teachers are fond of manipulating, provides us with both descriptions and characteristics of biblical faith. Verse 1 tells us that "Faith is the assurance of things hoped for, the conviction of things not seen" (NASB95), which corrects the false idea taught by the faith teachers that faith is an invisible substance or the "basic stuff" out of which the universe is made.

Faith is not a force because the writer here clearly tells us that faith is the *assurance* of the hope—"Faith gives substance to what is hoped for" in the objective sense rather than in the subjective sense. Faith is therefore being assured that the object of what is hoped for (God's promises) will come to pass. Another way of putting it is that faith is being assured that God making good on his promises is based on absolute certainty rather than uncertainty. Faith is trusting that God's promises are true even when we don't see them. It is the evidence or the conviction of things not seen. We are convinced that the unseen realities are true because they are rooted in God's trustworthiness.

It is therefore by faith that we understand that the universe was created by the word of God (Heb. 11:3). It is not faith that gives reality to creation here but rather God. The overarching view of faith in Hebrews 11 is reliance upon and trust in God *in the sense of fidelity and firmness.*[74] Absolutely nothing in Scripture speaks of faith as a force or even a container for our words; this is an invention rooted in New Thought, not God's Word. Faith is not invisible stuff that creates what we speak. Rather, faith is trusting God, period, regardless of the outcome.

IS HEALTH AND WEALTH A RIGHT GUARANTEED ALL BELIEVERS IN THE ATONEMENT?

Prosperity gospel preachers fallaciously teach, based on Galatians 3:14, that the blessings of Abraham are material blessings that every believer inherits by faith in Christ. The second clause of that same verse explains that the blessing is the promise of the Spirit, which we receive through faith. The promise is the Spirit, the new birth or regeneration—by which God promised to Abraham that all nations would be blessed (Gen. 18:18) through Abraham's seed. Paul explains that this refers not merely to Israel, but more specifically to Christ. The blessing here refers to salvation, not to an inheritance of material blessings that we have a right to claim from God. This is confirmed by Paul in Ephesians 1:3–14, where we are taught that the spiritual blessings are not as the Prosperity teachers claim—material blessings in spiritual form waiting to manifest upon positive faith confession—but rather the promised Spirit, which we receive when we believe the gospel.

Additionally, the curse of the law referred to in Galatians 3:13, "*Christ redeemed us from the curse of the law*" (NASB95), does not, as Hagin taught, refer to the specific curses mentioned in Deuteronomy 28 but rather, as Paul argued, to the judgment of God as a consequence of human sin. This is a curse which those who rely upon works of the law rather than faith are clearly under because of their moral inability to do everything commanded in the law. What we have been redeemed from is the incurred judgment of God that comes along with failure to be perfectly obedient to Him, which is why Paul argues in Galatians 3:11 that those who are righteous live by faith (Hab. 2:4). Our faith in the person and faithful life/work of Christ rather than our reliance upon the law is the basis of our redemption from the curse. As redeemed believers, we are freed from the penalty of sin, but the effects of the fall (the moral influence/presence of sin, sickness, disease, and death) remain with us until Christ returns a second time to establish a new heavens and new earth and to bring about our physical glorification (Rom. 8:21, 23, 25; Rev. 21:1–5). Further, the curses and blessings of Deuteronomy 28 were placed upon Israel as a corporate nation not upon specific individuals, and those were applied by God not by Satan.

The problem with the prosperity gospel's insistence that wealth and health is our right as guaranteed by the atonement is *not* the idea that this provision is made in the atonement. The redemptive metanarrative of Scripture tells us that everything we will ever receive from God was secured in the work of Christ at the cross. This includes the promise that the believer will ultimately have health and prosperity. However, the full scope of redemption won't be realized until we experience glorification in our bodies and live in the new earth (1 Cor. 15:42–45; 51–54). Until then, the healing presently provided in the atonement is our justification and forgiveness of our sin. This is what is in the immediate purview of Isaiah 53:4–6. While Prosperity teachers claim that healing, heath, and wealth is our entitlement right now because the curse has been lifted, they never include death as part of the curse that has been lifted. Why? Because it is evident that death is the final form of sickness and all still die, including the redeemed. Just as the redemptive work of Christ does not prevent the physical death of believers, it does not guarantee that all believers will be healed, be healthy, or have wealth in abundance prior to the second coming of Jesus.

There are several other passages that Prosperity teachers commonly cite or refer to, but a careful examination of their context reveals that these passages are being misused.

- *"Dear friend, I pray that you are prospering in every way and are in good health, just as your whole life is going well" (3 John 2 CSB).*

  John here is expressing his hope that his friend Gaius is doing well in every way, which is not a promise of God or even a doctrine expressing that this is God's will for every believer. The expression "I pray that you are prospering in every way" is a standard letter-writing greeting not only in antiquity but also in our contemporary world.
- *"For you know the grace of our Lord Jesus Christ: Though he was rich, for your sake he became poor, so that by his poverty you might become rich" (2 Cor. 8:9 CSB).*

  In context, Paul is here testing the authenticity of the Corinthian believers' love for him by their willingness to be sacrificial in their giving by appealing to the example of the Macedonian church and to the merciful love of Christ toward humanity as exhibited in his incarnated life. The richness of Christ does not refer to Jesus wearing designer clothing and having material wealth, but rather to his preexistent state in the "form of God" with the Father and Holy Spirit, which he did not exploit or hold onto for his own advantage (Phil. 2:6 CSB). Instead, Jesus gives up that state of existence so that he can serve the needs of humanity (2:7). The glory and equality he shared with the Father (Phil. 2:6; John 17:5) are the riches of which Paul speaks. His poverty refers not to his economic status on earth but to his incarnation—his taking on the form of a servant and the likeness of humanity (Phil. 2:7). It is precisely because Christ empties himself that we receive the riches of spiritual blessings (1 Cor. 1:4–5; Eph. 1:3–8).
- *"Truly I tell you," Jesus said, "there is no one who has left house or brothers or sisters or mother or father or children or fields for my sake and for the sake of the gospel, who will not receive a hundred times more, now at this time—houses, brothers and sisters, mothers and children, and fields, with persecutions—and eternal life in the age to come" (Mark 10:29–30 CSB).*

What Jesus means here could not possibly be that if we sow into the kingdom a certain amount of money, we receive one hundred times that amount in return. A wooden literal interpretation is impossible here without concluding that believers who have lost houses can expect one hundred houses in return. The idea here is that Jesus makes up the sufficiency of everything that we sacrifice here in this life as a result of following him, which was the core of Peter's concern in Mark 10:28. Jesus provides one hundred times the affection and love that we lose from family members and one hundred times the security from loss of land and houses—not only in this life but also in the age to come. Jesus states that what comes along with this promise is persecution (10:30), which is far from the ideal that WF teachers attempt to communicate using this verse.

- *"For the thing I feared has overtaken me, and what I dreaded has happened to me" (Job 3:25 CSB).*

The case of Job stands in sharp repudiation and condemnation of the prosperity gospel. WF proponents cite this text as support for the idea that the sufferings of Job were brought upon him by his own negative confession. However, this is the furthest thing from the truth. First, it is not Satan who causes Job's sufferings; it is God who approaches Satan and employs him to test the faithfulness of Job (1:6–12). Second, Prosperity teachers claim that negative confessions are doubts, which are the result of a lack of faith, which in turn is sin. However, the Bible tells us that Job at no point during his testing sins against God (1:21–22; 2:10). In fact, Job's response to his grief-stricken wife's advice to "curse God and die!" is quite instructive here to Word of Faith teachers and their followers. Job says, "Should we accept only good from God and not adversity?" (CSB). The teaching that believers are redeemed from having to experience sickness and poverty denies not only the sovereignty of God but the actual experiences of God's faithful children who went about, as the writer of Hebrews states, "in sheepskins, in goatskins, destitute, afflicted" (Heb. 11:37 CSB). What the Prosperity teachers want in reality is to accept only the good that comes from God while denying adversity, which they claim comes from the devil. Interestingly, the word "destitute" in Hebrews 11:37 means "to lack or to be in want or need"—the very thing the Faith teachers claim that you never need to experience because you have legal rights and entitlement to wealth so long as you work the faith formula successfully.

- *"Brothers and sisters, take the prophets who spoke in the Lord's name as an example of suffering and patience. See, we count as blessed those who have endured. You have heard of Job's endurance and have seen the outcome that the Lord brought about—the Lord is compassionate and merciful. . . . Is anyone among you suffering? He should pray. Is anyone cheerful? He should sing praises. Is anyone among you sick? He should call for the elders of the church, and they are to pray over him, anointing him with oil in the name of the Lord. The prayer of faith will save the sick person, and the Lord will raise him up; if he has committed sins, he will be forgiven" (James 5:10–11, 13–15 CSB).*

As James points out, believers should expect to experience sufferings, which include sickness and disease, in this life, just as many of the Lord's prophets experienced. It is their suffering with endurance that James argues is worthy of imitation. James then uses Job's endurance as a second example, which strikes to the heart of his point. Prosperity teachers will argue that Christians can and will experience suffering such as persecution but should not accept poverty and sickness. Interestingly, part of Job's suffering is physical illness (Job 2:7–8). Again, Satan is merely the agent of the sufferings of Job, not the cause of Job's sufferings. God uses them as a means of testing Job's faithfulness (Job 1:8; 42:11). As indicated by James, believers should seek out the prayers of the elders when they are sick or suffering, and the elders will pray collectively over the believer. The text does not say that the elders "command" healing, nor does it say that believers are taught to confess healing Scriptures and believe that they will receive healing. It says the prayer of faith shall save the sick— that God, by means of prayer, heals the sick. Any true prayer of faith will always include acknowledgment of God's sovereignty in all situations. Believers should ask God in prayer earnestly for healing; they should also trust God's wisdom and sovereignty even when healing is not the result.

GETTING THE GOSPEL RIGHT

The good news is not material wealth, health, and healing as a benefit and right of the believer. The good news is that those deserving of God's wrath can, by faith in Jesus, have their sins paid for and removed and be declared righteous before God on the basis of Jesus's perfect obedience to the Father. Jesus was not born again, he never took on Satan's nature, he did not literally become sin, he did not die spiritually, and he did not actually suffer in hell as our substitute. To save us from spiritual death, Jesus died physically for our sins, and every reference to his death refers to his physical sufferings and expiration (1 Cor. 15:3; 1 Pet. 2:24; Heb. 9:28).

Jesus's nature was not changed from divine to Satanic. This is a blasphemous and heretical notion. Paul states in 2 Corinthians 5:21 that "he made the one who did not know sin to be sin for us, so that in him we might become the righteousness of God" (CSB) to explain that Christ was made our sin offering. In other words, Christ was made to bear the consequences of our sin, not to actually become sinful. If Christ had become sin and had his divine nature changed, then we no longer have a gospel, because at no time does Christ cease from being both fully God and fully man yet remain sinless (Heb. 4:15; 1 Pet. 2:22). Also, Jesus is not referred to by God the Father as being sinful but as his "righteous servant" (Isa. 53:11 CSB).

The false idea that Jesus was reborn in hell is taught nowhere in Scripture. A quick examination of the proof texts that Prosperity teachers use would make any responsible exegete of Scripture scratch their heads in bewilderment as to how they arrived at such wild conclusions. First Peter 3:18 says, *"He was put to death in the flesh but made alive by the Spirit"* (CSB). But this does not support the idea that Jesus was reborn after having died spiritually. Jesus's death is stated here to be physical. Being made alive by the Spirit does not refer to his spirit receiving life but to his physical body being raised to life by the Holy Spirit. The new birth is a regenerative work of the Holy Spirit for those who are spiritually dead, and if Jesus died spiritually, he could not have offered himself as a sacrifice for our sins, as he would've needed salvation himself.

If Jesus were in fact separated from the Father on the cross as Prosperity teachers allege, according to Matthew 27:46, Mark 15:34, Psalm 22:1–24, it refers not to actual separation but rather to Jesus's emotional suffering, which made him feel forsaken. The doctrine of the Trinity, particularly the *perichoresis* (mutual indwelling) of the persons of the Godhead (John 14:11, 20), means that at no time could Jesus ever be separated from the Father and the Holy Spirit, not during his incarnation and not even in death. In doing so, the eternal and unchanging God would cease to be God.

Finally, Jesus as the firstborn from the dead according to Colossians 1:18 does not refer to him being the first person born again. Rather, the word *prōtotokos* means that Christ is supreme and preeminent over all creation and, by way of his resurrection, preeminent even over those who have died and are awaiting resurrection from the dead. Teaching that firstborn from the dead means spiritual rebirth is as heretical as Arius's teaching in the fourth century that there was a time when Jesus did not exist but was the first created by God the Father.

CONCLUSION: AN ANTIGOSPEL

The prosperity gospel is no gospel at all. It's an antigospel that works against Christians who want to develop their character through a biblical lens. It creates an untenable works-based approach to God that overpromises and under delivers. Jesus calls Christians to deny ourselves and follow him. The prosperity gospel offers a promise that does not deal with the reality of brokenness, hurt, sickness, or pain. Instead, it produces greed and lust for consumption and self-satisfaction. This also creates cognitive dissonance for people and keeps them mired in poverty because they have to keep sowing and giving in the hopes of getting more. Many people walk away from God after suffering the disappointment and then anger of false and broken promises.

Any Christian would do well to avoid the prosperity gospel and churches associated with it, and Black Christians should be especially aware of the negative effects of these teachings within their communities. The erosion of true biblical faith is an inevitable result of the "Word of Faith" and replaces our trust in God and his sovereignty. It leads us to misuse and undervalue Scripture and results in an unorthodox understanding of the gospel and Christology, encouraging Christians to see themselves as little gods and incarnations of God. It wrongly leads us to believe we have God's ability to create by the power of faith-filled words and that somehow we can force God's hand rather than seeking God earnestly in prayerful supplication and humility.

TWELVE

DETOXING FROM CULTS

ERIC MASON

In the movie *New Jack City*, Chris Rock plays the iconic role of a crackhead named Pookie. Pookie is the quintessential neighborhood guy swept into the smoking base during the 80s crack pandemic. Deep on drugs, he is given an opportunity to get clean with the help of an undercover cop named Scotty. It is painful to watch him go through the agony of detoxing from crack cocaine. He is in constant misery, craving the very thing he knows is destroying him. Entering detox, he utters an iconic statement: "It be calling me."

When you leave a cult, it can feel a bit like detoxing from an addictive drug: it's possible, but very painful. *Detoxing* is a term that refers to the removal of material that is poisonous or harmful to the body, such that it can lead to death or serious debilitation. Those who belong to a cult have often been wooed into turning off their critical alarms and the voices of those in their community in order to embrace something that seems to supply a need or satisfy an intense longing. Like a drug, it affects the way we perceive reality, often lulling us into a state of thinking things are great, when in reality our minds and hearts are being deceived. Having our sensibilities replaced and retrained in this way is not the way God designed us to operate. To escape from a cult, our brain must be emotionally and psychologically rewired, and that is deep— and often painful—work.

PARTNERING WITH GOD IN THE PROCESS OF DETOXING

A bug was imbedded under the scalp of a young man. When his family found out, they immediately wanted to get some tweezers and pull it out. However, a family member who is a nurse practitioner stopped them. She explained that, because of the type of creature it is, they needed to go to the emergency room. The medical team in the ER began to investigate, and as they began to work, they said they must do the extraction slowly to ensure the insect didn't bore even more deeply into the body. Additionally, they wanted to be able to extract the entire thing. If they pulled it out too quickly, they might leave parts behind, and while the outside would heal up there was a risk the inside would be infected.

Cult detoxing must also be done with an enormous amount of care. Preferably, we want to take a noninvasive approach. What does that mean? People will engage their fight-or-flight response if the process is too much for them. They may even be aware that they are in need of help, but they are still deeply programmed by the cult's philosophy. Always remember that detoxing is a process, not a one-time event.

People who are lost in cults have often been brainwashed through a process of grooming and spiritual manipulation. They may have grown numb to God's truth in the gospel and to other biblical truths, and they likely need God to supernaturally intervene. They need God's Holy Spirit by the power of the gospel to break the bonds in which they are tied. Without the presence of the Spirit to enable divine breakthrough, helping people separate themselves from a cult can be futile work.

I've had a taste of this firsthand. During my college years I was sucked into some Black mystery ideologies and spiritualities. Though I didn't fully commit to any of them, I knew they promoted the idea that Christianity wasn't compatible with being Black. At the time, several of us were feeling drawn to their message. At our college we felt the "dignity gap" and were discovering our "Blackness" for the first time, and it was exhilarating. But there was something that held me back. I never felt fully comfortable in the conscious community. Their affirmation of Black dignity was amazing and powerful, but there was so much obvious misinformation and fallacious reasoning. Through my reading and relationships at the time, I could sense the Lord nurturing me and holding me back from becoming invested in their message. On November 15, 1992, I trusted Jesus despite all of the obstacles still clinging to my soul. Another, even deeper encounter in the Lord's presence later sealed it for me.

In Acts 19:18–20 we read about the Ephesians having an encounter with God. Prior to this section, God had used Paul to confound the spiritual evil in that city. Some Jewish exorcists had attempted to use the name of Jesus, and the spirits had turned on them. Luke records: "When this became known to everyone who lived in Ephesus, both Jews and Greeks, they became afraid, and the name of the Lord Jesus was held in high esteem" (Acts 19:17 CSB). Those who participated in the Ephesian mystery cults had their wills broken because they witnessed the might of God's power in the gospel. Again, Luke describes what happened,

> And many who had become believers came confessing and disclosing their practices, while many of those who had practiced magic collected their books and burned them in front of everyone. So they calculated their value and found it to be fifty thousand pieces of silver. In this way the word of the Lord spread and prevailed. (Acts 19:18–20 CSB)

In his letter to the Ephesian church, Paul seems to be reminding the Ephesians in 5:8–13 about this experience. He challenges and warns them about it, writing: "Don't participate in the fruitless works of darkness, but instead expose them. For it is shameful even to mention what is done by them in secret" (Eph. 5:11–12 CSB). Paul provides yet more context for the deliverance of the Ephesians who were practicing magic, telling us that many were demon possessed in connection with some form of divination. Keener provides some helpful cultural background:

> Jewish texts often used "light" and "darkness" to contrast good and evil, and Paul milks this image here. Some Greek religious groups known as "mystery cults" emphasized night initiations, and some of them were also connected with sexual immorality; because some Roman critics of all foreign religions associated Christians with immoral cults, Paul has all the more reason to wish to dissociate Christianity from cults he already regards as pagan. People could enact deeds in darkness of which they would have been ashamed in public (cf. Is 29:15; 47:10).[1]

These mystery cults were complex groups within Roman society. Many who converted to Christianity were deeply embedded in these cults, and even after transitioning out of them they still needed to detox from their influence. The process of initiation into the church, including their baptism, would have had a powerful effect on them, and the gospel broke the connection with their past, but there would have still been memories and habits of thinking that needed to be transformed. Many of these cults utilized rituals and reenactments. Again, Keener helpfully provides some background:

"Mystery cults" or "mystery religions" refer to a pattern of religious expression in the Greco-Roman world. The "mysteries" were initiation rituals in which the initiate (*mýstēs*) had an extraordinary experience about which participants were forbidden to speak afterwards. Elements of these rituals (*teletaí*, "completions") could include: *legómena* ("things spoken"), recitations or enactments of ritual words or the myth of the cult deities; *deiknýmena* ("things shown"), cult objects often hidden in a basket; and *dr̂mena* ("things performed"), ritual actions or dramatic enactments. . . . Cult worship was not confined to initiation rituals but also included public ceremonies and personal devotional acts. Initiation was an individual choice, but most cults did not require exclusive loyalty.[2]

Like all forms of religious expression, much of life was oriented around the group, shaping their identity. Detoxing—or transitioning out of that group—would have been a difficult and painful journey for many. While the gospel would redeem them, in Roman society leaving the group would have caused a great amount of loss and reorientation: leaving behind friends, habits, and a lifetime of experiences.

Jesus taught his followers that "the kingdom of God is among us," saying, "Your kingdom come, your will be done, on earth as it is in heaven" (Matt. 6:10). In order to reorient their will and establish a new identity, the people would need *kingdom* experiences. Never forget that in addition to the intellectual and doctrinal component of detoxing, something more is needed. Head knowledge alone isn't enough to transform us. Looking over biblical history—Adam, Eve, Sarah, Abraham, Moses, Gideon, the Twelve, Paul, and many others—God's people were exposed to God's words, but they also had an encounter with him. To change, people need new kingdom experiences.

Our hope is rooted in God's kingdom and his promise of a new age. We eagerly anticipate eternal life with our Lord Jesus Christ. There is much more to our present experience, however, than finding a secure place to wait until Christ returns. The turn of the ages has already dawned with the coming of the Lord Jesus, and the good news is that we can experience some of the blessings of the age to come right now. Eternal life is just as much a present experience as a future aspiration (cf. John 17:3). Some of these kingdom manifestations include the following:[3]

- The empowering presence of the Holy Spirit in our lives
- Union and close relationship with the Lord Jesus Christ
- Reception and manifestation of the gifts of the Holy Spirit
- Ability to break free from the bondage of sin
- Authority over evil spirits

Much of Western apologetics—and even our efforts at urban apologetics—have often overemphasized the intellect rather than comprehensively addressing the whole person. Detoxing the will means retraining the mind, but it cannot be done in a lasting way without new experiences in a new kingdom community. This is what forms our new identity in Christ.

Entering a relationship with Christ means being supernaturally rescued from the kingdom of Satan and installed as a member of Christ's kingdom (Col. 1:13). Believers truly have a new citizenship in a heavenly kingdom (Phil. 3:20). Our identity is wrapped up in Christ; our allegiance is to the kingdom of God; the eschatological reality is that we are now participants in the age to come and part of the new creation; we are joined to the people of God and we are indeed children of God.[4]

STEPS FOR DETOXING THE MIND AND EMOTIONS

The "heart" in the Old Testament was used to refer to the immaterial faculties that make up the human inner self. The heart functions as a metonymy encompassing mind, emotions, and will. The mind often refers to where the values are, while the emotions were the seat of the affections, and the will is where the commitment to what is valued and felt lies. If you change someone's thinking, often their affections will change and then what they do will follow as well. Once the values and affections are co-opted, the will or volition comes with it.

Cults connect with the longings of the unassuming by luring them with knowledge or insight that leads them away from being whom God created them to be to becoming a mental, emotional, and practical slave to the interests of the cult. Indoctrination is often coupled with a felt need being met. The person is told that this ideology or group or spiritual community is the only solution to their need.

Changing the thinking of someone in a cult is like breaking a stronghold. My working definition of a stronghold is a mindset, value system, or thought process that hinders your growth and your exalting Jesus above everything in your life.[5] Strongholds aren't merely things that hold on to us—they are the things we hold on to.[6] A stronghold is a pattern of unrighteousness that holds you hostage outside of the will of God. Strongholds result from something invisible in the spiritual realm cooperating with something visible in the physical realm, keeping a person trapped in an addiction or negative life pattern. Overcoming a stronghold in the physical realm always involves a spiritual solution, because strongholds always have a spiritual cause.[7]

In detoxing, you may need to explore apologetical entryways into each aspect of a person's identity through a variety of activities, habits, and practices. Those who have been under the influence of a cult for a long period of time will have a more difficult time escaping from the effects of the cult on their hearts and identities. For others, it may be easier, especially if they are able to see their obedience to the cult as a form of abuse, if they can recognize the ideologies as illogical, and see the activities of the cult as abhorrent. These all open the door to helping people detox. Never forget that praying and fasting are an important part of helping people begin the detoxing process as well.

In what follows, I want to elaborate on the process of leaving a cult—detoxing—by covering several steps I've modified from chapter 10 of *Combating Cult Mind Control* by Steven Hassan.[8] As helpful as Hassan's book is, it has no theological connections. He draws his principles from general revelation and mental psychology, but they are spot on. The primary difference in what I provide is that our goal in detoxing is more than mere behavioral modification. We want gospel transformation. Here are the seven steps we'll briefly cover.

1. Be prayerful.
2. Build rapport and trust.
3. Engage them with facts and sources and God's truth.
4. Get to the core heart need that the cult attempted to fulfill.
5. Show how the gospel answers their greatest yearnings.
6. Get permission to connect others to help in the engagement process.
7. Let them know that they have a safe place to land.

1. BE PRAYERFUL

Romans 12:12 says to "be persistent in prayer" (CSB). The word translated "persistent" is a present active participle with imperatival force. This portrays an action in process or a state of being with no assessment of the action's completion—meaning this should be our constant disposition.[9] Since the work of helping someone out of a cult is an act of spiritual warfare, we must be consciously dependent on God. Some will only come out by prayer. The idea Paul is communicating to us here is that you are actively doing this, but it's something that will also characterize the believer in all of life. Being prayerful means that we always remember this cannot be done in our own strength.

2. BUILD RAPPORT AND TRUST

Don't make the center of every interaction with the individual about the issues you disagree on. I have family members I've engaged with for many years on a variety of difficult and controversial issues, and one of the ways of practically loving them is simply being a good family member to them. Birthday shout-outs, selfies, encouragement, aid when they need it—all of these things are ways to love them and build rapport and trust. Colossians 4 says, "Devote yourselves to prayer. . . . Act wisely toward outsiders, making the most of the time. Let your speech always be gracious, seasoned with salt, so that you may know how you should answer each person" (Col. 4:2, 5–6 CSB). These verses remind us that in addition to prayer, we should act wisely toward people in our words and actions. Words "seasoned with salt" refer to interesting, stimulating, and enjoyable conversation or discourse.[10] Salt not only flavors, but it slowly breaks things down. It was used to redeem manure as a fertilizer. Loving engagement listens, engages slowly but surely, and utilizes what is learned to help engage the person with the gospel.

3. ENGAGE THEM WITH FACTS AND SOURCES AND GOD'S TRUTH

Godly reasoning means using original sources from history, experiences from your own life, and the sciences where helpful. First Peter 3:15 lets us know we have a reasonable faith. In one cult group, I'm aware of their belief that the earth is flat. While our every conversation shouldn't focus on that issue, there are times when it will need to be touched on as you work through various conspiracies. Don't be surprised to find that most cults have extravagant conspiracy theories. This can be exhausting, but don't lose faith. You will get through it all. But it might take time. Keep pressing the truth.

4. GET TO THE CORE HEART NEED THAT THE CULT ATTEMPTED TO FULFILL

In many cults, especially many in the Black community, the core issue is identity: Who am I? It's a huge life question. Many of those engaged in urban apologetics are good at answering the "what" questions, but then they miss the "who." It is important, particularly with African Americans, to remember that they need the answer to "who" as well. What does this cult reinforce about their identity? What does it teach that meets a need for them in answering the question: Who am I? The doctrines many believe are often driven by identity questions, and you need to understand how the cult answers that question. The doctrine may merely be the caboose, with identity driving the train.

5. SHOW HOW THE GOSPEL ANSWERS THEIR GREATEST YEARNINGS

Ecclesiastes 3:11 tells us that "he has made everything beautiful in its time. He has also set eternity in the human heart; yet no one can fathom what God has done from beginning to end." He has put eternity in their hearts. What does this mean? The NET Bible provides some helpful commentary. Clearly, God has endowed mankind with some form of knowledge ("he has put eternity in [their] heart"), yet God has either somehow obscured man's knowledge or man has been plagued with forgetfulness. There is "knowledge" but not sufficient knowledge to fully understand God's plan. Mankind is plagued with trying to make sense of life and meaning. Only Jesus brings about meaning on every level of life. This is where we have to point people: to the revelation of God's answer to human life and our quest for meaning in the gospel of Jesus Christ.

Listen to the longings they express. Find out what their unique desires and unmet needs are. And then pray that God would help you share how Jesus meets and exceeds those desires. He is better in every way.

6. GET PERMISSION TO CONNECT OTHERS TO HELP IN THE ENGAGEMENT PROCESS

Don't do this work alone. Getting others involved helps in so many ways. There will be times when you have belief gaps or you don't know what to say or how to respond. Others can help you share the love and engagement load. Paul always did his mission work in teams. Even his solo efforts often turned into team mission, like his work in Athens. But do this respectfully, and get permission. The cult member you are working with should be asked if you can have others to connect to talk with them. And don't be afraid of the reverse request. Talk to others from the cult who may be influencing the person you are engaging with. Just make sure you have a spiritual and theological equivalent with you so you won't get destroyed. You don't need to know the answer to every question, but if you are repeatedly defeated and confounded, that will only build confidence in the lost person that the cult is true.

7. LET THEM KNOW THAT THEY HAVE A SAFE PLACE TO LAND

Coming out of cult philosophies and groups can be extremely painful, confusing, and disorienting for people. The pain of manipulation and the loss of time and life can hit hard. People will need support. Some people begin coming out on their own sometimes. They may not need as much help. But others may need massive support, including professional therapy. I've seen many people come out of cultic churches, and they need months or years of therapy just to find a spiritual normal. Also, they need help decluttering what is true from what is false. Something healthy in a healthy environment communicated in a healthy way could still be a trigger for them. Whether its money, marriage, serving, sacrifice, submitting to authority—when you've been in a cult, there are so many things that can trigger you. Detoxing can be a life journey of Jesus helping the person see him as their safe place. We need to help them find healthy community in the local church. They need to be known and to know others as they become a viable kingdom citizen.

CARING FOR THE PERSON

Coming out of a cult can be just as traumatizing—if not more so—than being in the cult. When someone is coming to terms with the fact that their heart, mind, and soul have been enslaved to a huge lie it can be very painful. We have to be patient as people work through it all with God to relearn what is real and what is not. The good news is that God is able to restore anyone to their right mind. We must help those coming out of a cult to deal with their guilt in a healthy way as they progress onward toward recovery.

IT'S SPIRITUAL WARFARE

Though we've mentioned it several times already, never forget that this work is spiritual warfare. In helping bring a person out of a cult or ideology, you may experience mild to intense spiritual attack. Paul states, "Now the Spirit explicitly says that in later times some will depart from the faith, paying attention to *deceitful spirits and the teachings of demons*" (1 Tim. 4:1 CSB, italics added). From Paul's perspective, heterodoxy, heresy, mythology, and other deceitful teachings are promoted by evil spirits that cause people to fall away from the faith. The word "demon" would not have necessarily sounded bad to people in the first century. People used the word to refer to various spiritual beings to whom they sacrificed and who might provide direction. But Paul is clear, stating that such teaching or direction is categorically bad. Instead, he points people to the work of the Spirit.[11] Clinton Arnold states, "Paul's original readers were accustomed to hearing about *daimonia* teaching and guiding people through oracles, prophecy, or in other ways. . . . Paul says that the Holy Spirit himself has *expressly* provided a warning against the teaching of *daimonia*, which are deceiving spirits (see also 1 John 4:1–3)."[12]

Merely engaging at the intellectual, psychological, or emotional level is futile without also recognizing the spiritual reality as well. Treat these issues with a great deal of prayer and fasting. While we must be holistic, we should minimally address spiritual problems with spiritual solutions. While being involved in the work of urban apologetics and engaging individuals who are in Black mystery cults and ideologies, many of us working on challenging and restoring these groups have experienced warfare and attacks, including death threats, our children having night terrors, and unexplained afflictions (often happening to many of us at the same time).

Jesus described the work of engaging the fallen unseen powers as the coming of the kingdom of God. He says, "If I drive out demons by the Spirit of

God, then the kingdom of God has come upon you" (Matt. 12:28 CSB). Robert Stein notes that "Jesus's power to cast out demons proved that the kingdom of God was overthrowing Satan's kingdom. Jesus was tying up the strong man (Satan) so he could plunder his house, or claim Satan's captives as citizens of his own kingdom."[13] But don't be afraid. Acts 1:8 tells us that we will receive power to be Jesus's witnesses. Being a witness of Jesus means more than just speaking; it is the deployment of God's power through his people. We must be dependent on God's power, using the spiritual weapons he has given us for combat. Our hope is that these weapons, properly used in concert with one another, will aid in the release of the bound individual.

KEEP THE LAMP BURNING BRIGHT

ERIC MASON

This book, *Urban Apologetics: Cults and Cultural Ideologies* is a sequel to a previous volume titled *Urban Apologetics*. In that first volume, we sought to deal with the issue of Black dignity and how the gospel restores it. We engaged several means that Blacks seek to use for dignity restoration and showed why many of them appeal to people—even if they only offer a false gospel.

In this volume we've looked at several cults and cultural ideologies that Christians today—especially Black Christians—are encountering. There are so many ideologies and movements, and it is easy to feel overwhelmed. And while we've only given a brief introduction to these topics, our hope is that each essay provides a starting point for discussion and further engagement. The church has to have its eyes wide open today because many of these cultural movements are defining the way people think and act. They are discipling the people in our churches with beliefs that are not aligned with the truth of God's Word.

Today, the LGBTQ movement is saturated into everything we read and view, from art, to entertainment, to education, science, politics, and even our faith. It is here to stay—and its influence is only going to grow more and more mainstream.

Of the movements covered in this book, white Christian national-ism is probably one of the oldest ideologies, dating to the emergence of the evangelical movement in Europe and the founding of America. But today, Christian nationalism—in various forms around the world—has become the face of Christianity in the West for many non-Christians. And again, that is not changing any time soon.

Critical race theory is another topic that is in the news every day, and it is important for us to know what is worth affirming and what is not aligned with the Bible. There are elements of CRT that are helpful in diagnosing problems with systemic racial injustice—especially in the legal sphere. But there are also elements—of critical theory in particular—that cannot be affirmed without serious reservations.

As we saw in the excellent chapter on Black liberation theology, this ideology is not fundamentally wrong or bad. There are parts of it that need to be seriously considered, yet other portions need to be challenged and sifted out. At one time, Blacks who went to get their theological education could sift through some of the more faith-shaking and unorthodox teaching in mainline divinity schools and come out holding to a historic Christian faith. Today, however, we are seeing a different turn in the Black church. Among the many conferences in the Black church community, you see how varied and nonmonolithic the theological thinking in the Black community has become.

In addition to these cultural ideologies, we've looked at several movements that are derivative of the Christian faith—what we might refer to as "cults." Several of these have been gnawing at Blacks in the church I lead and among other churches I know. My reason for choosing these specific cults and cultic ideologies was largely because of their presence in our local urban community. Though we've placed the Seventh-day Adventists and promoters of the prosperity gospel in the section on cults, they aren't typically viewed that way. My hope is that after reading and examining the information provided in these chapters, you will see why I've labeled them this way.

With any cult, the church needs to not only be aware of what that cult is and what it teaches, but how to challenge and defend against it. For many years, I was not aware of the more obscure and hidden teachings of the Seventh-day Adventists. But as we began working on the previous volume, *Urban Apologetics*, several close friends raised some concerns. People started sending me information about the history and present-day beliefs of the movement, and I was floored by what I learned. I had been invited to work with several people in that movement and even invited to speak at an event. Several people warned me that this is all part of their strategy of infiltration. Many groups don't present themselves as a threat, but as a dearly beloved friend.

And the teachings of the prosperity gospel, while perhaps not as clearly a cult, are just as dangerous. They lead people to reject the real gospel and result in massive distrust of the church and its teachings. Just recently, a Prosperity pastor and his wife were robbed at gunpoint on Sunday morning. They were wearing jewelry valued at somewhere between $400,000 and $1,000,000. To make matters worse, a video of the pastor went viral showing off an extravagant prayer closet with multiple rooms. It looked more like a boutique than a place to meet with God. Of course, because our culture loves to see confusion in the church, this video was viral for over a month.

For too long the church in the Black community has allowed certain ideologies to fester. Because we are a grace-heavy community, at times we will apply grace where a robust defense is really what is needed. Churches that are influenced by urban culture—where most of these cults and cultic ideologies dwell—must work to engage them and be able to defend against them.

REBRANDING THE CHURCH

Now is a time when we have to speak clearly and honestly. Our goal is to rebrand the church. When I say "rebrand," I mean the task of re-presenting the church to the world, so those in the world know who she is and so that we represent the name of Jesus well. In the mind of many people, when they think of the church, there are countless caricatures that come to mind. They think "hypocritical," "judgmental," "money-hungry," "womanizing," "racist," "sheepish," and so much more—instead of "loving," "generous," "peacemaking," "hardworking," "sacrificial," "gracious," "kind," and "gentle."

As we rebrand the church, we are working on imaging Jesus well to those who don't know him. My intent isn't to give the impression that we are somehow perfect. I don't think that's what people expect at all. But they do expect us to be real and honest about our failures and to be consistent in practicing what we preach—even when that means confessing our sins and repenting.

Rebranding is something that must be done intentionally not haphazardly. In this I mean that we must ask ourselves the tough questions and put in the hard work.

- What is the church's purpose and mission?
- Whom do we represent?
- What are we trying to accomplish?
- What spells a win?
- Whom does our target audience perceive us to be?
- What qualities should our target audience associate with us?
- What is our product?
- What are our services?

The key question we need to ask is, *How do those we are trying to reach perceive us?* This is the question the body of Jesus in general needs to answer, but also the question each local community needs to answer. We ask this, not in an attempt to play to their desires or give them what they want, but to measure their perception against what God has said the church should be in his Word. Jesus asks his disciples in Matthew 16:13, "Who do people say that the Son of Man is?" (CSB). Even Jesus asked what people thought about him and the work he did. If people get it wrong, we want it to be because they are rejecting the real Jesus, not a misrepresentation of the faith.

We are called to be his witnesses (Acts 1:8). We are the brand ambassadors of Jesus (2 Cor. 5:17–21), tasked with helping people transfer their citizenship from the kingdom of darkness to the kingdom of the Son (Col. 1:11–13). We keep score based on God's desired ends. Our product must lead to life change at *every* level of life, and our service must be rooted in love. My hope in all of this is that God's people are once again inspired to contend for the faith that was delivered to the saints once for all (Jude 3). We must not shrink back from today's cults or cultural ideologies, but lovingly and courageously communicate and walk in biblical convictions by the power of the Holy Spirit. Upon the return of our Savior, may we each be found with our lamp burning bright, bringing light to a dark world.

NOTES

INTRODUCTION

1. Martin Luther King Jr., *Strength to Love* (Boston: Beacon), 11, Kindle.
2. King, *Strength to Love*, 2, Kindle.
3. King, *Strength to Love*, 13, Kindle.
4. King, *Strength to Love*, 16, Kindle.
5. William Arndt, Frederick W. Danker et al., *A Greek-English Lexicon of the New Testament and Other Early Christian Literature* (Chicago: University of Chicago Press, 2000), 202.
6. Timothy Friberg, Barbara Friberg, and Neva F. Miller, *Analytical Lexicon of the Greek New Testament*, Baker's Greek New Testament Library (Grand Rapids: Baker Books, 2000), 100.
7. James Swanson, *Dictionary of Biblical Languages with Semantic Domains: Greek (New Testament)* (Oak Harbor, WA: Logos Research Systems, Inc., 1997).
8. Tony Evans, *Oneness Embraced* (Chicago: Moody, 2015), 218, Kindle.
9. Carl F. Ellis Jr., *Free at Last? The Gospel in the African American Experience*, The IVP Signature Collection (Downers Grove, IL: InterVarsity, 2020), Kindle.

CHAPTER I: REDEEMING THE CULTURE

1. Brittany DiCologero, "Edutainment: What It Means and Why I'm Happy It Exists at Walt Disney World," *The Disney Outpost*, July 1, 2016, https://the disneyoutpost.com/2016/07/01/edutainment-what-it-means-and-why-im-happy -it-exists-at-walt-disney-world/.
2. Harvie Conn, "Genesis as Urban Epilogue," in *Discipling the City: A Comprehensive Approach to Urban Ministry*, ed. Roger S. Greenway (Eugene, OR: Wipf & Stock, 2000), 15.
3. Manuel Ortiz and Harvie M. Conn, *Urban Ministry: The Kingdom, the City & the People of God* (Downers Grove, IL: IVP Accademic), loc. 1009–1011, Kindle.
4. Ortiz and Conn, *Urban Ministry*, loc. 1016, Kindle.

5. Ellis, *Free at Last?*, 26.

6. "Cultural Intelligence: Core vs. Flex," *What Is Culture?*, https://whatisculture .org/?page_id=32.

7. "Cultural Imperialism," *Definitions.net*, https://www.definitions.net/definition /cultural+imperialism#:~:text=Cultural%20imperialism%20is%20defined%20 as%20the%20cultural%20aspects,relationships%20between%20civilizations %20favoring%20the%20more%20powerful%20civilization.

8. Tony Evans, *The Kingdom Agenda: Life under God* (Chicago: Moody, 2013), Kindle.

9. Lois Barrett, *Missional Church: A Vision for the Sending of the Church in North America*, The Gospel and Our Culture Series (Grand Rapids: Eerdmans, 1998), 127, Kindle.

10. Barrett, *Missional Church*, 128, Kindle.

CHAPTER 2: EVALUATING CRITICAL RACE THEORY

1. Jemar Tisby, *The Color of Compromise: The Truth About the American Church's Complicity in Racism* (Grand Rapids: Zondervan, 2019).

2. Scot McKnight, *The King Jesus Gospel: The Original Good News Revisited* (Grand Rapids: Zondervan, 2011), 28–34.

3. Brandon Washington, *A Burning House: Redeeming American Evangelicalism by Examining Its History, Mission, and Message* (Grand Rapids: Zondervan, 2023).

4. Ben Shapiro, "Ep. 29 – Pastor John MacArthur," on *The Ben Shapiro Show*, produced by *The Daily Wire*, December 1, 2018, https://www.dailywire.com /episode/sunday%20special%20ep-29-pastor-john-macarthur.

5. Carl F. H. Henry, *God, Revelation and Authority: God Who Speaks and Shows*, vol. 4 (Wheaton, IL: Crossway, 1999), 551.

6. My colleague Thabiti Anyabwile's astute take can be found in chapter 3 of this volume.

7. Anya Steinberg, "Lawmakers Want to Ban Discomfort in School. But Black History Isn't Always Comfortable," *NPR*, February 24, 2022, https://www .npr.org/2022/02/19/1081987384/teaching-black-history-month-schools-bans -lawmakers-politics.

8. Jacey Fortin, "Critical Race Theory: A Brief History," *The New York Times*, November 9, 2021, https://www.nytimes.com/article/what-is-critical-race -theory.html.

9. Richard Delgado and Jean Stefancic, *Critical Race Theory: An Introduction* (New York: New York University Press, 2017), 3.

10. Delgado and Stefancic, *Critical Race Theory*, 3–4.

11. Richard Delgado and Jean Stefancic, "Introduction," in *Critical Race Theory: The Cutting Edge*, 3rd ed. (Philadelphia: Temple University Press, 2013), 2.

12. See Anthony E. Cook, "Beyond Critical Legal Studies: The Reconstructive

Theology of Dr. Martin Luther King, Jr.," in *Critical Race Theory: The Key Writings that Formed the Movement* (New York: The New Press, 1995), 85–102.

13. See Douglas A. Blackmon, *Slavery by Another Name: The Re-enslavement of Black Americans from the Civil War to World War II* (New York: Doubleday, 2008).

14. Victor Ray, *On Critical Race Theory: Why It Matters & Why You Should Care* (New York: Random House, 2022), xxi.

15. Kenneth B. Nunn, "Law as Eurocentric Enterprise," in *Critical Race Theory: The Cutting Edge*, 555–61.

16. Ray, *On Critical Race Theory*, xix–xxxix.

17. Ray, *On Critical Race Theory*, xxi.

18. Ray, *On Critical Race Theory*, xiv.

19. Brandon Washington, "Philosophy and Worldviews," in *Urban Apologetics: Restoring Black Dignity with the Gospel*, ed. Eric Mason (Grand Rapids: Zondervan, 2021), 191.

20. W. E. B. Du Bois, *Black Reconstruction in America: 1860–1880* (New York: The Free Press, 1998), 702.

21. Kimberlé W. Crenshaw, "Race, Reform, Retrenchment: Transformation and Legitimation in Antidiscrimination Law," in *Critical Race Theory: The Key Writings That Formed the Movement*, ed. Kimberlé W. Crenshaw et al. (New York: The New Press, 1995), 106.

22. Gary Peller, "Race Consciousness," in *Critical Race Theory: The Key Writings That Formed the Movement*, 127–57.

23. Crenshaw, "Race, Reform, Retrenchment," 106.

24. Neil Gotanda, "A Critique of 'Our Constitution is Color Blind,'" in *Critical Race Theory: The Key Writings That Formed the Movement*, 270–71; italics mine.

25. Raymond Geuss, *The Idea of Critical Theory: Haberman and the Frankfurt School* (Cambridge: Cambridge University Press, 1981), 1–3.

26. Steinberg, "Lawmakers Want to Ban Discomfort in School."

27. John Fea, *Why Study History: Reflecting on the Importance of the Past* (Grand Rapids: Baker Academic, 2013), 1–24; Carl R. Trueman, *Histories and Fallacies: Problems Faced in the Writing of History* (Wheaton, IL: Crossway, 2001).

28. Thomas Kidd, *American History: 1492–1877*, vol. 1 (Nashville: B&H Academic, 2019), 106, 200, 212.

29. Delgado and Stefancic, *Critical Race Theory*, 172–72.

30. Alas, women would not receive the right to vote until the nineteenth amendment, ratified in August 1920.

31. Derrick Bell, *Silent Covenants: Brown v. Board of Education and the Unfulfilled Hopes for Racial Reform* (Oxford: Oxford University Press, 2004), 11–12.

32. Ray, *On Critical Race Theory*, xix–xx; Delgado and Stefancic, *Critical Race Theory*, 3.

33. Du Bois, *Black Reconstruction in America*, 30.
34. Nikole Hannah Jones, "Choosing a School for My Daughter in a Segregated City: How One School Became a Battleground over Which Children Benefit from a Separate and Unequal System," *The New York Times Magazine*, June 9, 2016, https://www.nytimes.com/2016/06/12/magazine/choosing-a-school-for -my-daughter-in-a-segregated-city.html?.
35. Bell, *Silent Covenants*, 5.
36. Allen C. Guelzo, *Reconstruction: A Concise History* (Oxford: Oxford University Press, 2018), 124.
37. Paul Johnson, *A History of the American People* (New York: HarperCollins, 1997), 549.
38. Kidd, *American History*, 1:318–321.
39. Alan Greenblatt, "The Racial History of the 'Grandfather Clause,'" *NPR*, October 22, 2013, https://www.npr.org/sections/codeswitch/2013/10/21/2390 81586/the-racial-history-of-the-grandfather-clause.
40. Du Bois, *Black Reconstruction in America*, 30.
41. David Hackett Fischer, *Historians' Fallacies: Toward a Logic of Historical Thought* (New York: Harper Perennial, 1970), 155–57.
42. Martin Luther King Jr., *Why We Can't Wait* (New York: Signet Classic, 1963, 2000), 85–112.
43. Frederick Douglass, *Narrative of the Life of Frederick Douglass and the Fourth of July Speech* (Orinda, CA: SeaWolf Press, 2020), 116.

CHAPTER 3: EVANGELICALISM AND WHITE CHRISTIAN NATIONALISM

1. David W. Bebbington, *Evangelicalism in Modern Britain: A History from the 1730s to the 1980s* (London: Unwin Hyman, 1989).
2. This section draws heavily from the magisterial work of American historian Mark A. Noll and British historian David Bebbington. The five-volume opus they edited offers a rich, readable history of the movement. Specifically, I draw from Mark A. Noll, *The Rise of Evangelicalism: The Age of Edwards, Whitefield and the Wesleys*, vol. 1 of *A History of Evangelicalism: People, Movements and Ideas in the English-Speaking World* (Downers Grove, IL: IVP Academic, 2018).
3. J. I. Packer, "Physicians of the Soul," *Christian History* 89 (2006), https://www .christianitytoday.com/history/issues/issue-89/physicians-of-soul.html.
4. For Jonathan Edwards as an Old-World aristocrat, see George M. Marsden, *Jonathan Edwards: A Life* (New Haven, CT: Yale University Press), 2003.
5. Noll, *Rise of Evangelicalism*, 233.
6. Rebecca Anne Goetz, *The Baptism of Early Virginia: How Christianity Created Race* (Baltimore: Johns Hopkins University Press, 2016), 3.
7. Goetz, *Baptism of Early Virginia*, 10.
8. For an excellent analysis of Du Bois's view of whiteness as dominion and its

connection to global colonialism and racial capitalism, see Ella Myers, "Beyond the Psychological Wage: Du Bois on White Dominion," *Political Theory* 47, no. 1 (2019): 6–31.

9. See Colin S. Kidd, *The Forging of Races: Race and Scripture in the Protestant Atlantic World, 1600–2000* (Cambridge: Cambridge University Press, 2006).

10. Noll, *Rise of Evangelicalism*, 108.

11. Noll, *Rise of Evangelicalism*, 175.

12. Noll, *Rise of Evangelicalism*, 255.

13. Noll, *Rise of Evangelicalism*, 256.

14. Noll, *Rise of Evangelicalism*, 262.

15. Noll, *Rise of Evangelicalism*, 292.

16. See Tisby, *The Color of Compromise.*

17. For this view of whiteness, see Du Bois, *Black Reconstruction in America: 1860–1880.*

18. Philip S. Gorski and Samuel L. Perry, *The Flag and the Cross: White Christian Nationalism and the Threat to American Democracy* (New York: Oxford University Press, 2022), 1; italics added.

19. Andrew L. Whitehead and Samuel L. Perry, *Taking America Back for God: Christian Nationalism in the United States* (New York: Oxford University Press, 2020), 10.

20. I borrow this phrase from Claudine Rankin, *The Racial Imaginary: Writers on Race in the Life of the Mind* (Albany, NY: Fence Books, 2015). For an illustration of the racial imaginary, see also the adapted foreword by Claudia Rankine and Beth Loffreda, "On Whiteness and the Racial Imagination: Where Writers Go Wrong in Imagining the Lives of Others," *Literary Hub*, April 9, 2015, https://lithub.com/on-whiteness-and-the-racial-imaginary/.

21. Gorski and Perry, *Flag and the Cross*, 43–44.

22. Gorski and Perry, *Flag and the Cross*, 8.

23. Gorski and Perry, *Flag and the Cross*, 4–5.

24. Thomas S. Kidd, *Who Is an Evangelical? The History of a Movement in Crisis* (New Haven, CT: Yale University Press, 2019), 1.

25. Kidd, *Who Is an Evangelical?*, 2.

26. According to the *World Christian Encyclopedia*, global evangelicalism represents an incredibly diverse movement. For example, evangelical Christians number 22.3 million in Nigeria, 27.7 million in Brazil, 116 million in Britain, and 40.6 million in the United States. That demographic diversity suggests that theology is no hindrance to inclusion. Rather, other factors tend to strain unity and stratify the movement into clusters and groups.

27. For a thorough look at differences in Black and white views on a range of issues, see Whitehead and Perry, *Taking America Back for God* and Gorski and Perry, *The Flag and the Cross.*

28. See, for example, Glenn E. Bracey II and Wendy Leo Moore, "'Race Tests': Racial Boundary Maintenance in White Evangelical Churches," *Sociological Inquiry* 87, no.2 (2017): 282–302.

29. See, for example, Kori L. Edwards, *The Elusive Dream: The Power of Race in Interracial Churches* (New York: Oxford University Press, 2008).

30. Campbell Robertson, "A Quiet Exodus: Why Black Worshipers Are Leaving White Evangelical Churches," *The New York Times*, March 9, 2018, https://www.nytimes.com/2018/03/09/us/blacks-evangelical-churches.html.

CONVICTION: FAITH, HOPE, AND LOVE

1. John Perkins, "Why We Can't Wait for Economic Justice," in *Letters to a Birmingham Jail*, ed. Brian Loritts (Moody: Chicago, 2013), 42.

2. John Perkins, *One Blood* (Moody: Chicago, 2018), 65.

3. John Perkins, *Dream with Me* (Grand Rapids: Baker Books, 2017), 199–200.

CHAPTER 4: UNDERSTANDING BLACK LIBERATION THEOLOGY

1. James H. Cone and Gayraud S. Wilmore, eds., *Black Theology: A Documentary History, Volume I: 1966–1979* (Maryknoll, NY: Orbis Books, 1979), 101.

2. James Cone, *My Soul Looks Back* (Maryknoll, NY: Orbis Books, 1986), 37; italics original.

3. Black liberation theologian Kelly Brown Douglas writes, "The Bible does not present as clear a position on homosexuality as is often self-righteously asserted. . . . Jesus made no pronouncement and certainly no condemnation concerning homosexuality . . . as is the case with the Old Testament, the New Testament provides no indisputable position on homosexuality." Kelly Brown Douglas, "Homophobia and Heterosexism in the Black Church and Community," in *African American Religious Thought: An Anthology*, ed. Cornel West and Eddie S. Glaude, Jr. (Louisville: Westminster John Knox, 2003), 999.

4. Studying the details of Cone's theological orientation goes a bit beyond the scope of this study, although locating Cone within the appropriate theological school may help readers understand him better. James Cone's early theological texts are highly dependent on the theology of Karl Barth, which is likely the result of the topic of his PhD dissertation, "The Doctrine of Man in the Theology of Karl Barth." In general, Cone's perspective, which can be easily placed within the twentieth-century liberal and neo-orthodox Protestant traditions, is primarily derived from philosophers and theologians such as Immanuel Kant, Jean-Paul Sartre, Friedrich Schleiermacher, Albert Ritschl, Karl Barth, Paul Tillich, Rudolf Bultmann, Reinhold Niebuhr, Dietrich Bonhoeffer, Jürgen Moltmann, Wolfhart Pannenberg, and other neo-orthodox theologians.

5. James Cone, *A Black Theology of Liberation* (Maryknoll, NY: Orbis Books, 1990), 1.

6. See James H. Evans Jr., *We Have Been Believers: An African American Systematic Theology* (Minneapolis: Fortress, 1992).

7. Cone, *A Black Theology of Liberation*, 1.

8. Harry H. Singleton, *Forever in Thy Path: The God of Black Liberation* (Maryknoll, NY: Orbis Books, 2022), 7

9. Singleton, *Forever in Thy Path.*

10. Singleton, *Forever in Thy Path*, 7.

11. Singleton, *Forever in Thy Path*, 8.

12. Anthony Bradley, *Liberation Black Theology: The Bible and the Black Experience in America* (Wheaton, IL: Crossway, 2010), 33.

13. Cone, *A Black Theology of Liberation*, 2–3.

14. In fact, white Christianity was known to be a fraud. See James Cone, *The Cross and the Lynching Tree* (Maryknoll, NY: Orbis, 2011), 181.

15. Cone, *The Cross and the Lynching Tree*, 9.

16. Bradley, *Liberation Black Theology*, 23.

17. Singleton, *Forever in Thy Path*, 11.

18. Singleton, *Forever in Thy Path*, 11.

19. Singleton, *Forever in Thy Path*, 13.

20. James H. Cone, *Speaking the Truth: Ecumenism, Liberation, and Black Theology* (Grand Rapids: Eerdmans, 1986), 4.

21. Cone, *Speaking the Truth*, 5.

22. Albert J. Raboteau, *Slave Religion: The "Invisible Institution" in the Antebellum South* (Oxford: Oxford University Press, 2004), 96–288. See also Albert J. Raboteau, *Canaan Land: A Religious History of African Americans* (Oxford: Oxford University Press, 2001), 3–20.

23. Cone, *Speaking the Truth*, 83.

24. Cone, *Speaking the Truth*, 85.

25. Cone, *Speaking the Truth*, 87.

26. Peter J. Paris, "The Public Role of the Black Churches," in *The Church's Public Role: Retrospect and Prospect*, ed. Deiter T. Hessel (Grand Rapids: Eerdmans, 1993), 49.

27. Slavery and white supremacy were the Puritan pattern, and this tradition was carried on by Jonathan Edwards. See Joseph R. Washington Jr., *Anti-Blackness in English Religion 1500–1800* (New York: Edwin Mellon, 1984), 309–311. This book chronicles white supremacy in Puritan and Reformed religious thought. For a more directed look at white supremacy in the Calvinist tradition, particularly in the Northern states, see Joseph R. Washington Jr., *Puritan Race Virtue, Vice, and Values 1620–1820: Original Calvinist True Believers' Enduring Faith and Ethics Race Claims (In Emerging Congregationalist, Presbyterian and Baptist Power Denominations)* (New York: Peter Lang, 1987).

28. Washington, *Puritan Race Virtue, Vice, and Values*, 133–134.

29. Anne H. Pinn and Anthony B. Pinn, *Fortress Introduction to Black Church History* (Minneapolis: Fortress, 2001), 138.

30. Cone, *Speaking the Truth*, 120.

31. Cone, *Speaking the Truth*, 121.

32. Cornel West, "Black Theology of Liberation as Critique of Capitalist Civilization," in *Black Theology: A Documentary History, Volume II: 1980–1992*, ed. James H. Cone and Gayraud S. Wilmore (Marynoll, NY: Orbis Books), 416.

33. Sharon D. Welch, *Reconstructing Christian Theology* (Minneapolis: Fortress, 1994), 173–74.

34. Welch, *Reconstructing Christian Theology*, 173–74.

35. Stephanie Mitchem, *Introducing Womanist Theology* (Marynoll, NY: Orbis Books, 2002), 23.

36. Mitchem, *Introducing Womanist Theology*, 47.

37. Mitchem, *Introducing Womanist Theology*, 57.

38. Myrna Thurmond-Malone, *Midwifing: A Womanist Approach to Pastoral Counseling Investigating the Fractured Self, Slavery, Violence, and the Black Woman* (Eugene, OR: Pickwick, 2019), 45.

39. See Delores S. Williams, *Sisters in the Wilderness*, 2nd ed. (Maryknoll, NY: Orbis Books, 1995); Delores S. Williams, "Searching for a Balm in Gilead," *Living Pulpit* 9, no. 4 (October–December 2000): 6; Delores S. Williams, "A Theology of Advocacy for Women," *Church & Society* 91, no. 2 (November–December 2000): 8; Katie G. Cannon, *Black Womanist Ethics* (Eugene, OR: Wipf & Stock, 1998), 4; Katie G. Cannon, "Womanist Perspectival Discourse and Cannon Formation," *Journal of Feminist Studies in Religion* 9 (Spring–Fall 1993): 30; Cheryl Sanders, "Ethics and the Educational Achievements of Black Women," *Religion and Intellectual Life* 5 (Summer 1988): 8; Cheryl Sanders, *Empowerment Ethics for a Liberated People: A Path to African American Social Transformation* (Minneapolis: Fortress, 1995), 7; Cheryl Sanders, "Afrocentrism and Womanism in the Seminary," *Christianity and Crisis* 52 (April 1992): 124; and Frederick L. Ware, *Methodologies of Black Theology* (Eugene, OR: Wipf & Stock, 2008), 24, 155–56.

40. Delores S. Williams, "Womanist Theology: Black Women's Voices," *Christianity and Crisis*, March 2, 1987, 270.

41. Mitchem, *Introducing Womanist Theology*, 64.

42. Singleton, *Forever in Thy Path*, 33.

43. Singleton, *Forever in Thy Path*, 35.

44. Singleton, *Forever in Thy Path*, 35.

45. Singleton, *Forever in Thy Path*, 41.

46. Singleton, *Forever in Thy Path*, 41.

47. Singleton, *Forever in Thy Path*, 41.

48. Singleton, *Forever in Thy Path*, 44.

49. Singleton, *Forever in Thy Path*, 44.
50. Singleton, *Forever in Thy Path*, 66.
51. Singleton, *Forever in Thy Path*, 72.
52. Singleton, *Forever in Thy Path*, 72.
53. Singleton, *Forever in Thy Path*, 76.
54. Singleton, *Forever in Thy Path*, 84.
55. Singleton, *Forever in Thy Path*, 93.
56. Singleton, *Forever in Thy Path*, 97, 99.
57. Singleton, *Forever in Thy Path*, 137.
58. Singleton, *Forever in Thy Path*, 138.
59. Singleton, *Forever in Thy Path*, 138.
60. Singleton, *Forever in Thy Path*, 138.
61. The questions are adapted from David Koyzis, *Political Visions and Illusions: A Survey and Christian Critique of Contemporary Ideologies*, 2nd ed. (Downers Grove, IL: IVP Academic, 2009), 25.
62. Singleton, *Forever in Thy Path*, 78.
63. E. O. Winstedt (1909), "Some Coptic Legends about Roman Emperors" *The Classical Quarterly* 3: 218–22. https://www.premierchristianity.com/interviews /archbishop-angaelos-the-world-needs-the-church-more-than-ever/12925.article.
64. In 2015, twenty-one Coptic Christians were beheaded by Muslims in Libya.
65. Theodore Stylianopoulos, "Scripture and Tradition in the Church," in *The Cambridge Companion to Orthodox Christian Theology*, ed. Mary Cunningham (Cambridge: Cambridge University Press, 2010), 21; The Coptic Church, "Man and Redemption," *The Coptic Church and Dogmas: Part III, Section 2*, https:// www.copticchurch.net/introduction-to-the-coptic-church/book/church3-2; Abba Melkesdek and Robert Olson, *The Handbook of the Ethiopian Church's Teaching* (North Haven, CT: n.p., July 2021).
66. See also Luke 4:18; 1 Cor. 2:6–9; Col. 1:13; 2 Tim. 2:25–26.
67. The Coptic Church teaches that Jesus came to do the following: "(1) To declare the Creator's goodness. He created man and He is able to renew his nature. (2) To join us with Himself (John 17:23). (3) To accomplish God's sentence of death (2 Cor 5:14) and to condemn sin (Rom 8:3). (4) To undergo death by his victory over death and his resurrection (1 Cor 15:21). (5) To conquer Satan, our enemy (1 John 3:1). (6) To raise us up to heaven (Eph 2:6). (7) To renew our nature in Him, and grant us participation in His divine nature (2 Pet. 1:4). (8) To realize universality of the Church, by joining the Gentiles together with the Jews through faith in one Body. (9) To grant us the true knowledge (Matt 11:27), for Jesus alone knows the Father." See Tadrous Y. Malaty, Samy Anis, and Nora El-Agamy, *Introduction to the Coptic Orthodox Church* (Alexandria, Egypt: St. George's Coptic Orthodox Church, 1993), 256. In fact, one of the critiques the Coptic Church has of Black theology is that it became "a sign of

revolution against injustice and the desire for freedom. The black man feels that he wants to be freed from the yoke of the white man. . . . This feeling created an exaggerated tendency against every order, looking at it as a kind of bondage. . . . In the Coptic Church, priesthood is looked upon as a sacrifice of love and service, and not as a means for power and authority, therefore there is no room for such struggle in the church" (282–283).

68. According to Ethiopian Christianity, "If a person is enslaved by desire, then this desire pulls him down and down and dominates him. Therefore, he loses part of this true inner freedom. . . . God's love liberates man from all desires and fears." See Pope Shenouda III, *God and Nothing Else* (Chicago: Saint Mark Coptic Orthodox Church of Chicago, 1991), 6.

69. Pope Shenouda, *The Life of Repentance and Purity*, trans. Bishop Suriel (Yonkers, NY: St. Vladimir's Seminary Press, 2016), 24. For example, one related question is, How does Black theology help Black Christians keep themselves from idols (1 John 5:21)? One could argue that spiritual formation is not the intended objective of Black liberation theology, but therein lies one of its limitations.

70. According to Coptic teaching, "The worst kind of knowledge is the knowledge without a relationship. You have to know God through experience and through living with him." See Pope Shenouda III, *God and Nothing Else*, 2.

71. Pope Shenouda III says, "A person who begins the spiritual path and grows for a while and abandons it is not rooted in Christ. . . . What then is the root? The root is a life of profound faith and true love. It is a personal relationship with God, communion with Him, and knowledge of Him." *Characteristics of the Spiritual Path* (Anaheim, CA: ACTS, 2020), 17–18.

72. For Ethiopian Christians, the second aspect of an active prayer life is petition, supplication, and intercession: "We make for our daily necessities. A man lacks many things; therefore, he must ask his Creator for all that he needs. Christ in his prayer has shown us how to make petition concerning our daily life: 'Give us this day our daily bread.'" In this view, righteousness is associated with acts of mercy like giving money to the poor or feeding the hungry and caring for those on the margins. Melkesdek and Olson, *Handbook of the Ethiopian Church's Teaching*.

CONVICTION: THE REVOLUTIONARY PULPIT

1. Warren Baker and Gene Carpenter, eds., *The Complete Word Study Dictionary: Old Testament*, Word Study Series (Chattanooga, TN: AMG, 2003), s.v. "*chadash*."

2. *The Soul of America*, directed by K.D. Davison (New York: HBO Documentary Films, 2020).

3. Len Sweet, *Giving Blood: A Fresh Paradigm for Preaching* (Grand Rapids: Zondervan, 2014).

4. I'm talking less than two or three hundred people in the assembly.

5. Kanye West, "Jesus Walks," written by Che Smith, Curtis Lundy, Kanye West, and Miri Ben-Ari (UMG Recordings, 2004).

CHAPTER 5: THE LGBTQ+ MOVEMENT: HISTORY, INFLUENCE, AND CHURCH RESPONSE

1. I have chosen to refer to the community consistently throughout this chapter as LGBTQ+, although many people prefer additional letters. No one, including individuals within the LGBTQ+ community, will agree on all the terms and how they should be used. I use "homosexuality" to refer to the practice of same-sex sexual expression, but I use the term same-sex attraction (SSA) to refer to people who acknowledge an attraction but do not as a lifestyle or identity express their sexual attraction. I will often use terms interchangeably, especially when trying to use the terms that fit within a specific time-period. While it is impossible to use terms that will suit the preference of everyone who reads this chapter, including people outside of the LGBTQ+ community, it is not my goal to trigger anyone who has been harmed by specific terms, nor do I desire to be intentionally offensive.

2. Jonathan Alexander, Deborah T. Meem, and Michelle A. Gibson, *Finding Out: An Introduction to LGBTQ Studies*, 3rd ed. (Los Angeles: SAGE, 2018).

3. Michael Bronski, *A Queer History of the United States: ReVisioning American History* (Boston: Beacon, 2011), "Introduction," Kindle.

4. Kamna Kirti, "History's First Gay Couple," *Medium*, August 13, 2020, https://medium.com/lessons-from-history/historys-first-gay-couple-f877be3a5b86.

5. Kirti, "History's First Gay Couple."

6. Sodomy is defined as sexual intercourse involving anal or oral copulation.

7. Alexander, Meem, and Gibson, *Finding Out*, 4.

8. Alexander, Meem, and Gibson, *Finding Out*.

9. Sarah Pomeroy, *Goddess, Whores, Wives, and Slaves: Women in Classical Antiquity* (New York: Shocken, 1975).

10. Bronski, *A Queer History of the United States*, "Introduction," Kindle.

11. Lillian Faderman, *The Gay Revolution: The Story of the Struggle* (New York: Simon & Schuster, 2015), xx.

12. People known as "intersex" were previously labeled "hermaphrodite" and are typically born with both male and female genitalia or sex organs or with genitalia that are not clearly male or female sex organs. Some have found a home among the "newest" members of the LGBTQ+ community, while other intersex persons don't believe their physicality neatly fits within the LGBTQ+ community or activism because intersex is a physiological reality not a sexual identity. See chapter 6 of Alexander, Meem, and Gibson, *Finding Out*, for a great overview of this unique group and their specific challenges. R. Martha Rhodes, "A Short History of the Word 'Bisexuality,'" *Stonewall UK*,

January 22, 2022, https://www.stonewall.org.uk/about-us/news/short-history
-word-bisexuality.

13. Alexander, Meem, and Gibson, *Finding Out*, 162–63.

14. Faderman, *Gay Revolution*, x.

15. Alexander, Meem, and Gibson, *Finding Out*, 166.

16. Gabrielle Marlowe, "The Experiences of Transgender Children: A Comparison
of Public Perception from the 1980s to 2018," November 14, 2018, https://
wgssfall2018.voices.wooster.edu/2018/11/14/research-based-opinion-piece-on
-transgender-children-now/.

17. "Questioning" is considered the state or process of discovering one's sexual
orientation.

18. Alexander, Meem, and Gibson, *Finding Out*.

19. Alexander, Meem, and Gibson, *Finding Out*.

20. For more in depth reading on intersex individuals See: Cox, A. Jennifer, *Intersex
in Christ: Ambiguous Biology and the Gospel* (Eugene: Cascade Books, 2018).

21. Michael G. Long, *Martin Luther King Jr., Homosexuality, and the Early Gay
Rights Movement: Keeping the Dream Straight?* (New York: Palgrave Macmillan,
2012).

22. Long, *Martin Luther King Jr., Homosexuality, and the Early Gay Rights
Movement*.

23. Alexander, Meem, and Gibson, *Finding Out*.

24. Accessed May 17, 2022: https://makinggayhistory.com/podcast/revisiting-the
-archive-episode-12-bayard-rustin/.

25. Long, *Martin Luther King Jr., Homosexuality, and the Early Gay Rights
Movement*.

26. Alexander, Meem, and Gibson, *Finding Out*, 68.

27. Branch, Alan J. *Born This Way?: Homosexuality, Science, & the Scripture*
(Bellingham: Lexham Press 2016), 32.

28. Alexander, Meem, and Gibson, *Finding Out*, 68.

29. Alexander, Meem, and Gibson, *Finding Out*, 69.

30. The Combahee River Collective is a collective of Black feminists from Boston;
the group began in 1974.

31. Alexander, Meem, and Gibson, *Finding Out*, 88.

32. Alexander, Meem, and Gibson, *Finding Out*, 86.

33. American Psychiatric Association, *Diagnostic and Statistical Manual of Mental
Disorders* (Washington, DC: APA, 1952), 34; Alexander, Meem, and Gibson,
Finding Out, 69.

34. Long, *Martin Luther King Jr., Homosexuality, and the Early Gay Rights
Movement*, 41.

35. Christopher Doyle, *The War on Psychotherapy: When Sexual Politics, Gender
Ideology, and Mental Health Collide* (Manassas, VA: Institute for Healthy

Families, 2019), 63, quoting Jack Drescher, "Out of DSM: Depathologizing Homosexuality," *Behav Sci* 5, no. 4 (2015): 565–75.

36. Doyle, *The War on Psychotherapy*, 63.

37. "In 'homosexuality's' place, the DSM-II contained a new diagnosis: Sexual Orientation Disturbance (SOD). SOD regarded homosexuality as an illness if an individual with same-sex attractions found them distressing and wanted to change. The new diagnosis legitimized the practice of sexual conversion therapies (and presumably justified insurance reimbursement for those interventions as well), even if homosexuality *per se* was no longer considered an illness. . . . SOD was later replaced in DSM-III by a new category called 'Ego Dystonic Homosexuality' (EDH). . . . Ego-dystonic homosexuality was removed from the next revision, DSM-III-R, in 1987." See Jack Drescher, "Out of DSM," doi: 10.3390/bs5040565.

38. Greg Johnson, *Still Time to Care: What We Can Learn from the Church's Failed Attempt to Cure Homosexuality* (Grand Rapids: Zondervan, 2021), 39.

39. Jonathan Merritt, "The Downfall of the Ex-Gay Movement," *The Atlantic*, October 6, 2015, https://www.theatlantic.com/politics/archive/2015/10/the -man-who-dismantled-the-ex-gay-ministry/408970/.

40. Conversion therapy is any emotional or physical therapy used to "cure" or "repair" a person's attraction to the same sex or their gender identity and expressions. For a detailed discussion of conversion therapy and a positive view of it from a professional counselor, see Doyle, *The War on Psychotherapy*.

41. Merritt, "Downfall of the Ex-Gay Movement." The cofounder of Exodus left the group in 1979 and entered a relationship with another Exodus leader, Gary Copper.

42. Merritt, "Downfall of the Ex-Gay Movement."

43. Greg Johnson, *Still Time to Care: What We Can Learn from the Church's Failed Attempt to Cure Homosexuality* (Grand Rapids: Zondervan, 2021), 185.

44. Joe Dallas and Nancy Heche, *The Complete Christian Guide to Understanding Homosexuality: A Biblical and Compassionate Response to Same-Sex Attraction* (Eugene, OR: Harvest House, 2010), 43.

45. Michael P. Dentato, ed., *Social Work Practice with the LGBTQ Community: Intersection of History, Health, Mental Health, and Policy Factors* (New York: Oxford, 2018), 16.

46. Alexander, Meem, and Gibson, *Finding Out*, 72.

47. The Mattachine and Daughters of Bilitis (DOB) groups were characterized by their mission to assimilate with mainstream society. The beginning of the homophile movement primarily advocated for the assimilation of gays and lesbians into the heterosexual mainstream. To assimilate, these groups would encourage gay men to wear business suits when they marched and women to wear skits. This strategy and others was implemented after early gay activists

began patterning their activism tactics after what was seen in the Black civil rights movement. See Long, *Martin Luther King Jr., Homosexuality, and the Early Gay Rights Movement*, 121–36.

48. Alexander, Meem, and Gibson, *Finding Out*, 72.
49. Alexander, Meem, and Gibson, *Finding Out*, 68, quoting Molly McGarry, *Becoming Visible: An Illustrated History of Lesbian and Gay Life in Twentieth-Century America* (London: Penguin Studio, 1998), 2.
50. Alexander, Meem, and Gibson, *Finding Out*, 68, quoting McGarry, *Becoming Visible*, 96.
51. Kelly Brown Douglas, *Sexuality and the Black Church: A Womanist Perspective* (Maryknoll: Orbis Books, 1999), 2.
52. Douglas, *Sexuality and the Black Church*, 5–6.
53. Bronski, *A Queer History of the United States*, 236.
54. Bronski, *A Queer History of the United States*, 237.
55. Sarah Elizabeth Adler, "Key Moments in LGBTQ Pride History," *AARP*, June 21, 2021, https://www.aarp.org/politics-society/history/info-2019/lgbt-pride-key-moments.html.
56. Alexander, Meem, and Gibson, *Finding Out*, 101.
57. Dentato, *Social Work Practice with the LGBTQ Community*, 3.
58. Alexander, Meem, and Gibson, *Finding Out*, 103.
59. Monique Moultrie, *Passionate and Pious: Religious Media and Black Women's Sexuality* (Durham, NC: Duke University Press, 2017), 83. Emphasis added.
60. Alice Walker, *In Search of Our Mothers' Gardens: Womanist Prose* (San Diego: Harcourt Brace Jovanovich, 1983), 11.
61. Moultrie, *Passionate and Pious*, 93.
62. Queer youth have a higher rate of suicide. See, e.g., https://www.thetrevor project.org/resources/article/facts-about-lgbtq-youth-suicide/.
63. Transgendered individuals are more likely to be victims of hate crimes than anyone else. See, e.g., https://williamsinstitute.law.ucla.edu/press/ncvs-trans -press-release/.
64. Derrick Sherwin Bailey, *Homosexuality and the Western Christian Tradition* (North Haven, CT: Archon, 1975).
65. Kevin DeYoung, *What Does the Bible Really Teach about Homosexuality?* (Wheaton, IL: Crossway, 2015), 38.
66. "Paul's sexual ethic" refers to beliefs that the passages in Scripture condemning homosexuality in the New Testament are Paul's opinions and not the views of Jesus because Jesus doesn't have any identifiable words condemning homosexuality in the New Testament.

CHAPTER 6: A BIBLICAL APOLOGETIC FOR GENDER, SEX, AND MARRIAGE

1. Michael Bird, *Evangelical Theology: A Biblical and Systematic Introduction*, 2nd ed. (Grand Rapids: Zondervan, 2020), 764.

2. Michael P. Dentato, ed., *Social Work Practice with the LGBTQ Community: Intersection of History, Health, Mental Health, and Policy Factors* (New York: Oxford, 2018), 31.

3. Dentato, *Social Work Practice with the LGBTQ Community*.

4. The biological conditions of being intersex (having both male and female genitalia), chromosomally atypical (people whose chromosomes don't match their genitalia or who have XXY or just an X chromosome), as well as the condition of gender dysphoria (psychological trauma resulting from the perception that their biological sex does not match their gender identification), after the fall, "call into question the integrity of a gender binary of male and female." See Bird, *Evangelical Theology*, 761.

5. Bird, *Evangelical Theology*, 760.

6. Merriam-Webster defines "cisgender" as "someone whose internal sense of gender corresponds with the sex that the person had or was identified as having at birth. Most people can be described as cisgender. If the pronouncement your mom heard at your birth—*It's a girl!* or *It's a boy!*—still feels like it was accurate." https://www.merriam-webster.com/words-at-play/cisgender-meaning.

7. Bird, *Evangelical Theology*, 762.

8. Andrew T. Walker, "Gender and Sexuality," *The Gospel Coalition*, 2022, https://www.thegospelcoalition.org/essay/gender-and-sexuality/. Walker provides an example, saying, "Cross-dressing is sinful because it violates the creational boundaries between male and female that come to be expressed in culturally-appropriate gender norms."

9. Walker, "Gender and Sexuality."

10. Simon Turpin, "The Apostle Paul's Use of Genesis 1–3 in Romans 1," *Answers in Genesis*, October 9, 2018, https://answersingenesis.org/the-word-of-god/apostle-pauls-use-genesis-13-romans-1/.

11. Walker, "Gender and Sexuality."

12. Abstaining from sex in marriage should not be the norm. Married couples are more vulnerable to Satan's temptations when they don't have sex for long periods.

13. David had sex with his wife when she was grieving. There is a lot of social science evidence suggesting the positive psychological impact of healthy sexual relationships in marriage.

14. Janet Boynes, *God and Sexuality: Truth and Relevance without Compromise* (Shippensburg, PA: Harrison House, 2016).

15. See Scriptures under section "Homosexual sin defined in Scripture." Additionally, pro-gay theologians suggest that Johnathan and David were a homosexual couple, Ruth and Naomi, the centurion and the man he asked Jesus to heal. These attempts to show Scripture affirming homosexuality are weak and not biblically supported. For a more comprehensive discussion of responses to pro-gay theology, see Joe Dallas and Nancy Heche, *The Complete*

Christian Guide to Understanding Homosexuality: A Biblical and Compassionate Response to Same-Sex Attraction (Eugene, OR: Harvest House, 2010), chapters 6 and 7; and see Kevin DeYoung, *What Does the Bible Really Teach about Homosexuality?* (Wheaton, IL: Crossway, 2015).

16. Rachel J. Welcher, *Talking Back to Purity Culture: Rediscovering Faithful Christian Sexuality* (Downers Grove, IL: InterVarsity Press, 2020), 129.

17. Welcher, *Talking Back to Purity Culture*, 129.

18. Questions about the categories to consider and talk through in community: (1) Which category best represents how you function today? (2) Can you remember a time when you were in another category, and if you shifted, what was the cause of that shift? (3) What descriptions would you add to the categories? Can you think of a different category I didn't mention, and how would you describe it? (4) What thoughts and feelings came up for you as you read through the categories?

19. See chapter 6 in Yana Conner and Sherelle Ducksworth, *Courageous Conversations: Tools you Need for the Conversations in the Culture* (Jacksonville, FL: Jude 3 Project, Inc., 2022), esp. p. 77.

20. Corey Dade, "Blacks, Gays and the Church: A Complex Relationship," *NPR*, May 22, 2012, https://www.npr.org/2012/05/22/153282066/blacks-gays-and -the-church-a-complex-relationship.

21. "Now these three remain: faith, hope and love. But the greatest of these is love" (1 Cor. 13:13).

22. See, for example, Moultrie, *Passionate and Pious*.

23. Jackie Hill Perry, *Gay Girl, Good God: The Story of Who I Was and Who God Has Always Been* (Nashville: Broadman & Holman, 2018), 178: "The 'heterosexual gospel' is one that encourages SSA men and women to come to Jesus so that they can be straight or that coming to Jesus ensures that they will be sexually attracted to the opposite sex."

24. Greg Johnson, *Still Time to Care: What We Can Learn from the Church's Failed Attempt to Cure Homosexuality* (Grand Rapids: Zondervan, 2021), 32.

25. See https://www.gotquestions.org/Bible-consecration.html.

26. Johnson, *Still Time to Care*, 29.

CHAPTER 7: FAITH DECONSTRUCTION

1. Alycia Wicker, "Crystals and Christianity: Are You Going to Hell?," *Alycia Wicker* (blog), https://www.alyciawicker.com/blog/crystals-and-christianity.

2. Gordon D. Fee, *God's Empowering Presence: The Holy Spirit in the Letters of Paul* (Grand Rapids: Baker Academic, 2011), 768.

3. Clinton E. Arnold, *Romans to Philemon*, vol. 3 of *Zondervan Illustrated Bible Backgrounds Commentary* (Grand Rapids: Zondervan, 2002), 463.

4. Jamin Andreas Hübner, *Deconstructing Evangelicalism: A Letter to a Friend and*

a Professor's Guide to Escaping Fundamentalist Christianity (Rapid City, SD: Hills), 20, Kindle.

5. Brandon Briscoe, "On Christian Deconstruction," *Living Faith Fellowship* (blog), August 8, 2019, https://www.lffellowship.com/blog/2019/8/7/on -christian-deconstruction#:~:text=Deconstruction%20is%20a%20systematic %20approach%20for%20casting%20doubt,doctrinal%20claims%20held%20 to%20be%20holistic%20and%20absolute.

6. Briscoe, "On Christian Deconstruction."

7. Hübner, *Deconstructing Evangelicalism*, 19, Kindle.

8. Frederick Douglass, *Narrative of the Life of Frederick Douglass, an American Slave* (Boston: Anti-Slavery Office, 1845), 118.

9. Peter Suciu, "Americans Spent on Average More Than 1,300 Hours on Social Media Last Year," *Forbes*, June 24, 2021, https://www.forbes.com/sites /petersuciu/2021/06/24/americans-spent-more-than-1300-hours-on-social -media/?sh=154041822547.

10. Jerome Gay Jr., *The Whitewashing of Christianity: A Hidden Past, a Hurtful Present, and a Hopeful Future* (Chicago: 13th & Joan, 2020), 243, Kindle.

11. Gay, *Whitewashing of Christianity*, location 3571, Kindle.

12. Barna Group, "Millennials and the Bible: 3 Surprising Insights," *Barna*, October 21, 2014, https://www.barna.com/research/millennials-and-the-bible -3-surprising-insights/.

CONVICTION: TEN PRINCIPLES FOR CREATING ONLINE CONTENT

1. Jennifer Herrity, "What Is Content Creation? (Plus How-To and List of Tools)," *Indeed* (blog), March 30, 2022, https://www.indeed.com/career-advice/career -development/content-creation.

2. Ed Hindson and Ergun Caner, *The Popular Encyclopedia of Apologetics: Surveying the Evidence for the Truth of Christianity* (Eugene, OR: Harvest House, 2008), 50–51.

CHAPTER 8: WHAT IS A CULT?

1. I believe in and at times operate in the gifts, so I'm not a cessationist. "Cessationism, in Christian theology, is the view that the miraculous gifts of the Spirit, such as healing, tongues, and prophetic revelation, pertained to the apostolic era only, served a purpose that was unique to establishing the early church, and passed away before the canon of Scripture was closed (comp. 1 Cor. 13:8–12 with Heb. 2:3–4)." "Cessationism," *Theopedia*, https://www.theopedia .com/cessationism#:~:text=Cessationism%2C%20in%20Christian%20theology %2C%20is%20the%20view%20that,closed%20%28comp.%201%20Cor.%20 13%3A8-12%20with%20Heb.%202%3A3-4%29.

2. "Cult," *The Free Dictionary*, https://www.thefreedictionary.com/cult.

3. Charles S. Braden and John C. Schaffer, *These Also Believe* (New York: Macmillan Company, 1949), xii.

4. Walter Martin, *The Kingdom of the Cults: The Definitive Work on the Subject*, 6th ed. (Grand Rapids: Baker, 2019), 13–14, Kindle.

5. Eric Mason, *Urban Apologetics: Restoring Black Dignity with the Gospel* (Grand Rapids: Zondervan, 2019), 70, Kindle.

6. Judith Weisenfeld, *New World A-Coming: Black Religion and Racial Identity during the Great Migration* (New York: New York University Press, 2017).

7. "Gabriel, Angel," *Bible.ca, Massive Online Encyclopedia of Islam*, https://www .bible.ca/islam/dictionary/G/gabriel.html

8. "Totalitarianism," *The Free Dictionary*, https://www.thefreedictionary.com /totalitarianism.

9. Rick Alan Ross, *Cults Inside Out: How People Get In and Can Get Out* (Charleston, SC: CreateSpace Independent Publishing, 2014), 99, Kindle.

10. Robert Jay Lifton, *Thought Reform and the Psychology of Totalism: A Study of 'Brainwashing' in China* (Chapel Hill: University of North Carolina Press, 1989), 5, Kindle.

11. Eric Mason, *Unleashed* (Nashville: B&H, 2015). Kindle Edition.

12. I first heard this quote from Dr. Tony Evans. Ed Silvoso, *That None Should Perish: How to Reach Entire Cities for Christ through Prayer Evangelism* (Ventura, CA: Chosen, 1995), 155.

13. Ross, *Cults Inside Out*, 103, Kindle

14. Elijah Muhammad, *Message to the Blackman in America* (Phoenix: Secretarius MEMPS, 1973), 137, Kindle.

15. Ross, *Cults Inside Out*, 128–129, Kindle.

16. Ross, *Cults Inside Out*, 128–129, Kindle.

CHAPTER 9: SEVENTH-DAY ADVENTISTS

·1. Walter Martin, Kingdom of the Cults (Bethany House, 1965), p. 517. Martin equivocated on the question of classifying Adventism as a cult, encouraged by the movement toward orthodoxy he saw in the 1950s and 60s. Yet according to a May 2006 email referenced on https://christinprophecy.org/articles/the -seventh-day-adventists/ Martin's close friend, Ron Carlson, admits that despite the hope Martin had for the SDA church, in subsequent decades nearly 50 percent of the SDA pastors and leaders who were seeking to move it to an evangelical position left the SDA and the movement largely returned to following the teachings of Ellen G. White and denying basic doctrines of Biblical Christianity. Carlson himself still classified the SDA church as a cult at the time of the email.

2. http://www.sdanet.org/atissue/books/qod/

3. https://adventist.news/news/world-church-questions-on-doctrine-book -annotated-republished

4. Arthur Beem and Teresa Beem, *It's Okay Not to Be a Seventh-Day Adventist* (North Charleston, SC: BookSurge, 2008), 36–37.

5. Ellen G. White, *Early Writings* (Washington, DC: Ellen G. White Estate, 2008), 233.

6. White, Early Writings, p. 13.

7. Academia Apology, "Defeating Adventism #20 – Seventh-Day Adventists and Ascension Robes," January 20, 2021, YouTube video, https://www.youtube.com/watch?v=-nYGK9S0My8&t=49s.

8. Beem, *It's Okay Not to Be a Seventh-Day Adventist*, 43–44.

9. Beem, *It's Okay Not to Be a Seventh-Day Adventist*, 45.

10. The Ellen G. White Estate, *Advent Pioneers Biographical Sketches and Pictures* (Washington, DC: Ellen G. White Estate, Inc., 2020), p. 10–11.

11. White, *Life Sketches of Ellen G. White*, p. 64, par. 1.

12. White, *The Great Controversy*, p. 409.

13. White, *Early Writings*, p. 74.

14. White, *Selected Messages, Book I*, p. 206–207.

15. White, *Last Day Events*, p. 52, par. 2–3.

16. White, *Testimonies for the Church*, Vol. 9, p. 19.

17. White, *Testimonies for the Church*, Vol. 3, p. 417 (1875).

18. Ibid, p. 492.

19. White, *Review and Herald*, May 25, 1905.

20. White, *Life Sketches of Ellen G. White*, p. 198, par. 1.

21. The Secretariat, General Conference of Seventh-day Adventists, *Seventh-day Adventist Church Manual* (Doral, FL: Inter-American Division Publishing Association, 2005, 2007), 32.

22. "What Adventists Believe about the Prophetic Gift," *Seventh-day Adventist Church*, accessed March 3, 2022, https://www.adventist.org/beliefs/fundamental-beliefs/church/the-gift-of-prophecy/.

23. White, *Selected Messages, Book I*, p. 161, par. 2.

24. "Statement of Confidence in the Writings of Ellen G. White," *Seventh-day Adventist Church*, accessed March 27, 2021, https://www.adventist.org/articles/statement-of-confidence-in-the-writingsof-ellen-g-white/?fbclid=IwAR2qu7nRPtBZLrJ-S6rN6B_xHooj9CrrsnjW4U8W-eVTyNsXlaVdtmJUvVY.

25. White, *Selected Messages*, Book I, p. 48.

26. White, *Testimonies for the Church*, Vol. 4, p. 211.

27. The amount of issues that surround Ellen White are too numerous to cover in this chapter. I have published three thorough, definitive volumes on SDA false doctrines, in which I prove what I have briefly discussed here. I also refute their false doctrines, arguments, and interpretations of Scripture and defend biblical, orthodox Christian teachings. Elce-Junior Lauriston, *Hiding in Plain Sight: The False Doctrines of Seventh-day Adventism*, 3 vols. (Montego Bay, Jamaica: Elce-Junior Lauriston, 2021–2022).

28. A pivotal text of the SDA Church is a sizable book by Ellen G. White entitled *The Great Controversy*. It explains this worldview of theirs in great detail.

29. White, *Testimonies for the Church*, Vol. 2, p. 426, par. 2.

30. White, *Spiritual Gifts*, Vol. 3, p. 36, par. 1, "The Temptation and Fall."

31. White, *Patriarchs and Prophets*, p. 761

32. White, *Sermons and Talks*, Vol. 1, p. 241, par. 1.

33. White, *The Signs of the Times*, September 14, 1882, par. 9.

34. White, *The Spirit of Prophecy*, Vol. 1, p. 17, par. 2.

35. White, *Spiritual Gifts*, Vol. 4b, p. 84, par. 1.

36. White, *Spiritual Gifts*, Vol. 3, Chap. 2 "The Temptation and the Fall."

37. White, *Manuscript Releases*, Vol. 16, p. 115, par. 1–2.

38. White, *The Signs of the Times*, November 5, 1896, "Be Ye Therefore Perfect."

39. White, *Review and Herald*, June 10, 1890, "Conditions for Obtaining Eternal Riches."

40. *Seventh-day Adventists Believe*, p. 296.

41. White, *The Great Controversy*, p. 480, par. 1.

42. Ibid, p. 483.

43. Ibid, p. 482, par. 1.

44. Ibid, p. 486, par. 1.

45. Ibid, p. 489, par. 3.

46. Ibid, p. 486, par. 2.

47. Ibid, p. 490, par. 1.

48. Ibid, p. 489.

49. Ibid, p. 490, par. 2.

50. *Seventh-day Adventists Believe*, p. 353.

51. White, *The Great Controversy*, p. 422, par. 2.

52. White, *The Faith I Live By*, p. 213, par. 4.

53. White, *My Life Today*, p. 287, p. 5–6.

54. White, *Testimonies for the Church*, Vol. 6, p. 349, par. 1.

55. White, *Last Day Events*, p. 220, par. 5.

56. White, *Pamphlet 086*, "Special Testimony to the Battle Creek Church (1898)," p. 6, par. 1.

57. White, *Review and Herald*, Dec. 20, 1898, par. 16.

58. White, *A Word to the Little Flock*, p. 18, par. 4.

59. White, *A Word to the Little Flock*, p. 19.

60. White, *Manuscript 16*, 1890, p. 21.

61. White, *Selected Messages*, Book 3, p. 380, par. 2.

62. *Seventh-day Adventists Believe*, p. 196.

63. White, *Evangelism*, p. 235 (1900).

64. White, *Testimonies for the Church*, Vol. 5, p. 451.

65. White, *Maranatha*, p. 268, par. 4.

66. White, *Review and Herald*, July 13, 1897.

67. White, *Review and Herald*, May 27, 1902, par. 2.

68. White, *Medical Missionary*, p. 259.

69. White, *Testimonies for the Church*, Vol. 9, p. 112–113.

70. White, *Testimonies for the Church*, Vol. 6, p. 229.

71. White, *General Conference Bulletin*, April 6, 1903, par. 24.

72. White, *Child Guidance*, p. 383, par. 1.

73. White, *Review and Herald*, May 27, 1902, par. 2.

74. White, *Counsels on Diet and Foods*, p. 399, par. 3.

75. White, *Counsels for the Church*, p. 105, par. 6.

76. White, *Counsels on Diets and Foods*, p. 425, par. 3.

77. See *Seventh-day Adventists Believe*, Fundamental Belief 22, "Christian Behavior," p. 311–323.

78. White, Selected Messages, Vol. 1, p. 256; White, *Signs of the Times*, May 29, 1901, par. 11; White, *Testimonies for the Church*, Vol. 2, p. 509.

79. White, *Youth's Instructor*, Dec. 20, 1900; White, *Review and Herald*, Feb. 24, 1874; White, *Desire of Ages*, p. 112.

80. White, *Testimonies for the Church*, Vol. 4, p. 294, par. 2.

81. White, *Review and Herald*, May 3, 1898, par. 13.

82. White, *Review and Herald*, April 1, 1902.

83. White, *Testimonies for the Church*, Vol. 5, p. 214.

84. White, *Review and Herald*, June 11, 1889, par. 8.

85. White, *Counsels to Parents, Teachers, and Students*, p. 324.

86. White, *Review and Herald*, January 17, 1907, par. 4.

87. White, *Daughters of God*, p. 272, par. 6; White, *Pacific Union Recorder*, April 29, 1915, par. 7–8.

88. *Seventh-day Adventists Believe*, p. 91.

89. Ibid, p. 94.

90. Ibid, p. 95

91. Ibid, p. 387–397.

92. White, *Testimonies for the Church*, Vol. 1, p. 224, par. 1.

93. White, *Spiritual Gifts*, Vol. 4b, p. 54, par. 4.

94. White, *Early Writings*, p. 116, par. 1.

95. Ibid, p. 274.

96. William G. Johnson, "Seventh-day Adventists and Other Churches: The Never-ending Quest for Understanding," *Adventist Review*, October 24, 2013, https://www.adventistreview.org/2013-1517-p16.

97. Stephen D. Pitcher, "Did Adventist Leaders Lie to Walter Martin? A Look Back at the Adventist/Evangelical Dialogues in the Mid 1950s," *Proclamation! Magazine*, July, August, September 2010, vol. 11, issue 3, https://www.life assuranceministries.org/proclamation/2010/3/waltermartin.html.

98. White, *Review and Herald*, January 21, 1896, par. 4.

99. White, *Review and Herald*, December 3, 1895, par. 3.

100. White, *Review and Herald*, January 21, 1896, par. 1.

101. White, *Spiritual Gifts*, Vol. 3, p. 64.

102. White, *Testimonies for the Church*, Vol. 9, p. 223, par. 3.

103. Ibid, p. 214.

104. Ibid, p. 208.

105. White, *Selected Messages*, Book 2, p. 343, par. 2; White, *Letter 36*, 1912; White, *The Southern Work*, p. 15.

106. White, *Testimonies for the Church*, Vol. 9, p. 213, par. 4.

107. White, *Gospel Herald*, March 1, 1901, par. 20.

108. Samuel Koranteng-Pipim, "Separate Black and White Conferences -- Part 1: The Sin We Don't Want to Overcome," *Dr. Pipim: A Biblical Look at Contemporary Issues* (blog), accessed March 3, 2022, http://drpipim.org/index.php/features /racially-separate-conferences/97-separate-black-and-white-conferences-part-1.

109. Mia Lindsey, "Separate, but United? The Conundrum of Race-Based Conferences," *Spectrum*, November 15, 2012, https://spectrummagazine.org/article /mia-lindsey/2012/11/15/separate-united-conundrum-race-based-conferences.

110. White, *Selected Messages*, Book 2, p. 36–37.

111. *Seventh-day Adventists Believe*, p. 317.

112. *Seventh-day Adventist Church Manual*, p. 180.

113. Ivor Myers, "Escape from the Black Hole," Xola Theodore Meki, February 13, 2014, YouTube video, https://www.youtube.com/watch?v=bGhK_QgAxPg.

114. See a ten-part music series by popular SDA musician and music expert Christian Berdahl, "Distraction Dilemma 1 – Overture: Our Personal Journey," ShepherdsCallMedia, December 17, 2014, YouTube video, https://www.youtube.com/watch?v=2gEkGwxa0Ls&list=PLNomdEoen 2NU3QS5OCJFhSclfNDTv4d6x.

115. White, *The Adventist Home*, p. 499–500, 518; White, *Counsels on Health*, p. 195.

116. CVM TV, "FTB Ministries Members Building Commune in St. Mary," *Live*, November 11, 2021, https://www.cvmtv.com/news/major-stories/ftb -ministries-members-building-commune-in-st-mary/.

117. Shanel Lemmie, "Religious Convert Insists She Has Not Been Brainwashed," *Jamaica Star*, October 20, 2021, http://jamaica-star.com/article/news/20211020 /religious-convert-insists-she-has-not-been-brainwashed.

118. Tiffany Taylor, "Sabbath Keepers Warn Sunday Worshippers," *Jamaica Star*, July 13, 2021, http://jamaica-star.com/article/news/20210713/sabbath-keepers -warn-sunday-worshippers.

119. White, *God's Amazing Grace*, p. 142, par. 2.

CONVICTION: DEVELOPING BIBLICAL CONVICTIONS IN DISCIPLES

1. See David D. Ireland, *One in Christ: Bridging Racial and Cultural Divides* (Washington, DC: Regnery Faith, 2018), 49.
2. H. E. Jacobs, "Convict, Conviction," in *The International Standard Bible Encyclopaedia*, ed. James Orr et al. (Chicago: The Howard-Severance Company, 1915), 708.
3. "What Is the Conviction of Sin?," *Got Questions*, https://www.gotquestions.org /conviction-of-sin.html.
4. "What Is the Conviction of Sin?," *Got Questions*.
5. See https://www.be1make1.org/.
6. "Ten Core Convictions," *Calvin Institute of Christian Worship*, June 22, 2021, https://worship.calvin.edu/resources/resource-library/ten-core-convictions/.

CHAPTER 10: JEHOVAH'S WITNESSES

1. For a more detailed discussion of the Seventh-day Adventist church, see chapter 9.
2. *Watchtower*, Sept. 15, 1910, p. 298.
3. John H. Gerstner, *The Teachings of the Jehovah's Witnesses: A Comparison of the Tenets of the Jehovah's Witnesses with Traditional Christian Doctrines* (Grand Rapids: Baker, 1960), 8.
4. Ibid.
5. *Jehovah's Witnesses: Proclaimers of God's Kingdom* (Watch Tower Bible and Tract Society, 1993), 200; *1975 Yearbook of Jehovah's Witnesses*, p. 147–149; J. F. Rutherford, *Riches: Information Which Will Enable Every Person to Realize in Fullness the Greatest Desire and Fondest Hopes of Humankind* (Brooklyn, NY: Watch Tower Bible and Tract Society, 1936), 27.
6. *Jehovah's Witnesses: Proclaimers of God's Kingdom*, 89.
7. "Kew Gardens: Transplant Center for the World," *Awake!*, 1989. p. 17.
8. *The Truth Shall Make You Free* (Brooklyn, NY: Watchtower Bible and Tract Society, 1943), 47; *The Kingdom Is at Hand* (Brooklyn, NY: Watchtower Bible and Tract Society, 1944), 46–47; https://www.jw.org/en/jehovahs-witnesses /faq/jehovah-witness-beliefs/; New World Translation of the Holy Scriptures (NWT) John 1:1; Col. 1:15; *Reasoning from the Scriptures* (Brooklyn, NY: Watchtower Bible and Tract Society, 1985), 218; *You Can Live Forever in Paradise on Earth* (Brooklyn, NY: Watchtower Bible and Tract Society, 1982), 58; *The Truth That Leads to Eternal Life* (Brooklyn, NY: Watchtower Bible and Tract Society, 1968), 47; *Aid to Bible Understanding* (Brooklyn, NY: Watchtower Bible and Tract Society, 1971), 918; *What Has Religion Done for Mankind?* Brooklyn, NY: Watchtower Bible and Tract Society, 1951), 231.
9. *Knowledge That Leads to Everlasting Life* (Brooklyn, NY: Watchtower Bible and

Tract Society, 1995), 65, 68; *You Can Live Forever in Paradise on Earth*, 60, 62; *The Truth That Leads to Eternal Life*, 51; https://www.jw.org/en/bible-teachings /questions/original-sin/; *Let God Be True* (Brooklyn, NY: Watchtower Bible and Tract Society, 1946), 40–41;114; 118–19; 276; *New World Translation of the Holy Scriptures (NWT)* Matt. 27:32; 1 Pet. 3:18.

10. *United in Worship of the Only True God* (Brooklyn, NY: Watchtower Bible and Tract Society, 1983), 111; *True Peace and Security: How Can You Find It?* (Brooklyn, NY: Watchtower Bible and Tract Society, 1986), 65; *Watchtower*, August 15, 1996, p. 31; *Examining the Scriptures Daily*, November 28, 2007, 117; *You Can Live Forever in Paradise on Earth* (Watch Tower Bible and Tract Society, 1982); *Watchtower*, December 1, 1901; *Cast Not Away Therefore Your Confidence, Zion's Watchtower*, Feb. 1881; *The Watchtower*, March 1, 1922; *The Time Is at Hand*; 1889.

11. *Watchtower*, Feb.15th, 1983, p.12; *Let God Be True* (Brooklyn, NY: Watchtower Bible and Tract Society, 1946), 74, 121; *Watchtower*, October 1, 1967, p. 591; · https://www.jw.org/en/bible-teachings/questions/what-is-salvation/; *Watchtower*, Mar. 1, 2016, p. 4.

12. *Watchtower*, 1983.

13. *Watchtower*, 2016.

14. *Let God Be True*, 108; *The Truth That Leads to Eternal Life*, 24; *Reasoning from the Scriptures*, 381.

15. *You Can Live Forever in Paradise on Earth*, 77; *Let God Be True*, 68.

16. E.g., Bruce M. Metzger, "The New World Translation of the Christian Greek Scriptures," *The Bible Translator*, July 1964; Robert H. Countess, *The Jehovah's Witnesses' New Testament: A Critical Analysis of the New World Translation of the Christian Greek Scriptures* (Phillipsburg, NJ: P&R, 1982); Walter Martin, The Kingdom of the Cults (Minneapolis: Bethany House, 2003); Ron Rhodes, *The Ten Most Important Things You Can Say to a Jehovah's Witness* (Grand Rapids: Zondervan, 2013).

17. Raymond V. Franz, *Crisis of Conscience* (Atlanta: Commentary Press, 1983)

18. *Watchtower*, December 15, 1974, p. 768.

19. M. James Penton, *Apocalypse Delayed: The Story of Jehovah's Witnesses* (Toronto: University of Toronto Press, 1985).

20. Franz, *Crisis of Conscience*, 50; *The Watchtower*, December 15, 1974, p. 768; Penton, *Apocalypse Delayed*, 174; Metzger, "The New World Translation of the Christian Greek Scriptures"; Robert McCoy, "Jehovah's Witnesses and Their New Testament," *Andover Newton Quarterly* 3, no. 3 (January 1963): 15–31; Countess, *The Jehovah's Witness' New Testament*, 91–93; Rhodes, *The Challenge of the Cults and New Religions*, 94.

21. Richara Heyward, "Witnessing in Black: Jehovah's Witnesses, Textual

Ethnogenesis, Racial Subjectivity, and the Foundational Politics of Theocracy," *Black Theology: An International Journal* 10, no. 1 (2012): 93–115.

22. *The Time Is at Hand*, 101; *Millions Now Living Will Never Die*, 89; *Why Are You Looking Forward to 1975?*, 494.

CONVICTION: THE GLOBAL CHURCH

1. *Merriam-Webster Dictionary* (online), s.v. "conviction," https://www.merriam -webster.com/dictionary/conviction.

2. Philip Jenkins, *The Lost History of Christianity: The Thousand-Year Golden Age of the Church in the Middle East, Africa, and Asia—and How It Died* (New York: HarperCollins, 2008), 3.

3. Jenkins, *The Lost History of Christianity*, 25–26.

4. William Bennett, *Tried by Fire: The Story of Christianity's First Thousand Years* (Nashville: Nelson, 2016), 7.

5. Gene L. Green, Stephen T. Pardue, and K. K. Yeo, eds., *The Church from Every Tribe and Tongue: Ecclesiology in the Majority World* (Carlisle, Cambria, UK: Langham Global Library, 2018).

6. Veli-Matti Kärkkäinen, "Ecclesiology and the Church in Christian Tradition and Western Theology," in *The Church from Every Tribe and Tongue*, ed. Green, Pardue, and Yeo, 20.

7. Kärkkäinen, "Ecclesiology and the Church," 30.

8. Stephanie Lowery, "Ecclesiology in Africa: Apprentices on a Mission," in *The Church from Every Tribe and Tongue*, ed. Green, Pardue, and Yeo, 75.

9. Lowery, "Ecclesiology in Africa," 84.

10. Lowery, "Ecclesiology in Africa," 85–6.

11. Kärkkäinen, "Ecclesiology and the Church," 33.

CHAPTER 11: THE PROSPERITY GOSPEL

1. Moore, 1972.

2. Bowler, 2013; Bowman, Jr., 2001; Kopiec, 2020; McConnell, 1995; Simmons, 1997; Smith, 1995

3. Kenneth Copeland, "Image of God in You" #3, audio, KCM.

4. Frederick K. C. Price, "Prayer: Do You Know What Prayer Is . . . and How to Pray?" in *The Word Study Bible* (Tulsa, OK: Harrison House, 1990), 1178; see also Price, "Ever Increasing Faith", TBN, May 1, 1992.

5. Kenneth E. Hagin, *New Thresholds of Faith* (Broken Arrow, OK: Faith Library, 1985), 30.

6. Kenneth Copeland, "Following the Faith of Abraham", audio, KCM.

7. Kenneth Copeland, "Spirit, Soul, and Body", audio, KCM.

8. Kenneth Copeland, *The Force of Faith* (Tulsa, OK: Harrison House, 1983), 16–17.

9. See, e.g., E. W. Kenyon, *Jesus the Healer*, 1940, p. 7; Essek William Kenyon, *The Two Kinds of Faith: Faith's Secret Revealed* (Lynnwood, WA: Kenyon Gospel Publishing Society, 1969), 20.

10. Frederick K. C. Price, *How Faith Works* (Tulsa, OK: Harrison House, 1976), 99, 101; see also Hagin, *New Thresholds of Faith*, 85–86.

11. Essek William Kenyon, *The Bible in the Light of Our Redemption* (1943), p. 21.

12. Kenneth E. Hagin, *The Believer's Authority* (Broken Arrow, OK: Kenneth Hagin Ministries, 1985), 19.

13. Bowman, 2001, p. 133.

14. Essek William Kenyon, *The Hidden Man* (1955), p. 7.

15. Kenneth E. Hagin, *Zoe: The God-Kind of Life* (Broken Arrow, OK: Faith Library, 1989), 35–36, 41.

16. "The Force of Love", 1987, audio, KCM.

17. Kenneth Copeland, *Our Covenant with God* (1987), p. 7.

18. Copeland, "Praise the Lord," TBN, Feb. 6, 1986.

19. Authority of the Believer IV, 1987, audio, KCM.

20. Kenyon, *The Bible in the Light of Our Redemption*, 17–18.

21. Kenneth E. Hagin, *Redeemed from Poverty, Sickness, and Spiritual Death* (Broken Arrow, OK: Faith Library, 1983), 56.

22. Essek William Kenyon, *Claiming Our Rights* (Crossreach, 2017), 1.

23. Essek William Kenyon, *The Father and His Family* (Spencer, MA: Reality, 1916), 36.

24. Kenyon, *The Father and His Family*, 42.

25. Kenyon, *The Father and His Family*, 57.

26. Hagin, *The Believer's Authority*, 19.

27. Charles Capps, *Authority in Three Worlds* (Tulsa, OK: Harrison House, 1982), 50–51.

28. "What Happened From the Cross to the Throne", 1990, audio, KCM.

29. Praise-a-Thon, TBN, April 1988.

30. "Faith in the Blood of Jesus," 1982, audio 01–4402, KCM.

31. "The Image of God in You" part 3, 1989, audio 01–1403, KCM.

32. Charles Capps, "Jesus: The Word Made Flesh," *Capps Ministries*, https://capps ministries.com/pages/jesus-the-word-made-flesh.

33. Bowman, 2001, p. 160.

34. Essek William Kenyon, *What Happened from the Cross to the Throne?* (Lynnwood, WA: Kenyon Gospel Publishing Society, 1946), 41.

35. Kenyon, *What Happened from the Cross to the Throne?*, 43.

36. Kenyon, *What Happened from the Cross to the Throne?*, 46.

37. Kenneth E. Hagin, *The Name of Jesus* (Broken Arrow, OK: Faith Library, 1979), 31.

38. "What Happened From the Cross to the Throne", 1990, audio, KCM.

39. *Identification #3*, 1980, audio #FP545 Ever Increasing Faith Ministries.

40. Kenneth Copeland, "Jesus—Our Lord of Glory," *Believer's Voice of Victory*, 10(4), April 1982.

41. Ever Increasing Faith Messenger [June 1980] 7; as cited in D. R. McConnell, *A Different Gospel*, 1988, p. 120.

42. Ibid.

43. Kenyon, *What Happened from the Cross to the Throne?*, 47, 68, 71.

44. Hagin, *The Name of Jesus*, 29–30.

45. "What Happened From the Cross to the Throne", 1990, audio, KCM.

46. *Substitution and Identification*, 1989, audio #00–0202, KCM.

47. *The Two Kinds of Life*, 1943, p. 2.

48. Kenyon, *The Bible in the Light of Our Redemption*, 151.

49. Creflo Dollar, *World Changers Magazine*, 2002, p. 6.

50. "The Force of Love", 1987, audio, KCM.

51. Hagin, *New Thresholds of Faith*, 60–62.

52. Kopiec, 2020.

53. Essek William Kenyon, *The Two Kinds of Knowledge* (Lynnwood, WA: Kenyon Gospel Publishing Society, 1938), 14–15.

54. Kenyon, *Jesus the Healer*, 11.

55. Kenyon, *The Hidden Man*, 98.

56. Hagin, *New Thresholds of Faith*, 47.

57. Kenneth E. Hagin, *Having Faith in Your Faith* (Kenneth Hagin Ministries, 1988), pp. 1, 3.

58. Frederick K. C. Price, *Three Keys to Positive Confession* (Los Angeles: Faith One, 1994).

59. Kenneth Copeland, *The Laws of Prosperity* (Tulsa, OK: Harrison House, 1974), 18–19.

60. Copeland, *The Power of the Tongue*, 15.

61. Capps, *Authority in Three Worlds*, 24.

62. Kenyon, *Jesus the Healer*, 24.

63. Kenyon, *Jesus the Healer*, 25.

64. Hagin, *Seven Things You Should Know about Divine Healing*, 21.

65. Frederick K. C. Price, *Praise the Lord*, TBN, September 21, 1990, taken from Documentation for Christianity in Crisis by Hank Hanegraaff.

66. Copeland, *Laws of Prosperity*, 51.

67. "Why Do Bad Things Happen?," *Kenneth Copeland Ministries*, https://www.kcm.org/real-help/spiritual-growth/learn/why-do-bad-things-happen?language_content_entity=en-US.

68. "Faith for Healing Is Based on Knowledge," *Andrew Wommack Ministries*, https://www.awmi.net/reading/teaching-articles/healing_knowledge/.

69. "Faith for Healing Is Based on Knowledge," *Andrew Wommack Ministries*.

70. "Prayer: Your Path to Success," March 2, 2009, http://www.creflodollar ministries.org/BibleStudy/Articles.aspx?id=329.

71. Gloria Copeland, *God's Will Is Prosperity* (Tulsa, OK: Harrison House, 1978), 54.

72. Joel Osteen, *Your Best Life Now: 7 Steps to Living at Your Full Potential* (Brentwood, TN: FaithWords, 2004), 132.

73. Milmon Harrison, *Righteous Riches: The Word of Faith Movement in Contemporary African American Religion* (Oxford: Oxford University Press, 2005).

74. Allen, 2010.

CHAPTER 12: DETOXING FROM CULTS

1. Craig S. Keener, *The IVP Bible Background Commentary: New Testament* (Downers Grove, IL: InterVarsity, 1993), Eph. 5:8–13.

2. Susan Elliott, "Mystery Cults," in *Eerdmans Dictionary of the Bible*, ed. David Noel Freedman, Allen C. Myers, and Astrid B. Beck (Grand Rapids: Eerdmans, 2000), 931.

3. Clinton E. Arnold, *3 Crucial Questions about Spiritual Warfare*, Three Crucial Questions (Grand Rapids: Baker Academic, 1997), Kindle.

4. Arnold, *3 Crucial Questions about Spiritual Warfare.*

5. Eric Mason, *Unleashed: Being Conformed to the Image of Christ* (Nashville: B&H, 2015), Kindle.

6. James MacDonald's definition is very helpful as well: "Fortified patterns of thinking that are stubbornly resistant to God's Word and God's will for us."

7. Tony Evans, *Victory in Spiritual Warfare: Outfitting Yourself for the Battle* (Eugene, OR: Harvest House, 2011), 169.

8. Steven Hassan, *Combating Cult Mind Control: The #1 Best-Selling Guide to Protection, Rescue, and Recovery from Destructive Cults*, 30th anniversary ed. (Newton, MA: Freedom of Mind, 2018), 247, Kindle.

9. Michael S. Heiser and Vincent M. Setterholm, *Glossary of Morpho-Syntactic Database Terminology* (Bellingham, WA: Lexham, 2013).

10. Clinton E. Arnold, *Zondervan Illustrated Bible Backgrounds Commentary: Volume 3, Romans to Philemon* (Grand Rapids: Zondervan, 2002), 399.

11. Ray Van Neste, "1–2 Timothy, Titus," in *The Baker Illustrated Bible Background Commentary*, ed. J. Scott Duvall and J. Daniel Hays (Grand Rapids: Baker Books, 2020), 1210.

12. Arnold, *Romans to Philemon*, 463.

13. Robert H. Stein, "Differences in the Gospels," in *CSB Study Bible: Notes*, ed. Edwin A. Blum and Trevin Wax (Nashville: Holman Bible Publishers, 2017), 1521.

SUBJECT INDEX

abstinence, 289n. 12
ahistoricism, 21
AIDS epidemic, the, 96–97
Ali, Nobel Drew, 156
Allen, Patrick, 165
Allen, Richard, 59
ally, 88
Anglicans, High Church, 41–42
annihilation, 180, 208, 211
anointed class, the, 205, 209
Arius, 205, 259
Arnold, Clinton E., 130, 269
asexual, 88
assimilation, 19
Baker, Josephine, 79
Bantu, Vince, 137
Barbour, Nelson, 197–98, 200
Barrett, Lois, 11
Barry, Marion, 96
Barth, Karl, 280n. 4
Bates, Joseph, 169, 170
Bell, Derrick, 16, 23, 24, 25
Bennett, William, 220
Benson, George, 197
Bird, Michael, 108, 109
bisexuals, 88
Black, Barry, 165
Black liberation theology
    aims of, 65
    and contemporary faith, 72–73
    definition of, 63–64
    development of, 64–65
    evaluation of, 74–77
    liberation as starting point of, 65–68, 73, 75
    limitations of, 75–77, 284n. 69
    as microcultural movement, 10
    role of the Black experience in, 67–70
    source of salvation of, 75
    and white supremacy as source of evil, 75, 76
    within the Christian Church, 77
    womanist, 70–71
Black Religious Identity Cults (BRICS), 157, 159, 161
Black theology. *See* Black liberation theology
Blackness, meaning of, 65
Bobbington, David, 39
Bonhoeffer, Dietrich, 280n. 4
Braden, Charles S., 155

Briscoe, Brandon, 131
Bultmann, Rudolf, 280n. 4
Campbell, Naomi, 197
Cannon, Katie, 71
Canright, D. M., 189
Capps, Charles, 229, 235–36, 237, 245
Carson, Ben, 165
cessationism, 291n. 1
Chambers, Alan, 95
Childish Gambino, 197
Christadelphians, the, 197
Christian nationalism 10, 28, 38, 44–48, 134–35.
    See also white Christian nationalism
Christian Scientists, the, 155, 229
church, the. *See:* global church, the
Churches of Christ, the, 197
cisgender, 109, 289n. 6
color blindness, 17–18, 19
Combahee River Collective, the, 94, 286n. 30
Cone, James, 64–66, 67, 68, 69, 280n. 4
Conn, Harvie, 5, 6
conversion therapy, 95, 287n. 37, 287n. 40
conviction
    biblically rooted, xviii–xix, 218
    definition of, xviii, 190–91, 218
    developing biblical, 193–95
    experiential, xix
    role of, 192–93
    when it occurs, 191
Copeland, Gloria, 248
Copeland, Kenneth, 229, 231, 233, 236–37, 238, 239, 240, 244–45, 247
Copper, Gary, 287n. 41
Coptic Christians
    critiques of black theology of, 283–84n. 67
    persecution of, 76, 283n. 64
    and prayer, 284n. 72
    teachings of, 283n.67, 284n. 68, 284n. 70, 284n. 71, 284n. 72
creation mandate, 5, 11, 111
Crenshaw, Kimberlé, 17, 18
critical race theory
    and the American legal system, 16, 20, 26
    and the civil rights movement, 17–19, 24
    and color blindness, 17–18
    complexity of evaluating, 15, 26
    and critical theory, 20, 21, 23, 27–28
    and deconstruction, 21, 22–23, 27, 29, 33

SCRIPTURE INDEX